MW00909389

THE HESSIANS

AND THE OTHER

GERMAN AUXILIARIES OF GREAT BRITAIN IN
THE REVOLUTIONARY WAR

BY
EDWARD J. LOWELL

WITH MAPS AND PLANS

NEW YORK
HARPER & BROTHERS, FRANKLIN SQUARE
1884

PREFACE.

THE history of the German auxiliaries, who fought for Great Britain in the Revolutionary War, has not received from American writers the amount of attention which its importance would seem to deserve. Much has been made of the fact that seven thousand French soldiers and nineteen thousand French seamen assisted the United States in the siege of Yorktown, but we have forgotten that a force of between fifteen and twenty thousand Germans served for seven years against us; that more than twenty-nine thousand were brought to America for this purpose; that more than twelve thousand never returned to Germany. I know of no American historian but Bancroft, who has made any thorough study of this subject in the original authorities, and the general nature of his work does not call on him, and, indeed, would hardly permit him, to write the history of the German troops in detail. Doctor George Washington Greene has published interesting reviews of three of Kapp's books, and the narrative of Baroness Riedesel has been translated into English by William L. Stone,

Esq., who has also translated that part of Eelking's "Life of Riedesel" which relates to the Revolutionary War.

In preparing the following book, I cannot claim to have used nearly all the very voluminous stores contained in the libraries and archives of Germany. I have, however, found original German accounts of every important engagement, and of almost every skirmish of the Revolutionary War, from the year 1776 to the end, except of some of those battles which occurred in the Carolinas and Georgia, and in which few, if any, Germans were engaged. Some of these accounts, I believe, had never yet fallen under the eye of an American writer.

In Germany the treaties for the letting of soldiers to Great Britain, and the history of those soldiers have received more attention than in America. Two writers are especially prominent among those who have dealt with these subjects. One of these writers is Friedrich Kapp, now a member of the Reichstag, and formerly an exile in America. To his books I am largely indebted, both directly and indirectly, for information embodied in this volume, and especially in the first five chapters. The other writer is Max von Eelking, captain in the service of Saxe-Meiningen, and corresponding member of the New York Historical Society. His two works, "Die deutschen Hülfstruppen im nordamerikanischen Befreiungskriege," and "Leben und Wirken des Herzoglich Braunschweigischen General Lieutenants Friedrich Adolph von Riedesel," constitute a history of the war from the German point of view. Captain von Eelking had access to a very rich store of material. His list of manuscripts for the first-mentioned work alone (many of them the property of private persons) comprises thirty-eight numbers. In writing the life of Riedesel he was allowed to consult or copy all the letters and papers left by that general. Had Captain von Eelking shown as much care in the use of materials as he did industry in their collection, his works would be very valuable contributions to American history. Unfortunately the results of his labors are marred by inaccuracies. I have often been obliged to depend upon him, but I have done so with caution.

The reader will find in this book many passages which belong rather to biography or to anecdote than to history. The adventures of comparatively unimportant persons, such as Wiederhold, Ewald, or Baroness Riedesel are related at some length. It has been my object to give an idea of what sort of people the auxiliaries were, and of what impression America and the Americans made upon them. To this end I have not hesitated to introduce apparently trivial matter, where it has seemed characteristic, nor to quote opinions or descriptions which, though genuine, were mistaken.

I take this opportunity heartily to thank Doctor Duncker, Librarian of the Ständische Landesbibliothek at Cassel, and the secretary, Herr Schultheiss; Doctor Könnecke, Keeper of the Archives at Marburg, and his assistants; and Doctor Speyer, Court Librarian to his Most Serene Highness the Prince of Waldeck, through whose kindness I have obtained copies of manuscripts in their respective keeping.

A part of the contents of this volume appeared in the form of letters to the *New York Times* in the winter of 1880–1881.

CONTENTS.

MAPS AND PLANS.

THE HESSIANS.

CHAPTER I.

THE PRINCES.

THE little city of Cassel is one of the most attractive in North Germany to a passing stranger. Its galleries, its parks and gardens, and its great palaces are calculated to excite admiration and surprise. Here Napoleon III. spent the months of his captivity amid scenes which might remind him of the magnificence of Versailles, which, indeed, those who planned the beautiful gardens had wished to imitate. For the grounds were mostly laid out and the buildings mainly constructed in the last century, when the court of France was the point towards which most princely eyes on the Continent were directed; and no court, perhaps, followed more assiduously or more closely, in outward show at least, in the path of the French court than that of the Landgraves of Hesse-Cassel. The expense of all these buildings and gardens was enormous, but there was generally money in the treasury. Yet the land was a poor land. The three or four hundred thousand inhabitants lived chiefly by the plough, but the Landgraves were in business. It was a profitable trade that they carried on, selling or letting out wares which were much in demand in that century, as in all centuries, for the Landgraves of Hesse-Cassel were dealers in men; thus it came to pass that Landgrave Frederick II. and his subjects played a part in American history, and that "Hessian" became a household word, though not a title of honor, in the United States.

The Landgraves were not particular as to their market or their customers. In 1687 one of them let out a thousand soldiers to the Venetians fighting against the Turks. In 1702 nine thousand Hessians served under the maritime powers, and in 1706 eleven thousand five hundred men were in Italy. England was the best customer. Through a large part of the eighteenth century she had Hessians in her pay. Some of them were with the army of the Duke of Cumberland during the Pretender's invasion in 1745; but it is stated that they refused to fight in that campaign for want of a cartel for the exchange of prisoners.* It would have been well for many of them had they declined to go to America for the same reason. So little was it a matter of patriotism, or of political preference, with the Landgraves, that in 1743 Hessian stood against Hessian, six thousand men serving in the army of King George II. of England, and six thousand in the opposing force of the Emperor Charles VII.

The Landgraves of Hesse were not the only princes who dealt in troops. In the war of the American Revolution alone, six German rulers let out their soldiers to Great Britain. These were Frederick II.,

* Letter of Sir Joseph Yorke to the Earl of Suffolk, quoted in Kapp's "Soldatenhandel," 1st ed. p. 229.

Landgrave of Hesse-Cassel; William, his son, the independent Count of Hesse-Hanau; Charles I., Duke of Brunswick; Frederick, Prince of Waldeck: Charles Alexander, Margrave of Anspach-Bayreuth; and Frederick Augustus, Prince of Anhalt-Zerbst. The action of these princes was opposed to the policy of the empire and to the moral sense of the age: but the emperor had no power to prevent it, for the subjection of those parts of Germany which were outside of his hereditary dominions was little more than nominal.

The map of Germany in the last century presents the most extraordinary patchwork. Across the northern part of the country, from its eastern to its western side, but not in an unbroken line, stretch the territories of the King of Prussia. The Austrian hereditary dominions, in a comparatively compact mass, occupy the southeastern corner. Beyond the boundaries of these two great powers, all is confusion. Electorates, duchies, bishoprics, the dominions of margraves, landgraves, princes, and free cities are inextricably jumbled together. There were nearly three hundred sovereignties in Germany, besides over fourteen hundred estates of Imperial Knights, holding immediately of the empire, and having many rights of sovereignty. Some of these three hundred states were not larger than townships in New England, many of them not larger than American counties. Nor was each of them compact in itself, for one dominion was often composed of several detached parcels of territory. Yet every little princedom had to maintain its petty prince, with his court and his army. The princes were practically despotic. The remnants of what had once been constitutional assemblies still existed in many places, but they represented at best but a small part of the population.* The cities and towns were governed by privileged classes. In the country some little freedom remained with the peasants of some neighborhoods as to the management of their village affairs, but in general the peasantry were not much better off than serfs, and subject to the tyranny of a horde of officials, who intermeddled in every important action of their lives. Trade was hampered by tolls and duties, for every little state had its own financial system. Commerce and manufactures were impeded by monopolies. In certain places sumptuary laws regulated the dress or the food of the people.

Before the last quarter of the century some improvement had taken place in the political condition of Germany. Frederick the Great of Prussia and Joseph II. of Austria were, in their different ways, enlightened princes, and their example had stimulated many of the better sovereigns to exert themselves in some measure for the good of their people. The influence of the Liberal movement in France was also felt. But the idea of political freedom had hardly taken shape in the most cultivated of German minds. The good or evil disposition of the prince was no more under the control of the ordinary subject than the state of the weather. The doctrine of passive obedience was in fashion, though not entirely uncon-

* The Landstände had more influence in Hesse than elsewhere. They are said to have tried in vain to obtain for the country a share in the money received by the Landgrave for letting out troops.—Biedermann, "Deutschland im Achtzehnten Jahrhundert," vol. i. p. 114.

tested. If, as one writer on politics explained, it was the duty of the subject to submit in case his prince should take his life in mere wantonness, it was to be hoped that another writer was equally correct in saying that "in princely houses all virtues are hereditary."*

Let us now look a little nearer at those special inheritors of all the virtues who sent mercenaries to America. The most important of them was Frederick II., Landgrave of Hesse-Cassel (not to be confounded with his great namesake and contemporary of Prussia). This prince was the Catholic ruler of a Protestant country. His first wife had been an English princess, a daughter of George II. She had separated herself from the Landgrave on his conversion to Catholicism, and had retired to Hanau, with her precious son, of whom I shall presently speak.

Frederick had led a merry life of it at Cassel. He had taken unto himself a cast-off mistress of the Duc de Bouillon, but set up no pretensions to fidelity, and is said to have had more than a hundred children. A French theatre and opera, with a French *corps de ballet*, were maintained. French adventurers with good letters obtained a welcome and even responsible positions in the state. The court was ordered on a French model. French was, moreover, then, and has remained almost to our own day, the language of princes, courtiers, and diplomatists. In that language Frederick the Great corresponded with many of his relations, in it his sister wrote her private memoirs, and French was spoken at the court of that smaller Frederick whom we have in hand.

* Biedermann, vol. i. pp. 161, 163, n.

At the time of the American Revolution, the Landgrave was living with his second wife. He was about sixty years old, and seems to have become comparatively steady in his habits. He was a good man of business. His troops, drilled on the Prussian system, and recruited in a measure among his own subjects by conscription, were good soldiers. His army in 1781 numbered twenty-two thousand, while the population of his territories was little above three hundred thousand souls; but many foreigners were enticed into the service, and a few of the regiments were not kept permanently under the banners, but spent the larger part of the year disbanded, and met only for a few weeks of drill.* Frederick took a personal interest in his army, and corresponded with his officers in America, making the hand and eye of the master usefully felt. He took pains with the internal affairs of his country, leaving, indeed, a full treasury at his death. He founded schools and museums, and, like all his family, loved costly buildings. When he sent twelve thousand men to America he diminished the taxes of his remaining subjects, and though these were sad and down-trodden, though they mourned their sons and brothers sent to fight in a strange quarrel beyond the sea, we may linger for a moment regretfully over Frederick of Hesse-Cassel, for he dealt in good wares, he showed some personal dignity, and he was one of the least disreputable of the princes who sent mercenaries to America.

William, the eldest son and heir apparent of Landgrave Frederick, governed at the time of the Revolu-

* "Briefe eines Reisenden."

tion the independent county of Hanau, which lay a few miles to the eastward of the city of Frankfort. William was his father's inferior in dignity and his equal in cupidity. As early as August, 1775, when the news of the battle of Bunker Hill must have been very fresh in Germany, the hereditary prince hastened to offer a regiment to George III., "without making the smallest condition." In spite of his protestations of disinterested devotion, he obtained in the end a larger price per man furnished than any one of his competitors, except his most serene father.

The courts of Cassel and of Hanau were not on good terms. The Landgrave, since his change of religion, had quarrelled with his wife and his heirs. But the mode of life of his eldest son was not very different from his own. When William had a natural child to provide for, he added a kreutzer (about one cent) to the price of every bag of salt which his subjects brought from the salt-mines, and gave the revenue thus obtained to the infant. As his left-handed children numbered seventy-four, the poorer of his subjects must have learned to be sparing of their salt. One of his bastards was that General von Haynau who, in the service of Austria, committed terrible cruelties in Italy in 1849, causing women to be whipped in Brescia, and who was afterwards mobbed in London. William's mistress for years was a Fraulein von Schlotheim, who at first ran away from him, but was sent back to him by her own parents. In the words of a lady of Cassel, "The Hessian nobility could not spare this advantage." Though the prince received some £12,000 a year as subsidy for sending troops to America, he is believed by Kapp to have remitted no taxes except to the wives and parents of soldiers with the expedition, or such taxes as were levied on the property of these soldiers themselves, where they had no wives or parents. As for the princes to be mentioned hereafter, I do not learn that they remitted any taxes at all, but my sources of information may be defective.

Duke Charles I. reigned over Brunswick-Luneburg, and the hereditary Prince Charles William Ferdinand was associated with him in the government. The latter had married a sister of King George III. The land had but one hundred and fifty thousand inhabitants, and the princes were deeply in debt. Charles was extravagant and the Seven Years' War had been expensive. Attempts had been made to help out the finances by alchemy, but the gold had all flown up the chimney or made its way into the pockets of the alchemists, and none was found in the melting-pots. An Italian theatrical director received a salary of 30,000 thalers a year, while Lessing, already the author of "Emilia Gallotti" and "Minna von Barnhelm," served as librarian for a pittance. Prince Charles William Ferdinand was a better economist than his father. The lottery, a fashionable means of raising money at that time, was established under the direction of a minister of state, and made to bring in a good income, and, although the Duke of Brunswick received less per head in the shape of subsidy for the soldiers sent to America than any other of the princes, he was able, for his corps of forty-three hundred men, to pocket more than £160,000 before the end of the war.

The little territories of Anspach and Bayreuth, containing together about four hundred thousand souls, had lately been united under the government of Margrave Charles Alexander. Neither land had been fortunate in its previous sovereign. Both countries had belonged to branches of the great Hohenzollern family, the main line of which had already laid in Prussia the foundations of that power which has given it to-day the foremost place in Europe. But the Margraves of Anspach and of Bayreuth lacked the ability which underlay the roughness of King Frederick William, father of Frederick the Great. Of this Frederick William we have a lively picture in the memoirs of his daughter Wilhelmina. How he chased his children about the room with his stick, how Wilhelmina hid under the bed and Frederick in the closet, how the king loved tall soldiers and bullied his wife are there graphically narrated. With the express object of making her story more cheerful, the princess tells how her father, in general the most chaste of monarchs, tried to kiss a lady of honor on the stairs, and how she struck him in the face and made his nose bleed. This Wilhelmina married a Margrave of Bayreuth, and her sister, Frederika Louisa, married a Margrave of Anspach, but did not live on good terms with him.

This Margrave of Anspach was good-natured, in his way, and kindly, when not out of temper. He liked to do small favors to his servants, and to inform these of them with his own lips. He gladly allowed dainties to be sent to the sick from his kitchen. When not in liquor, he was inclined to commute the death penalty to criminals in civil life, unless they had been guilty of such heinous offences as persuading his soldiers to desert, thieving about his court, or poaching; but his military executions were barbarous. The Margrave was regular in his attendance at church, and given to endowing churches, schools, and hospitals. He might, therefore, have been beloved of his subjects, but for his ungoverned temper, and for the excesses into which it led him. Thus, having heard that his dogs were not well fed, he rode to the house of the man who had them in charge, called him to the door, and shot him on his own threshold. An inn-keeper, having complained of some petty theft, the Margrave had the thief hanged before mine host's door. In 1747 a servant-girl was hanged without trial for having helped a soldier to desert. As the Margrave was riding out of his castle one day, he stopped and asked the sentinel on guard, who happened to be one of the city watch, and not a regular soldier, for his musket. The poor fellow, unsuspectingly, gave it up; whereupon the Margrave called him a coward and a scoundrel, and had two hussars drag him through the mill-pond at their horses' tails, of which treatment he died. One of his equerries, Von Reitzenstein by name, although avaricious and corruptible, was a favorite with the people for sometimes moderating these excesses. On one occasion a shepherd with a flock of sheep did not clear the road for the Margrave quickly enough, and made his Most Serene Highness's horse shy. The Margrave asked the equerry for his pistols to shoot the fellow. "They are not loaded," answered Von Reitzenstein. When the party got near home, however, the equerry took out both pistols and fired them into the air. Bang! bang! "What's the matter?" cried the startled

Margrave. "My gracious master," answered the other, "I think you will sleep far better to-night for having heard the crack of the pistols now, rather than an hour ago."

It was far from safe to criticise the Margrave's conduct. In 1740 one Christoph Wilhelm von Rauber was accused of posting up caricatures and lampoons. For this he was sentenced to strike himself on the mouth, under penalty of having it done for him by the executioner; to see the latter burn his lampoons; and finally to have his head cut off; which last punishment was graciously commuted to perpetual imprisonment and confiscation.*

Charles Alexander, son of this murdering Margrave, appears to have been more humane than his father. He was sent in his youth to Utrecht to learn republican virtues, and then to Italy, probably to learn princely graces. He returned worn out with dissipation, the blame of which his father found it convenient to lay on his travelling companion, Councillor Mayer. The latter was imprisoned at Zelle, and his subsequent fate is unknown. According to another story, he was executed at Altenkirchen.

In 1777, Charles Alexander, who had become Margrave both of Anspach and of Bayreuth, was deeply in debt, and delighted with the chance to let out two regiments of his subjects for foreign service. Recruits and additional soldiers were sent out from time to time until a total of two thousand three hundred and fifty-three men had been reached, for whose services

* "Geschichte des vorletzten Markgrafen von Brandenburg-Ansbach," von Karl Heinrich Ritter von Lang.

the Margrave received more than £100,000 sterling. Charles Alexander was the last Margrave of Anspach and Bayreuth. In 1791 he sold both countries to Prussia, for a pension, on which he afterwards lived in England, where he died in 1806.

Beside the Margraves of Anspach, the Princes of Waldeck seem almost respectable. To be sure, they used their little country (it lies westward from Cassel) principally as a stock-farm to raise men for the Dutch market, but they themselves fought with distinction for the same country. The fitting-out of troops for America was merely a side speculation, and the whole number sent was only one thousand two hundred and twenty-five soldiers.

Frederick Augustus, Prince of Anhalt-Zerbst, may be looked on as the caricature of the little German princes of his day. He reigned over some twenty thousand subjects, but he cannot be said to have governed them, for the last thirty years of his life were spent in Basle and in Luxemburg. Even there did he find that his subjects could be troublesome, and he forbade, by a formal printed order, that any one of his servants should trouble him with the affairs of his principality, under pain of dismissal. He was not above being severe, however, for he had a gallows erected on the Island of Wangeroge for the terror of oyster stealers. His army of two thousand men, and these, I think, mostly on paper, numbered no less than eleven colonels, yet when it came to sending six hundred men to America he had to go out of his own dominions to find not only soldiers but officers. The little principality was, so to speak, in commission, and governed by a few privy-councillors. It had neither arts nor manufactures, and had suffered from war, famine, pestilence, and flood. But it was a land highly honored. The sister of its prince was the Empress Catherine II. of Russia. That prince himself, though he lived away from his country, was quite sensible to the glory of his position, and had a feeling heart for the sufferings of monarchs, if not of subjects. When he heard that impious Frenchmen had cut off the head of their king, Louis XVI., he was borne down with melancholy, refused food and drink, and died, as he had lived, a parody, the caricature of a royal martyr.

CHAPTER II.

THE TREATIES.

IN the negotiations between the court of Great Britain and the German princes for the hire of mercenaries to serve against the rebels in America, it is clear that both sides were eager to come to terms. England wanted the men, the princes wanted the money, and while the latter were anxious to receive as large subsidies as possible, the chief care of Lord North's cabinet was to obtain the greatest number of soldiers with the least possible delay. Friedrich Kapp, the German historian of these bargains, thinks that Colonel William Faucitt, the British commissioner and plenipotentiary in the whole matter, was extravagant in the terms he granted. This does not appear, however, to have been the opinion of the Earl of Suffolk, Lord North's Secretary of State for Foreign Affairs, who constantly expressed himself as well satisfied with his agent.

The British cabinet had been disappointed in the hope, which it had entertained in the summer and early autumn of 1775, of obtaining twenty thousand men from Russia. Its negotiations for the use of a so-called Scotch regiment, actually in the service of Holland, were destined to fail. Five battalions of the Hanoverian subjects of George III. were despatched to Gibraltar and Minorca, setting the Englishmen who had been in garrison in those fortresses free for other service. No further source of supply was left but the small independent principalities of Germany.

On the other hand, the hereditary Prince of Hesse-Cassel, actual reigning Count of Hesse-Hanau, had written to express to His Majesty of England his zeal and attachment to the best of kings, and to offer the services of his regiment of five hundred men, "all sons of the land which the protection of your Majesty alone insures to me, and all ready to sacrifice with me their life and their blood for your service." It must not be imagined, however, that the prince was thinking of putting his own precious blood in any danger, and the expression of the eagerness of his subjects may also be considered rhetorical. The Prince of Waldeck wrote in the same strain in November, 1775, offering six hundred men. His officers and soldiers, like their prince, asked nothing better than to find an occasion to sacrifice themselves for His Majesty.

The Duke of Brunswick-Luneburg and the Landgrave of Hesse-Cassel did not at first offer their services, but Colonel Faucitt found no difficulty in entering into negotiations with them. The Margrave of Anspach-Bayreuth made an offer of two battalions in the autumn of 1775, but the treaty with him was not entered into for more than a year afterwards, and finally, in October, 1777, an agreement was made with the Prince of Anhalt-Zerbst, who had long been doing all in his power to bring one about. Offers of troops on the part of the Elector of Bavaria and the Duke of Würtemberg led to no result, partly on account of the bad quality and equipment of the soldiers offered, and partly, in the case of the latter, on account of the trouble made by Frederick the Great about the passage of troops through his dominions. Proposals of several other small German princes came to nothing.

The treaty first concluded was that with the Duke of Brunswick. It is dated January 9, 1776. The Duke yields to his Britannic Majesty a corps of three thousand nine hundred and sixty-four infantry men, and three hundred and thirty-six unmounted dragoons. This corps is to be completely equipped at the expense of the Duke, except as to horses for the light cavalry. They are to march from Brunswick in two divisions in February and March, and the King is to take measures to prevent desertion while they pass through his electoral dominions of Hanover on their way to the sea. The King is to pay and feed them on the same scale as his own soldiers, and the Duke engages "to let his corps enjoy all the emoluments of pay that his Britannic Majesty allows them," that is to say, not to pay them on a lower scale and pocket the difference. The British government, however, did not trust him. From the time of the arrival of the troops in America their pay was sent direct to them there, and did not pass through his Most Serene Ducal Highness's hands. This precaution was adopted with all the German auxiliaries but those of Hesse-Cassel, whose landgrave succeeded in getting the handling of the money. The Brunswick soldiers were to be cared for in the British hospitals, and the wounded not in condition to serve were to be transported into Europe at the expense of the King, and landed in a port on the Elbe or the Weser. The Duke agreed to furnish the recruits that should be annually necessary for the corps, to discipline and to equip them, but if it should happen that any of the regiments, battalions, or companies of the corps should suffer a loss altogether extraordinary, either in a battle, a siege, or by an uncommon contagious malady, or by the loss of any transport vessel in the voyage to America, his Britannic Majesty was to make good the loss of the officer or soldier, and to bear the expense of the necessary recruits to reestablish the corps that should have suffered this extraordinary loss.

The Duke was to nominate the officers, and fill vacancies among them. He engaged that they should be expert persons. He reserved to himself the administration of justice. He stipulated that his troops should not be required to render any extraordinary services, or such as were beyond their proportion to the rest of the army.

The King of England agreed to pay to his Most Serene Highness, under the title of levy-money, for every soldier the amount of 30 crowns banco, equal to £7 4*s*. 4½*d*. He was to grant, moreover, an annual subsidy amounting to £11,517 17*s*. 1½*d*. from the day of the signature of the treaty so long as the troops should enjoy his pay, and double that amount (viz., £23,035 14*s*. 3*d*.) for two years after the return of the troops into his Most Serene Highness's dominions. In consideration of the haste with which the troops were equipped his Majesty granted two months' pay previous to their march, and undertook all expenses from the time of their leaving their quarters.

One more provision of this treaty deserves especial

notice, as it has excited the well-warranted indignation of all who have execrated these bargains for the sale of human blood. It runs: "According to custom, three wounded men shall be reckoned as one killed; a man killed shall be paid for at the rate of levy-money." This clause, which does not appear in the subsequent treaty with Hesse-Cassel, stands in the Brunswick treaty in the same article with, and immediately before, the provision for making good any extraordinary loss from battle, pestilence, or shipwreck. It may be taken to mean that the King of England undertook to bear the expense of a recruit to fill the place of a Brunswick soldier actually killed in battle, but that the Duke must replace at his own cost one who deserted from the ranks or died of sickness, unless in case of an "uncommon contagious malady." Yet if this be the interpretation, what is the meaning of the "three wounded men." Kapp, moreover, rejects this explanation, and asserts that new recruits were paid for by levy-money in addition to the 30 crowns received for the killed and wounded, and that this blood-money was pocketed by the prince and not by the family of the soldier, nor by himself, if wounded.* At any rate, the fact remains that the Duke of Brunswick contracted to receive a sum amounting to about $35 for every one of his soldiers who should be killed in battle, and $11.66 for every one who should be maimed. It is probably now impossible to discover how much England actually paid out on this account. The payments were not entered under their proper heading in the bills sent to Parliament from the War Office. Kapp

* Sÿbel's "Historische Zeitschrift," II. 6=42, 1879, p. 327.

suggests that the cabinet did not care to meet the criticism which this item in the accounts would have raised.

The treaty with Hesse-Cassel, dated January 15, 1776, differs from that with Brunswick principally as being more favorable to the German court. In the first place, the King of Great Britain was made to engage in a defensive alliance with the Landgrave of Hesse-Cassel. The Hessian troops were to be kept together under their own general, unless reasons of war should require them to be separated. Their sick were to remain in the care of their surgeons and other persons appointed for the purpose under the Hessian generals, and everything was to be allowed them which the King allowed to his own troops. Under this treaty the Landgrave of Hesse-Cassel was to furnish twelve thousand men, completely equipped, and with artillery if desired. He was to be paid levy-money at the same rate as the Duke of Brunswick, viz., 30 crowns banco, or £7 4*s*. 4½*d*. for every man. His subsidy, however, was larger in proportion, amounting to 450,000 crowns banco, or £108,281 5*s*. per annum, to be continued (but not doubled) for one year after the actual return of the troops to Hesse. The Landgrave subsequently furnished various smaller contingents, making special bargains for them, but his advantage over the duke may be roughly estimated from the fact that, barring the blood-money above spoken of, and concerning which we have no data, barring, also, whatever pickings and stealings the most serene rivals managed to gather in, and counting only levy-money and subsidies, the Landgrave of Hesse-Cassel received more than twice as much per man sent to America as the Duke of Brunswick. In addition to this, and outside of the treaty, the Landgrave insisted on the payment of an old claim, dating from the Seven Years' War, previously disallowed by England, and amounting to £41,820 14*s.* 5*d.*

The treaties with the smaller states, Hesse-Hanau, Waldeck, Anspach-Bayreuth, and Anhalt-Zerbst did not differ in their main features from those already described. None of them were quite so favorable to the princes as the treaty with Cassel, none quite so favorable to England as that with Brunswick. The blood-money clause is found in those of Hanau and Waldeck, but not in that of Anspach.*

From time to time bargains were made with several of the princes above mentioned for small additional bodies of troops. Chasseurs or sharpshooters were especially in request. From year to year recruits were sent out to America to the various divisions. The sum total of men, according to Kapp, was made up as follows:

Brunswick sent	5,723
Hesse-Cassel sent	16,992
Hesse-Hanau sent	2,422
Anspach-Bayreuth sent	2,353
Waldeck sent	1,225
Anhalt-Zerbst sent	1,160
Total	29,875

Of these, rather more than eighteen thousand sailed to America in 1776. Of this total of nearly thirty thousand men, twelve thousand five hundred and sixty-

* For the text of the treaties with Brunswick, Hesse-Cassel, Hesse-Hanau, and Waldeck, see "Parliamentary Register," 1st series, vol. iii.; for the treaty with Anspach, vol. vii.

two did not return to Germany.* Besides the contingents sent to America from Germany by agreement with the princes, a certain number of Germans served in the English regiments, some of which had recruiting stations on the Rhine.

It is difficult to say how the bargains between England and the German princes were regarded by public opinion in Germany at the time. Schlözer's *Briefwechsel*, the foremost German periodical of the period, was published at Göttingen, in the Hanoverian dominions of George III. It contains many articles on the American war, all written on the English side, with the single exception of a letter from Baron Steuben, who was fighting for the colonies. This letter is, moreover, annotated by the editor in a sense adverse to the Americans. This tone may perhaps have been forced upon Schlözer by circumstances, as the press in Germany was then tolerated rather than free. An interesting little book was published at Wolfenbüttel, near Brunswick, in 1778. It gives an account of America, its products, its geography, and its history, together with an excellent map. The author of the book is decidedly hostile to the colonists. The sending of more than seventeen thousand Germans to America is briefly, one might almost say incidentally, mentioned, though the earlier operations of the war and of these auxiliaries are described at some length. Yet the presence of so many Germans in the New World was undoubtedly the principal reason for the book's existence. It

* 6 Schlözer's "Staats-Anzeiger," 521, with the corrections made by Kapp in respect to the Anspach contingent. "Soldatenhandel," 2d edition, p. 209.

is fair, also, to consider that rebellion was in those days looked on with far sterner eyes than at present, and that, by people of a conservative turn of mind, at least, it was treated not as a political mistake, but as a heinous crime.

Quite different was the style in which the liberals of Europe spoke of the war and of the mercenaries. The principles which were to bring about the French Revolution were at work, and some of the actors of that great drama were already stepping upon the stage. Mirabeau, then a fugitive in Holland, published a pamphlet addressed "To the Hessians and other nations of Germany, sold by their Princes to England." It is an eloquent protest against the rapacity of the princes, a splendid tribute to the patriotism of the Americans. The genius of Mirabeau could look far enough into the future to recognize in the North American continent an asylum for the oppressed of all nations. His blow at the Landgrave of Hesse-Cassel struck home. Not only did the latter attempt to buy up the edition of the pamphlet, but he caused an answer to be published, which only had the effect of calling forth a rejoinder, in which the future tribune maintains that an offense against the freedom of nations is the greatest of crimes. In the same spirit wrote Abbé Raynal and others, some of them better known in Europe, at that time, than Mirabeau, and against them a paper warfare was kept up in the Dutch journals, then the most influential, because the freest, on the Continent. In the public library at Cassel is an interesting little pamphlet published in 1782 in French, and also in German. This pamphlet is attributed by Kapp to Schlieffen, the

Minister of Landgrave Frederick II.; but I do not know on what authority. The writer pointed out such novel facts as that men had in all ages slaughtered each other, that the Swiss had long been in the habit of fighting as mercenaries, that the ten thousand Greeks under Xenophon did the same, and he considered it unjust to blame his contemporaries for what seemed to be a natural instinct of mankind. He noticed that the present letting-out of troops by Hesse was perhaps the tenth occasion of the sort since the beginning of the century. He showed the benefits which the Landgrave had bestowed on his country, and the affection in which he was held by his people. He drew attention—and this was, perhaps, his best argument—to the fact that the Landgrave of Hesse and the Duke of Brunswick were so nearly connected with the English royal family that their descendants might be one day called to the throne of Great Britain.* As for the boasted Liberty of the Americans, she was but a deceitful siren, for all history proved that republican governments were as tyrannical and cruel as monarchies.

Meanwhile the Freiherr von Gemmingen, minister to the Margrave of Anspach, was a little ashamed of the business in which he found himself. "It always seems very hard to me to deal in troops," writes he to his agent in London, "but the Margrave is determined to set his affairs in order at any price, and to pay all his own debts and those of his predecessors. So the good that may come out of such a treaty of subsidy will far outweigh the hatefulness of the business."

* This argument was not mentioned in the British Parliament, where it might, perhaps, have been received with derision.

Later he writes: "The treaty which we have just made is much more favorable than we could have expected, especially when you think that the offer came from us, and that the royal arms have hitherto had such great success in America. The matter will naturally be looked on in the most unfavorable light possible by people who do not understand how to see an affair of state as a whole, and with its proper motives. But as soon as such people see foreign money flowing into our poor country, as soon as they see us paying its debts with the means which come pouring in, they and the whole world will be enchanted, and will acknowledge that the troops, whose business is to fight the enemies of the state, have conquered our worst enemy —viz., our debts. Even the lowest soldier shipped to America, well paid and provided with what is most necessary, will come back with his savings and be proud to have worked for his country and for his own advantage. . . . I am, in general, a declared enemy of such dealings in men; but there are cases in which the evil changes into a comparative benefit, and such, if I am not mistaken, is ours." *

Frederick the Great, in a letter to Voltaire (June 18, 1776), expressed his contempt for the men-selling princes, and found occasion at a somewhat later time to throw impediments in their way. "Had the Landgrave come out of my school," he writes, "he would not have sold his subjects to the English as one sells cattle to be dragged to the shambles. This is an unbecoming trait in the character of a prince who sets himself up as a teacher of rulers. Such conduct is

* Kapp's "Soldatenhandel," 2d ed. pp. 108, 123, 124.

caused by nothing but dirty selfishness. I pity the poor Hessians who end their lives unhappily and uselessly in America."* Napoleon, when thirty years afterwards he drove away the then Landgrave of Hesse-Cassel (the Count of Hanau of our treaties), expressed the feeling of a later age: "The House of Hesse-Cassel has for many years sold its subjects to England. Thus have the electors gathered such great treasures. This vile avarice now overthrows their house."

But the infamy of the man-selling princes is perpetuated in Germany more by the words of the best-beloved of her poets than by those of the two greatest generals of the last century. In his tragedy of "Cabale und Liebe," written during the progress of the American war, Schiller has left an eloquent protest against the vile traffic. "But none were forced to go?" says Lady Milford to the old chamberlain, who is telling her how his two sons, with seven thousand of their countrymen, have been sent off to America. "Oh, God! no," he answers—"all volunteers. It is true, a few saucy fellows stepped out of the ranks and asked the colonels how much a yoke the prince sold men; but our most gracious master ordered all the regiments to march on to the parade ground, and had the jackanapes shot down. We heard the crack of the rifles, saw their brains spatter the pavement, and the whole army shouted, 'Hurrah! to America!'

"*Lady.* Oh, God! oh, God! And I heard nothing? and I noticed nothing?

* Quoted by Kapp in Sybel's "Historische Zeitschrift," II. 6=42, 1879, p. 314.

"*Chamberlain.* Yes, madam! Why did you ride out to the bear-hunt with our master, just as the signal was given to march away? You should not have missed that imposing spectacle, when the loud drums told us the time was come, and shrieking orphans here followed a living father, and there a raving mother ran to impale her sucking babe on the bayonets. You should have seen how lovers were torn asunder with sabre strokes, and old graybeards stood still in their despair, and at last threw their very crutches after the young fellows who were starting for the New World. Oh! and through it all, the noisy rolling of the drums, so that the Almighty might not hear us pray!

"*Lady.* Be quiet, poor old man! They will come back. They will see their home again.

"*Chamberlain.* Heaven knows it! So they will! Even at the city gates they turned and cried, 'God help you, wife and children! Long live our father the duke! We shall be back for *the Day of Judgment!*'"

CHAPTER III.

THE TREATIES BEFORE PARLIAMENT.

THE aggressive or apologetic tone of the ministers of German despots was of little importance, when once the course of their masters had been determined on. The impassioned protest of a young German poet or of a French pamphleteer could hardly be reckoned among political forces. The King of Prussia, whose word might have been law in the matter of letting-out German soldiers for foreign service, preferred to sneer rather than to command. But in the Parliament of Great Britain the treaties between the King of England and the mercenary princes were discussed by responsible ministers of the crown on the one side, and by statesmen, some of whom might one day be called to power, on the other. It is true that the majority which supported the administration was so overwhelming that the opposition could not hope soon to overthrow it. But there can be little doubt that if the greater number of votes in Parliament was in 1776 on the Tory side, the weight of intellect was as decidedly with the Whigs.

On February 29, 1776, *Lord North* moved that the treaties entered into between His Majesty and the Landgrave of Hesse-Cassel, the Duke of Brunswick, and the hereditary Prince of Hesse-Cassel, be referred to the Committee of Supply.* He said that the troops were wanted as the best and most speedy means of reducing America to a proper constitutional state of obedience, because men could be readier had and upon much cheaper terms in this way than they could possibly be recruited at home; that the troops hired would cost less than could have been expected, referring to former times and taking all the circumstances together; and, lastly, that the force which this measure would enable them to send to America would be such as, in all human probability, must compel that country to agree to terms of submission, perhaps without further effusion of blood.

Lord North was supported by *Mr. Cornwall*, who assured the House that he had a better opportunity of knowing the means of treating with German princes and procuring troops than any man in it; that his situation for many years (as clerk in the German pay office during the last war) gave him this opportunity; and that he was astonished to hear any gentleman conversant with German connections call the present terms disadvantageous. He contended that the two months' previous pay allowed to the Duke of Brunswick was no more than a douceur; and insisted that the troops were all had on better terms than was ever known before, especially if the business should be effected within the year, of which he had no reason to doubt.

Lord George Germaine defended the measure on the ground of necessity. He quoted a number of precedents to show that in every war, or rebellion, England had had recourse to foreigners to fight her battles

* "Parliamentary Register," 1st series, vol. iii. pp. 341–360.

and to support her government; and *Lord Barrington*, who is known in his heart to have disapproved of the general conduct of the administration, and to have been in vain urging the king to accept his resignation, supported the motion on similar grounds. Recruits could be obtained on no other terms. He confessed that the bargain was not advantageous, but it was the best that could be made.

On the other side, *Lord John Cavendish* reprobated the measure in all its parts. Britain was to be disgraced in the eyes of all Europe. He objected to the terms of the treaties, particular by particular, and pointed out that a body of twelve thousand foreigners was to be introduced into the dominions of the British crown, under no control of either king or parliament; for the express terms of the treaty were "that this body of troops shall remain under the orders of the general to whom his Most Serene Highness [the Landgrave] shall have intrusted the command."

Lord Irnham doubted the competency of the princes to make such treaties. He held it inconsistent with their duty to the Empire, which must thereby be rendered vile and dishonorable in the eyes of all Europe, as a nursery of men reserved for the purpose of supporting arbitrary power, whenever grasped by those who had more money, though not more justice and virtue, than the others whom they could pay for oppressing. He compared the princes to Sancho Panza, who wished that if he were a prince all his subjects should be blackamoors, as he could by the sale of them easily turn them into ready money.

Mr. Seymour answered Mr. Cornwall, and defied him

to produce a single instance in which the same number of men, within the same time, had cost the nation so much.

The *Hon. James Luttrell* pointed out that there were already a hundred and fifty thousand Germans settled in America, and that the hired troops were likely to desert. *Edmund Burke* stated that for every thousand foreigners they were paying as much as for fifteen hundred natives. *Sir George Saville* insisted that this was the worst bargain of the kind ever made since the hiring of foreign troops had prevailed; and *Alderman Bull* closed the debate. "Let not the historian be obliged to say," he exclaimed, "that the Russian and the German slave was hired to subdue the sons of Englishmen and of freedom; and that in the reign of a prince of the House of Brunswick, every infamous attempt was made to extinguish the spirit which brought his ancestors to the throne, and in spite of treachery and rebellion seated them firmly upon it." The alderman's sentiments were better than his rhetoric, but both were equally unavailing. The motion was passed by two hundred and forty-two votes to eighty-eight.

On March 5, 1776, the Duke of Richmond moved in the House of Lords that a humble address be presented to his Majesty, praying that he would be graciously pleased to countermand the march of the foreign troops, and to give directions for an immediate suspension of hostilities in America.* The protest expressed the sense which the House entertained of the danger and disgrace of the treaties, which acknowl-

* "Parliamentary Register," 1st series, vol. v. pp. 174–216.

edged to all Europe that Great Britain was unable, either from want of men, or disinclination to this service, to furnish a competent number of natural-born subjects to make the first campaign. It was a melancholy consideration that the drawing off the national troops (though feeble for the unhappy purpose on which they were employed) would yet leave Great Britain naked and exposed to the assaults and invasion of powerful neighboring and foreign nations.

The document then pointed out that a reconciliation with the colonies would be preferable to the employment of foreigners, who, when they were at so great a distance from their own country, and suffering under the distresses of a war wherein they had no concern, with so many temptations to exchange vassalage for freedom, would be more likely to mutiny or desert than to unite faithfully and co-operate with his Majesty's natural-born subjects.

After showing the danger of foreign troops being brought into the realm, and complaining that they had already been introduced into two of the strongest fortresses,* the protest continues: "We have, moreover, just reason to apprehend that when the colonies come to understand that Great Britain is forming alliances, and hiring foreign troops for their destruction, they may think they are well justified by the example, in endeavoring to avail themselves of the like assistance; and that France, Spain, Prussia, or other powers of Europe may conceive that they have as good a right as Hesse, Brunswick, and Hanau to interfere in our domestic quarrels."

* Hanoverian troops had been sent to Gibraltar and Port Mahon.

The danger of being obliged to defend the Landgrave of Hesse in his quarrels in Europe was then pointed out, and the opinion was expressed "that Great Britain never before entered into a treaty so expensive, so unequal, so dishonorable, and so dangerous in its consequences."

In introducing the protest, the *Duke of Richmond* gave a short history of the several treaties entered into, since 1702, with the Landgraves of Hesse, and showed that the successive landgraves, from time to time, rose in their demands; and still, as they continued to extort better terms, never failed to establish their former extortion as a precedent for the basis of the new succeeding treaty, always taking care to make some new demand on Great Britain. This treaty was "a downright, mercenary bargain, for the taking into pay of a certain number of hirelings, who were bought and sold like so many beasts for slaughter. . . . But taking it on the other ground, that the treaties were formed on the basis of an alliance, what would be the consequence? That if any of these powers were attacked, or should wantonly provoke an attack, for the engagement was left general and unconditional, we should give them all the succor in our power. Thus, for the assistance of a few thousand foreign mercenaries, we are not only to pay double, but we are to enter into a solemn engagement to exert our whole force to give them all the succor in our power, if the Landgrave or the Duke shall be attacked or disturbed in the possession of his dominions."

The Duke of Richmond further remarked on the danger of keeping a body of twelve thousand foreigners together under the command of one of their own generals, on the possibility of such a general arriving at the supreme command, and on the confusion which might be created by a difference on this head between the foreign general and the commander-in-chief.

The *Earl of Suffolk* answered in behalf of the administration. "The tenor of the treaties themselves," he said, "is no other than has been usual on former occasions. The present, it is true, is filled with pompous, high-sounding phrases of alliance, but I will be so ingenuous as to confess to the noble duke that I consider them merely in that light; and if he will, I allow that the true object of those treaties is not so much to create an alliance as to hire a body of troops, which the present rebellion in America has rendered necessary."

Having thus made light of the terms of a treaty for which he was personally responsible, Lord Suffolk proceeded to point out that the conditions of that treaty were advantageous if the employment of the troops should only last one year, but that in any case, if they wanted the soldiers, they were obliged to acquiesce in the terms demanded. He expressed his belief that the commander-in-chief superseded all other generals, and on being pressed he asserted positively that such was the case.

The *Earl of Carlisle* was persuaded that the number of hands required to carry on manufactures, the little use of new levies, at least for the first campaign, and the desire that every friend of his country ought to have for putting a speedy termination to the unhappy troubles, united, created an evident necessity for the employment of foreigners in preference to native troops. He called on their lordships to consider the unwieldy bulk of the empire, and the operations necessary even in case of a defensive war, and asked if it were possible for such an inconsiderable spot as the island of Great Britain, in the nature of things, to furnish numbers sufficient to carry on operations the nature of such a service would necessarily demand.

The debate was continued at great length and with considerable violence. On the Whig side the *Duke of Cumberland* lamented "to see Brunswickers who once, to their great honor, were employed in the defence of the liberties of the subject, now sent to subjugate his constitutional liberties in another part of this vast empire." The *Duke of Manchester* pointed out that "that man must be deemed a mercenary soldier who fights for pay in the cause in which he has no concern." The *Earl of Effingham* suggested that by a decree of the Imperial Chamber the directors of the circle might be ordered to march into the Landgrave's country to compel him to some act of justice or retribution; in which case England would be obliged to excuse her breach of the treaty by her ministers' ignorance of the imperial constitutions, or else to enter into a war, like that in America, not to maintain, but to subvert, the liberties of the Germanic body. The *Earl of Shelburne* denied the necessity of employing foreigners, and was supported in this by *Lord Camden*, who also appealed to their lordships, if the whole transaction were not a compound of the most solemn mockery, fallacy, and gross imposition that was ever attempted to be put upon a House of Parliament. "Is there one of your lordships," he asked, "that does not perceive most clearly that the whole is a mere mercenary bargain for the hire of troops on one side, and for the sale of human blood on the other; and that the devoted wretches thus purchased for slaughter are mere mercenaries in the worst sense of the word?"

The Tory lords would seem to have done less than their share of the talking, perhaps, because it was unnecessary for them to speak, sure as they were of a majority. The motion was lost by thirty-two votes to one hundred.

It seems to me that their lordships were a little hard upon the German soldiers. Most of these poor fellows did not fight for pay at all, but fought because they could not help it. The people who were really "mercenaries in the worst sense of the word" were the Landgrave, the Duke, and the princes; but perhaps the noble lords could hardly be expected to say so.

As to the conduct of the British ministry in hiring the troops, it would seem that if the war were to be carried on energetically, no other course was possible. Owing to the distrust of regular soldiers that still lingered in English minds, the British army had not been maintained during peace of a strength equal to the demands now made upon it. Enlistments were made with difficulty, and could at best bring in but raw recruits. Conscription seems always to be out of the question in England. If men must be had, Lord North must seek them in Germany.

But the ministry and the empire paid a terrible price for the German auxiliaries. The answer to the treaty with the Landgrave was the Declaration of Independence. The employment of foreign mercenaries by the British government was largely instrumental in persuading the Americans to throw off their allegiance to the English crown, and to seek the alliance of their former enemies. The danger pointed out in the protest of the lords became a reality, and men of English blood held that France had as good a right as Hesse to interfere in their domestic quarrels.*

* See Leckey's "History of England in the Eighteenth Century," vol. iii. pp. 453 et seq. See also a clause in the Declaration of Independence (given in Appendix C).

CHAPTER IV.

THE SOLDIERS.

THE soldiers whom the German princes let out to England for the suppression of the American rebellion were brought together in various ways. In Hesse-Cassel the country had been cut up into districts, each of which was to furnish a given number of recruits to a certain regiment. Officers were, however, instructed to bring as many foreigners as possible into the service, in order to spare their own districts, whose inhabitants would always be at hand, to be called in case of need. It was announced in the army regulations that regimental chiefs, or captains, would best recommend themselves to favor, by striving to enlist foreign recruits.* Forcible recruiting was forbidden; but this rule was probably intended to apply only to natives. It certainly does not seem to have diminished the activity of the recruiting officers, and probably no such rule existed in the smaller states. In Anspach no subject could leave the country, or marry, without permission.† It is to be noted that in this case the country did not mean Germany, but the territories of the Margrave, and that the foreigners whom the Landgrave of Hesse wished to see recruited were the sub-

* Reglement von der Infanterie. Cassel, 1767. Theil ii. tit. v. art. 6.

† "Geschichte von Anspach," Fischer, 1786.

jects of the neighboring German princelings. Recruiting officers were active all over Germany. Spendthrifts, loose livers, drunkards, arguers, restless people, and such as made political trouble, if not more than sixty years old and of fair health and stature, were forced into the ranks. The present of a tall, strapping fellow was at that time an acceptable compliment from one prince to another, and in every regiment were many deserters from the service of neighboring states. Together with this mixed rabble served the honest peasant lads of Germany, forced from their ploughs. It may be noted, as a general rule, that the regiments sent to America in 1776 were made up of better material than were the bodies of recruits subsequently furnished.*

Johann Gottfried Seume, who afterwards attained some prominence as a writer, was a victim of the recruiting system, and has given an account of his adventures. Seume was a theological student at Leipsic, and having conceived religious doubts which he knew would be offensive to his friends, left that city on foot for Paris, with a sword at his side, a few shirts and a few volumes of the classics in his knapsack, and about nine thalers in his pocket. His journey, however, was destined to take a different direction. "The third night I spent at Bach," writes he, "and here the Landgrave of Cassel, the great broker of men of the time, undertook through his recruiting officers, and in spite of my protestations, the care of my future quar-

* In the autumn of 1777 Knyphausen complains to the Landgrave that since the new recruits have joined the army, pilfering within the regiments and plundering outside of them can hardly be restrained.

ters on the road to Ziegenhayn, to Cassel, and thence to the New World." *

"I was brought under arrest to Ziegenhayn, where I found many companions in misfortune from all parts of the country. There we waited to be sent to America in the spring, after Faucitt should have inspected us. I gave myself up to my fate, and tried to make the best of it, bad as it might be. We stayed a long time at Ziegenhayn † before the necessary number of recruits was brought together from the plough, the highways, and the recruiting stations. The story of those times is well known. No one was safe from the grip of the seller of souls. Persuasion, cunning, deception, force—all served. No one asked what means were used to the damnable end. Strangers of all kinds were arrested, imprisoned, sent off. They tore up my academic matriculation papers, as being the only instrument by which I could prove my identity. At last I fretted no more. One can live anywhere. You can stand what so many do. The idea of crossing the ocean was inviting enough to a young fellow; and there were things worth seeing on the other side. So I reflected. While we were at Ziegenhayn old General Gore ‡ employed me in writing, and treated me very kindly. Here was an indescribable lot of human beings brought together, good and bad, and others that were both by turns. My comrades were a runaway son of the Muses from Jena, a bankrupt trades-

---

* "Autobiography."

† Ziegenhayn was an unhealthy place, where most of the men fell sick, of scurvy or itch. Seume's article in *Archenholtz's Magazine*, 1789.

‡ Von Gohr.

man from Vienna, a fringemaker from Hanover, a discharged secretary of the post-office from Gotha, a monk from Würzburg, an upper steward from Meinungen, a Prussian sergeant of hussars, a cashiered Hessian major from the fortress itself, and others of like stamp. You can imagine that there was entertainment enough, and a mere sketch of the lives of these gentry would make amusing and instructive reading."

A plot was gotten up among this rabble. Seume was offered the command of the conspirators, but, by the advice of an old sergeant, declined the dangerous honor. The mutineers were to rise in the night, surprise the guard and take their weapons, cut down such as opposed them, spike the cannon, lock up the officers at headquarters, and march fifteen hundred strong across the frontier, which was only a few miles away. The plot was betrayed; the ringleaders were arrested, Seume among them. He was soon released, however, for too many were implicated to allow the punishment of all concerned. "The trial went on," he says; "two were condemned to the gallows, as I should certainly have been, had not the old Prussian sergeant-major saved me. The remainder had to run the gantlet a great many times, from thirty-six down to twelve. It was a terrible butchery. The candidates for the gallows were pardoned, after suffering the fear of death under that instrument, but had to run the gantlet thirty-six times, and were sent to Cassel to be kept in irons at the mercy of the prince. 'For an indefinite time,' and 'at mercy' were then equivalent expressions, and meant 'forever, without release.' At least, the mercy of the prince was an affair that no one wanted to have anything to do with. More than thirty were terribly treated in this way, and many, of whom I was one, were let off only because too many of the accomplices would have had to be punished. Some came out of prison when we marched away, for reasons which were easy to understand; for a fellow that is in irons at Cassel is not paid for by the British."*

With troops collected as these were, desertion was necessarily common. The military service was dreaded, and in the smaller states a successful run of a few miles would take the deserter beyond the frontier. The people sympathized with him, and would gladly have helped him had they not been restrained by severe punishments. These, however, were not wanting. In Würtemberg, when the alarm was given, the parish must instantly rise and occupy roads, paths, and bridges for twenty-four hours, or until the fugitive was caught. Should he escape, the place must furnish a substitute as tall as the deserter, and the sons of the principal man of the village were first liable. This order was to be read every month from the pulpit. Whoever helped a deserter lost his civil rights, and was imprisoned with hard labor and flogged in prison. The laws of Hesse-Cassel appear to have been a little less savage. Peasants arresting a deserter received a ducat; but if the fugitive passed through a village without being arrested, the village was liable to pay for him. Every soldier going more than a mile from his garrison was to be furnished with a pass, and all persons meeting him at a greater distance from home were required to de-

* Autobiography.

mand it.* A characteristic incident occurred in 1738. A Prussian recruiting officer and a Prussian soldier's wife induced an Anspach soldier to desert for the sake of re-enlisting in the Prussian army. They were intercepted by the Anspach authorities. The woman was hanged; the officer was obliged to be present at the execution and was then locked up in a fortress. The deserter seems to have escaped with his life, being a valuable merchantable commodity.†

Having enlisted his recruits, perhaps under a foreign jurisdiction, the officer, or under-officer, was obliged to get them to his garrison. This would afford, of course, opportunities for escape; and Kapp quotes, from a book printed in Berlin as late as 1805, the precautions to be taken against this danger. The under-officer who is escorting a recruit must wear sword and pistol. He must make the recruit walk in front of him, never let him come too near, and warn him that a single false step may cost him his life. He must avoid large towns, and places where the recruit has previously served, as much as possible. It is also desirable to avoid the place where the recruit was born. They must spend the night at inns where the landlord is known to be well-disposed to recruiting officers, and sure to side with them, and not with their victim. The recruit and the officer must both undress, and their clothes be given to the landlord for safe keeping. Inns where recruits are to spend the night must have a separate room for the purpose; if possible, up-stairs, and with barred windows. A light must be kept burning all

* Reglement von der Infanterie, Theil ii. tit. vi.

† Lang, "Geschichte des vorletzten Markgrafen," p. 92.

night, and the under-officer must give up his weapons to the landlord, lest the recruit should get them away from him and use them against him in the night. In the morning he must get them back, see to the loading and priming, dress himself, and be ready for his journey before the clothes of the recruit are brought to him. The recruit must enter a house, or a room, first; he must come out last. At meals he must sit behind the table, next the wall. If he shows signs of being troublesome, the straps and buttons must be cut from his breeches, and he must hold them up with his hands.

A good dog, trained to the business, will be very useful to an under-officer under such circumstances. If an under-officer is unfortunately obliged to kill or wound a recruit he must bring a paper from the local magistrate. But no document will excuse the escape of a recruit, an accident which the Prussian military imagination refuses to consider ever necessary.

The men collected to serve in America were of various qualities from a military point of view. They were all received and examined by an English commissioner, generally by Colonel Faucitt, who had negotiated the treaties, at the seaports before shipment, and while some of the regiments were pronounced excellent, others were found to be partly made up of old men and boys, unfit to endure the fatigues of a campaign. Some soldiers were rejected for these causes, especially in the latter years of the war, when good men were growing harder to get in many of the states.

It is not easy, from the documents before me, to judge what chance a private soldier had of promotion from the ranks. Seume writes that he himself had hopes of promotion, which were shattered by the ending of the war, as in time of peace no one who was not noble could aspire to be anything more than a sergeant-major. Kapp speaks of the officers as belonging mostly to the lower nobility. The list of Hessian officers in 1779 does not bear out these statements. It appears that at that time more than one half of the officers were not noble, nobility being judged by the presence, or absence, of the mystic particle *von*.

We come at last to the character of the officers. Their education was generally confined to a limited amount of writing and a little barbarous French. They understood neither the cause for which the Americans were fighting, nor, at first, the language in which the statesmen of both contending parties argued their different claims. But had they understood far more than they did, their feelings would still have been on the side of royal prerogative against popular rights. I can recall no instance in which one of the German officers engaged in this war uses any expression showing him to have been in sympathy with the liberal intellectual movement of the eighteenth century. This conservatism was not necessary to make them go where they were ordered, nor did it prevent some of them from heartily wishing themselves at home again after a campaign or two in America. Once there, we find them talking about the despotism of Congress. This absurd idea was probably suggested to them by the English, and was taken up by the anti-American press in Germany. There is little doubt, too, that many, both of the officers and soldiers, looked forward with pleasure to active employment in America, if only to break up the monotony of garrison duty.

In spite of the injustice with which the rank and file had been treated, there are signs that many of these involuntary volunteers were not such bad fellows after all. The Germans have their fair share of those virtues which every nation is fond of claiming as its peculiar birthright; honesty, courage, kindliness. The motley mass had been shaped and welded by a rigorous, if often cruel discipline. They could not wipe out, to American eyes, the shame of their mercenary calling. But the shame fairly belonged to their princes, and not to themselves. In the field, or in captivity, they often deserved and sometimes obtained the respect of their opponents. Many of them became, in the end, citizens of the republic they were sent to destroy.

CHAPTER V.

FROM GERMANY TO AMERICA.

THE first German troops to start for America were the Brunswickers. These marched from Brunswick on February 22d, 1776, two thousand two hundred and eighty-two strong, and were embarked at Stade, near the mouth of the Elbe. The second division of Brunswickers embarked at the end of May — about two thousand men. The first Hessians set out from Cassel early in March, and were shipped at Bremerlehe, near the mouth of the Weser. The second division was embarked in June. Together they numbered between twelve and thirteen thousand men. They were for the most part excellent troops and well equipped, for the Landgrave's little army was one of the best in Germany.

The march from Brunswick or Cassel to the port of embarkation was a comparatively simple matter. The troops passed from the territory of their own prince into the Hanoverian dominions of the King of England, and these reached to the sea. The Prince of Waldeck sent his regiment through Cassel without trouble. The Prince of Hesse-Hanau, the Margrave of Anspach-Bayreuth, and the Prince of Anhalt-Zerbst had a longer road and more difficulties before them.

The town of Hanau lies above Frankfort, on the river Main, about thirty miles from Mainz, where that river falls into the Rhine. The district of which Hanau was the capital was at this time governed by the heir-apparent of the Landgrave of Hesse-Cassel, as an independent county. The prince was not on good terms with his father, and was unwilling to send his troops through the territories of the latter, for fear of desertion. The soldiers were therefore shipped on boats and sent down the Rhine. The three spiritual electorates, the lands of the Elector of the Phalz, the free city of Cologne, and other less important districts bordered on that stretch of the river which the modern tourist passes in his steamboat between breakfast and dinner-time. Any one of the little states might make trouble if its permission for the passage of troops were not obtained, and after running the gantlet of them all, there was danger of still more serious hinderance when the flotilla came to Rhenish Prussia. Difficulties had already arisen between the local authorities and the English recruiting officers, and although the first regiment from Hanau, in the spring of 1776, was allowed to pass unmolested, trouble was brewing.

A detachment of chasseurs and recruits started from Hanau on March 7th, 1777. On the 8th the boats were stopped at Mainz, and eight men were taken from them. The archbishop claimed these either as his own subjects or as deserters from his service. The English government refused to interfere, and the complaints of the Prince of Hanau were unheeded. On March 25th, at S'Gravendael, in Holland, seven men sprang overboard, and three of them escaped, with the help of sympathizing peasants.

Meanwhile, two regiments of Anspach and Bayreuth, with one hundred and one chasseurs and forty-four artillerymen,* had marched from Anspach on March 7th, 1777, and were embarked at Ochsenfurth, a pretty little walled town lying on the Main about a hundred miles above Hanau, and belonging at that time to the Bishop of Würzburg. The men were embarked towards evening, and their boats remained at anchor through the night. The poor country lads were unused to their crowded quarters, shivering with cold, and sickened by the smell of the boats, in which, in their simplicity, they thought they were to sail to America. Their grumbling grew at last into a mutiny, a poor, helpless mutiny, without a plan, without a leader. At daybreak some of the soldiers of the Anspach regiment, whose boat lay near the bank, laid a plank to the shore and walked over it. They then dragged other boats to land, and in an hour the miserable crowd of cold and hungry men was on shore, storming with anger and refusing to yield to the threats and promises of its officers. These acted prudently. They sent for food and wood to warm and feed the starving mutineers. Unfortunately the inhabitants of Ochsenfurth brought drink as well. The insubordination increased. The soldiers began to wander away; but the chasseurs still obeyed orders. They were posted on the surrounding hills and told to fire at deserters, "to frighten them." The rioters returned the fire. Several men were wounded. The burghers of Ochsenfurth shut their gates and drew up their drawbridges to keep themselves out of harm's way. Towards evening the soldiers began to get sober again,

* In all twelve hundred and eighty-five men.

and were finally brought back into their ranks, some scores of them having succeeded in escaping. The Bishop of Würzburg sent hussars and dragoons to help quell the riot. He was afterwards officially thanked by the English government.

Meanwhile an express had been sent to warn the Margrave at Anspach. The Margrave was startled. Here were twelve hundred men, with eighteen thousand good English pounds, and next winter's little journey to Paris, all in danger of making off at once. His Most Serene Highness threw himself into the saddle, forgetting his watch and neglecting his carpet-bag; (he had afterwards to borrow some clean shirts of his princely neighbor of Hanau). He rode quickly through the night, and early morning found him at Ochsenfurth. The regiments were drawn up and the Margrave passed from man to man. He inquired into their grievances, and promised forgiveness to all who would go to America. He announced that any man might then and there leave the service, forfeiting his home, all his property, and the princely favor. No one stirred. The soldiers were re-embarked and taken down the Main. The Margrave accompanied them. The story that he sat in one of the boats, with a cocked rifle, ready for future deserters, seems to want authority.

The flotilla arrived at Mainz. About thirty officers and men had been sent by the Bishop-Elector to visit it and take off deserters. They were recalled, however, on account of the presence of the Margrave, and of the two Hessian princes who were with him. The Elector prepared a grand dinner for these distinguished guests, but they did not venture to accept it, and only sent an officer to demand that the bridge should be opened, threatening to blow it up in case of refusal. The bridge was opened in the night, without the formal consent of the Elector, and the boats went on their way. From this point, the voyage down the Rhine was unhindered, and the troops were mustered into the English service in Holland. Each regiment received a present of 100 ducats from the Margrave, and extra rations during the journey.

The Margrave had accomplished his purpose and could return with a light heart to Anspach. He set out for Paris on the 16th of October following, with his good friend Lady Craven, having arranged that a new body of about three hundred recruits and chasseurs should start down stream at the end of the month, taking with them uniforms for his regiments. He had taken the trouble to write to his uncle, the great Frederick of Prussia, asking that the passage of these troops might be permitted; but he looked on this request as a mere formality, and travelled off without waiting for an answer.* He was destined to be disappointed. His ministers at Anspach received and opened in due time the following letter, written, as was usual with diplomatic correspondence, in the French language:

"Potsdam, this 24th October, 1777.

"MONSIEUR MY NEPHEW!—I own to your Most Serene Highness that I never think of the present war in America without being struck

* Elliot, the English Ambassador at Berlin, had sent a like request, which also was refused. Elliot states in a letter to Suffolk that the German princes had felt obliged to ask the permission of the court of Berlin before letting out their soldiers to Great Britain, and that they had obtained this permission. Kapp, "Friedrich der Grosse und die Vereinigten Staaten," pp. 63–65.

with the eagerness of some German princes to sacrifice their troops in a quarrel which does not concern them. My astonishment increases when I remember in ancient history the wise and general aversion of our ancestors to wasting German blood for the defence of foreign rights, which even became a law in the German state.

"But I perceive that my patriotism is running away with me; and I return to your Most Serene Highness's letter of the 14th, which excited it so strongly. You ask for free passage for the recruits and baggage which you wish to send to the corps of your troops in the service of Great Britain, and I take the liberty of observing that if you wish them to go to England, they will not even have to pass through my states, and that you can send them a shorter way to be embarked. I submit this idea to the judgment of your Most Serene Highness, and am none the less, with all the tenderness I owe you, Monsieur my Nephew, your Most Serene Highness's good uncle, FRÉDÉRIC."

The ministers were perplexed. They thought it too late to keep back the troops, and hoped to gain their end by negotiation. In this they did not succeed. The soldiers were stopped on their passage down the Rhine, and after spending a month in their boats, lying, for the most part, off the little town of Bendorf, which belonged to the Margrave of Anspach, were finally brought back to winter at Hanau. Their sufferings while crowded on board the boats in the months of November and December, and only allowed occasional exercise on shore, must have been great; but there were but few desertions, for a cordon of troops lined the bank to prevent them. About two hundred and fifty recruits from Hanau lay alongside of the Anspachers, similarly detained, and these suffered much from fever. The whole party of five hundred and thirty-four men marched in February and March, 1778, overland to the coast, and was shipped in April for England and America. The passage was a long one, and these men, who had left Anspach early in November, 1777, were not landed in New York until September, 1778.

The sudden refusal of Frederick the Great to allow the passage of troops told most of all on the Zerbst regiment. In order to pass round the Prussian dominions, this body was obliged to march through seven different states and free cities. The result was disastrous. In the village of Zeulenrode a deserter chased by a corporal sought refuge in an inn. The corporal, in his anger and excitement, shot after him through the window and killed the innkeeper's wife, who was sitting quietly in the room. The peasants were enraged, and a riot shortly afterwards occurred, in which a lieutenant was mortally injured. Moreover, the Prussian recruiting officers saw their chance to pick up a few men, and once on the route there was a skirmish with them and bloodshed. Three hundred and thirty-four men deserted in the course of ten days, leaving only four hundred and ninety-four under the banners. The colonel succeeded, however, in enlisting about one hundred and thirty recruits, to take the place of the deserters, and six hundred and twenty-five men were thus shipped on April 22, 1778, at Stade. Making a quick passage, they arrived before Quebec towards the last of May; but they had not come to the end of their troubles. The commander of the place had received no orders concerning them, and would not allow them to land. For three months the poor fellows had to lie on shipboard in the St. Lawrence, before instructions could be received from England.

Frederick the Great has left in his memoirs his own account of his reasons for his conduct on this occasion.

"The King of England, who from caprice or obstinacy maintained Bute's system, stiffened himself against the obstacles which arose under his feet. With little consideration for the misfortunes which fell on his people, he became all the more ardent in the execution of his designs; and in order to obtain a superiority of force over the Americans, he had negotiations carried on with all the courts of Germany to obtain what little help they could still furnish. Germany already felt the evil consequences of sending so many of her men into those distant climes, and the King of Prussia did not like to see the Empire deprived of all its defenders, especially in case of a new war; for in the troubles of 1756, Lower Saxony and Westphalia alone had set on foot an army with which the progress of the French had been stopped and disorganized. For this reason he made difficulties about the passage of the troops of the princes allied to England when they had to pass through Magdeburg, Minden, and the district on the Lower Rhine. That was but a weak revenge for the bad attitude which the court of London had assumed towards him concerning the city and harbor of Dantzic. Nevertheless, the king did not care to push matters too far, for long experience had taught him that one always finds a host of enemies in the world, without taking the trouble to raise them wantonly against oneself."*

These troublesome measures of Frederick were but temporary, and in 1778 the business returned to its old channels. The war of the Bavarian Succession had then broken out, and Frederick was inclined to be

* "Œuvres de Frédéric le Grand," vol. vi. p. 117.

more conciliatory towards England. The whole relation of the King of Prussia to our Revolutionary War is hardly worth the attention that has been bestowed on it. It would appear that Frederick, owing to his dislike for the British, and on grounds of general policy, gave orders to his ministers to treat the American agents, Arthur and William Lee, with politeness, though he was prevented by his political judgment from according them the smallest advantage. "I propose," wrote he to his brother Henry, on June 17th, 1777, "to procrastinate in these negotiations, and to go over to the side on which fortune shall declare herself."* Seeing, however, in the autumn of 1777, a good opportunity to vent his spite against the English, to express his contempt for what he considered a disgraceful business, to diminish the drain of men from Germany, and, perhaps, to do a good turn to the Americans, with whom he sympathized as the enemies of his enemies, he adopted the measures above described. It is possible that Frederick was also influenced by a personal dislike for "Monsieur his Nephew," who had long before embraced the Austrian side in German politics.

As for the importance to America of the hinderance thus thrown in the way of the mercenary princes, it seems to me that Kapp overrates it. It may possibly have been the want of the reinforcements thus delayed and the uncertainty of obtaining more men in the future that prevented Sir William Howe from destroying Washington's army at Valley Forge, and completely stamping out the rebellion. But such a con-

* "Œuvres Frédéric le Grand," vol. xxvi. p. 393.

sequence of the delay in receiving fifteen hundred men, and of the abandonment of a scheme for obtaining a few thousands more from Würtemberg, seems to me too remote for serious consideration. Is there any reason to suppose that Sir William would have made a better use of the fifteen hundred German soldiers he expected than of the twelve or fifteen thousand he had already? The great king, as we have seen, confined himself to small annoyances. One authoritative word from him might probably have sufficed to put a stop to the whole disgraceful business.*

The march of the auxiliaries from their national headquarters to the sea can have been, at least after the first year, no cheerful or martial spectacle. The poor fellows travelled partially armed, escorted by picked men. The villages in which they slept were surrounded by a double chain of sentries.† If they went by the river Weser, a certain number of them had at most times, even when Prussia was not unusually troublesome, to march round her territory at Minden. We have seen how they were treated on the Rhine. For it was a peculiarity of these troops, that a regiment of them could hardly pass through any part

* Kapp's "Soldatenhandel," pp. 147–177; Kapp's "Friedrich der Grosse und die Vereinigten Staaten," part i. passim. Frederick subsequently encouraged the French court to enter into the American alliance, "Bancroft," vol. x. chap. iii. In January, 1778, Schulenberg, Frederick's minister, wrote to Arthur Lee that the King of Prussia would not delay to acknowledge the independence of the United States so soon as France should have done so (Kapp, "Friedrich," etc., p. 52). This promise was not fulfilled.

† MSS. of Regiment von Mirbach, in the Cassel Library.

of Germany where the authorities had not some claim on some of the soldiers.

Seume, the captive poet, has left a graphic description of his experiences on shipboard. The men were packed like herring. A tall man could not stand upright between decks, nor sit up straight in his berth. To every such berth six men were allotted, but as there was room for only four, the last two had to squeeze in as best they might. "This was not cool in warm weather," says Seume. Thus the men lay in what boys call "spoon fashion," and when they were tired on one side, the man on the right would call "about face," and the whole file would turn over at once; then, when they were tired again, the man on the left would give the same order, and they would turn back on to the first side. The food was on a par with the lodging. Pork and pease were the chief of their diet. The pork seemed to be four or five years old. It was streaked with black towards the outside, and was yellow farther in, with a little white in the middle. The salt beef was in much the same condition. The ship biscuit was often full of maggots. "We had to eat them for a relish," says Seume, "not to reduce our slender rations too much." This biscuit was so hard that they sometimes broke it up with a cannon-ball, and the story ran that it had been taken from the French in the Seven Years' War, and lain in Portsmouth ever since. The English had kept it twenty years or so, and "were now feeding the Germans with it, that these might, if it were God's will, destroy Rochambeau and Lafayette. It does not seem to have been God's will, exactly." Sometimes they had groats and barley, or, by way of a treat, a pudding made of flour mixed half with salt water and half with fresh water, and with old, old mutton fat. The water was all spoiled. When a cask was opened "it stank between decks like Styx, Phlegethon, and Cocytus all together." It was thick with filaments as long as your finger, and they had to filter it through a cloth before the could drink it. They held their noses while they drank, and yet it was so scarce that they fought to get it. Rum, and sometimes a little strong beer, completed their fare.

Thus crowded together, with close air, bad food, and foul water, many of them insufficiently clothed, these boys and old men, students, shopkeepers, and peasants tossed for months on the Atlantic. Much of the suffering of the voyage was doubtless inevitable, and many of the recruits were already inured to hardship. But much of what they underwent was the result of wanton carelessness or grasping avarice. What shall we say of the British Quartermaster's Department, which sent these men to sea without proper food or drink? What of the Duke of Brunswick, who despatched his subjects to Canada without shoes and stockings that would hold together, and without overcoats? Men have often borne such hardships cheerfully for a cause that they understood and loved. But these poor fellows suffered in a quarrel that was not their own, and simply to provide means to pay the debts, or minister to the pleasures of their masters. It is well for us to know something of their sufferings; to know what despotism means.

CHAPTER VI.

THE BATTLE OF LONG ISLAND, AUGUST, 1776.

THE first division of Hessians, some eight thousand strong, passed Sandy Hook on August 15, 1776, and landed at Staten Island amid salvoes of artillery and musketry. The division was under the command of Lieutenant-general Philip von Heister, a tough old soldier of the Seven Years' War. It is related that when Landgrave Frederick II. called him to command the Hessian expeditionary force, he did so in these terms: "Heister, you must go along to America." "Very well, your Most Serene Highness, but I take the liberty of making a few requests." "And what may they be?" "First, my debts must be paid, my wife and children must be taken care of until I come back, and if I should fall, my wife must have a pension." When the Landgrave had smilingly assented, Heister cried out: "Now your Serene Highness shall see what this old head and these bones can do."

The army collected on Staten Island under the command of Sir William Howe numbered, after the arrival of the Hessians, between twenty-five and thirty thousand soldiers. It was supported by a fleet under Sir William's brother, Lord Howe. The opposing army of Washington was composed of some thirteen or fourteen thousand men, not more than six thousand of whom had any military experience, and whose officers were taken from civil life.

The Hessians were much struck with the appearance of wealth and plenty which they found on Staten Island. The colonists lived in comfortable houses surrounded by gardens and orchards. Their light red wagons drawn by two small horses excited the wonder of the Germans. A colonist on Staten Island lived as comfortably as a German country gentleman, and it seemed extraordinary to the Hessians that people should revolt against a government under which they enjoyed so many blessings. Many of the Americans had fled from their homes on the approach of the Hessians, and those who remained were at first inclined to be surly when troops were quartered upon them; but when they saw that strict discipline was enforced, and that only regular requisitions were made, the fugitives returned, and relations of tolerance, if not of cordiality, were soon established. The British government still hoped to reconcile the colonists to the rule of the mother country, and strict orders had been given to prevent all excesses.

No sooner did Sir William Howe find his army collected than he prepared to attack the Americans. The British advanced guard, under Sir Henry Clinton, with the Hessian chasseurs and grenadiers, commanded by Colonel von Donop, crossed the Narrows to Long Island on August 22, 1776. A diary, published in a magazine at Frankfort-on-the-Main in the following year, gives a graphic account of this operation and of those that followed:

"*August* 22.—We weighed anchor and lay close

over against Long Island. The ships of war came within range of the shore and pointed their cannon at the beach. At eight in the morning the whole coast swarmed with boats. At half-past eight the admiral hoisted the red flag, and in a moment all the boats reached the shore. The English and Scotch, with the artillery, were first disembarked, and then the brigade of Colonel von Donop (the only Hessians there). Not a soul opposed our landing. This was the second blunder of the rebels since I have been in America. Their first mistake was when we disembarked on Staten Island, for they might then have destroyed a good many of our people with two six-pounders, and now they might have made it very nasty for us. We marched on, equally undisturbed, through Gravesend, and reached Flatbush towards evening. Three hundred riflemen had been there a little while before us. We sent a few cannon shots after them, set out our pickets, and slept quietly all night. I got two horses as booty, one of which I sent to the colonel and gave the other to my St. Martin for a pack-horse.

"*August* 23.—This morning early we were attacked on the right wing of the advanced guard. We brought up a cannon and drove them back. It rained bullets. Captain Congreve and one Constable were wounded by my side, and an Englishman was shot through. In the afternoon they attacked on the left side of the village and set fire to several houses, and we drew back into the village. Lieutenant von Donop, who stood on the left wing, was wounded in the breast; the ball glanced from his rib. I advanced on the right wing, where I occupied a big garden, with one hundred and fifty men, chasseurs and light infantry. As the enemy had fallen back from here, I relieved Lieutenant von Donop. The rebels were placing cannon on the highway, and our Scotch Highlanders had to make a battery across the road, with embrasures for two cannon. I had to cover the work, and so came to the advanced posts, where, however, I was little disturbed.

"*August* 24.—A hot day. The rebels approached twice, fired howitzers and used grape and ball, so that all our artillery had to come up. At noon I slept a little while, and was waked by two cannon-balls which covered me with earth. The rebels have some very good marksmen, but some of them have wretched guns, and most of them shoot crooked. But they are clever at hunters' wiles. They climb trees, they crawl forward on their bellies for one hundred and fifty paces, shoot, and go as quickly back again. They make themselves shelters of boughs, etc. But to-day they are much put out by our green coats,* for we don't let our fellows fire unless they can get good aim at a man, so that they dare not undertake anything more against us.

"*August* 25.—We barricaded ourselves in the village; and to-night our chasseurs were to take a good rest. About two o'clock the rebels roused us from our slumbers; we quickly quieted them, however, with two cannon and a few rifle-shots. To-day we were attacked again, but after several of them had bitten the dust they drew off. Long Island is a beautiful island, an Arcadia; a most delightful region, full of meadows, corn-fields, all kinds of fruit-trees and pleasantly built

* The chasseurs wore green coats with crimson trimmings.

houses. There were still a great many cattle there, although the rebels had taken many away with them. Most of the inhabitants had fled from the houses.* The rebels advanced in force. General Cornwallis wanted Colonel Donop to retire, but the colonel stayed where he was and intrenched himself.

"*August* 26.—During this day we had much trouble, and at night were continually awakened by alarms from the outposts. This was not caused by attacks of the rebels, but mostly by deserters who wanted to come to us; and when the English and the [Hessian] grenadiers heard them approach they at once fired by platoons, if they did not get an immediate answer. To-day General von Heister came over to us with six battalions.†

"*August* 27.—Our colonel had been promised that he should make the first attack, and he heard that the English were to attack to-day, but he had not received any orders either last evening or this morning. About ten o'clock we were all put under arms (the colonel having then spoken with General von Heister), and about eleven we were all in order of battle. On our left and right the English advanced on the flanks, and destroyed those that we drove back. On the left wing, where I commanded the advanced guards (thirty chasseurs and twenty grenadiers), stood Colonel Block, with his battalion. Behind me I had Captain Mallet

* For a particular description of this part of Long Island see "Schlözer's Briefwechsel," vol. ii. p. 103 et seq., by Lieutenant Hinrichs of the chasseurs.

† Of Hessians. According to Bancroft these regiments crossed on the 25th. For an account of the curious and complicated nomenclature of the Hessian regiments, and of the different regiments engaged in different battles, see Appendix A.

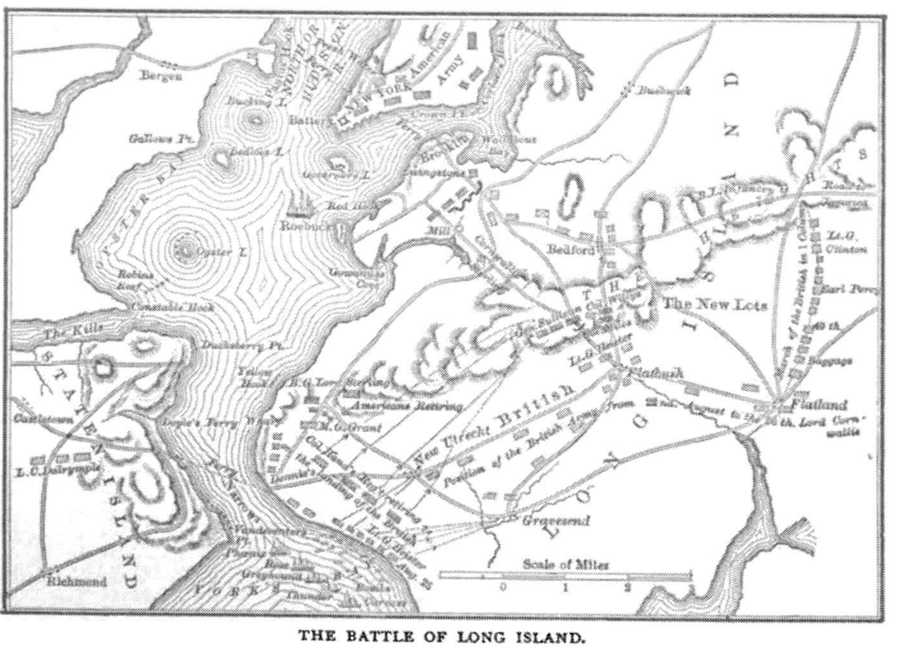

THE BATTLE OF LONG ISLAND.

with one company, as a reserve. In the centre Captain von Wrede attacked, and had the battalion von Minnigerode behind him. On the right Captain Lory pressed on, supported by the three remaining companies of Linsig's battalion" [Battalion von Linsingen].

In describing this arrangement of the troops, the writer refers only to the brigade in which he served. The Hessians, forming the centre of the British force, were posted on the Flatbush road. The right, under Clinton and Lord Percy, with Sir William Howe, had started early in the morning and succeeded in turning the left wing of the American position, near Bedford, and in getting in its rear. On hearing the cannon on his right, Heister ordered the Hessians to advance. The battle was substantially lost and won before the first shot was fired, the Americans having been outflanked. The latter saw themselves in danger of being cut off from their fortifications, and fled. A few of them were drowned in Gowanus Creek while trying to escape. Two whole regiments would probably have been captured but for the bravery of General Stirling, who selected five companies of Marylanders, with whom he covered the retreat of the rest. Of these five companies only eight men escaped death or capture. We return to our Hessian officer and his narrative.

"My chasseurs were so eager that I had hardly got into the wood when I found myself alone with my command. I came into the middle of the rebel camp, where they still were, saw on my left their great camp, on my right a fortification, and fifty or sixty men were forming in column before me. But we left them no time and beat them completely. Many were shot and still more taken prisoners. I did not lose a single man, so much had the rebels come to be afraid of the chasseurs. Things went equally well on the other wing. We lost few men, and, except one chasseur, who was shot in the village, not a single one was killed. On the other hand, we made on the first day more than five hundred prisoners, among whom were General Stirling and one other general, and Colonel Johnson was shot. General Stirling is one of the most important rebels, who, sword in hand, forced the people to fight against their king. As long as we had no horses, the prisoners were harnessed in front of the cannon, and they were afterwards sent aboard the ships of war. In two days we had taken eleven hundred men. The rebels looked ragged, and had no shirts on. Our Hessians marched like Hessians; they marched incorrigibly, and the English like the bravest and best of soldiers. They, therefore, lost more men than we. This was a lucky day for us. The rebels had a very advantageous position in the wood, and we had a very bad one in the village of Flatbush. At first they made good use of their position, burned down a house and set fire to the barns upon our outposts. But when we attacked them courageously in their hiding-places, they ran, as all mobs do."*

The editor of the Frankfort magazine, who publishes the above, remarks that many letters from Hessian officers have appeared in the newspapers; that

* "Die Neuesten Staatsbegebenheiten," 1777, Frankfurt a. M., pp. 110-116. The letter, of which the above is the largest part, would seem to have been written by an officer of chasseurs, probably either Major von Prueschenk or Lieutenant von Grothausen.

these officers ascribe a great part of the credit of the victory to themselves, and that, in view of the well-known valor of the Hessian soldiery, they undoubtedly deserve it, but that some of them make too little of the resistance and military knowledge of the Americans, "so that the honor of having gained a victory over an enemy numbering only one third as many as themselves almost suffers." The remark is certainly pertinent, and the odds do not appear to be overstated. Washington's army before the battle was occupying lines which extended from Kingsbridge to Flatbush. There were probably not more than eight thousand Americans on Long Island, while those actually engaged on the advanced lines numbered only four or five thousand, against twenty thousand Englishmen and Germans.

Sir William Howe, in his official report, sets the American loss in killed, wounded, prisoners and drowned, at three thousand three hundred men; but Bancroft believes this to be a gross exaggeration, and, relying on Washington's report and a careful inquiry, says that the total American loss did not exceed one thousand, of whom three quarters were taken prisoners. The English loss, according to Howe, was seventeen officers and three hundred and one non-commissioned officers and privates; the Hessians had two men killed, and two officers and twenty-three privates wounded.

"The enemy," writes Colonel von Heeringen, commanding a Hessian regiment, "had almost impenetrable thickets, lines, abattis, and redoubts in front of them. The riflemen were mostly spitted to the trees with bayonets. These frightful people deserve pity rather than fear. It always takes them a quarter of an hour to load, and meanwhile they feel our balls and bayonets." Among the prisoners taken by the Hessians were two generals—Sullivan and Stirling. Nothing can be more characteristic of the hatred and contempt felt at this time by the Hessian officers for the undisciplined troop of rebels to whom they were opposed, than Von Heeringen's account of these generals and of other officers of the American army. "John Sullivan was a lawyer, and previously a domestic servant, but a man of genius, whom the rebels will much regret. Among the prisoners are many so-called colonels, lieutenant-colonels, majors, and other officers, who, however, are nothing but mechanics, tailors, shoemakers, wig-makers, barbers, etc. Some of them were soundly beaten by our people, who would by no means let such persons pass for officers. Sullivan was brought to me. I had him searched and found the original orders of General Washington on him; from which it appears that he had the best troops under his command, that everything depended on his holding the wood, and that he was eight thousand men strong. The English have one hundred and fifty killed and wounded" [three hundred and eighteen, says Sir William Howe]. "This they owe more to their disorderly attack than to the valor of the enemy. It looked horrible in the wood, as at least two thousand killed and wounded lay there. Colonel John, of the rebels, is dead. A grenadier took him prisoner and generously gave him his life, only telling him to go back to the battalion which was following, for the grenadier was a skirmisher. The colonel wanted to murder him, slyly, from behind; secretly drew out a pistol, but only hit the grenadier in the arm, whereupon the latter treated him to three or four bayonet strokes."

"Among the officers taken I did not find a single one who had been in foreign service. They are nothing but rebels and citizens settled here. Tailor Graul would play a considerable part here." Colonel von Heeringen clearly considers it far more honorable to fight in other people's quarrels than in one's own. A man who had once been a mercenary could be more readily forgiven for being a rebel. "My Lord Stirling himself is only an *échappé de famille*, and does not pass for a lord in England. He looks as much like my Lord Granby as one egg does like another. General Putnam is a butcher by profession. I imagine him to be like Butcher Fischer at Rinteln. The rebels desert in great numbers, and it is nothing to see colonels, lieutenant-colonels, and majors come in with whole troops of men. The captured flag, which is made of red damask, with the motto, 'Liberty,' appeared with sixty men before Rall's regiment. They had all shouldered their guns upside down, and had their hats under their arms. They fell on their knees and begged piteously for their lives. No regiment is properly uniformed or armed. Every man has a common gun, such as the citizens in Hesse march out with at Whitsuntide. Stirling's regiment, however, was uniformed in blue and red, three battalions strong, and mostly composed of Germans recruited in Pennsylvania. They were tall, fine-looking fellows, and had extremely good English guns, with bayonets. This regiment met the English, and as the latter took them for Hessians in the bushes, they did not fire; but their error cost them Colonel Grant, several other officers, and eighty men. A volley was fired. The English gathered themselves together, attacked with the bayonet, knocked everybody head over heels, and those they did not massacre they took prisoners. In short, the whole regiment is ruined. The rebel artillery is miserable, mostly of iron, and mounted on ships' carriages."*

It is said that many times in this battle the English and Hessians did not give quarter when it was asked. Colonel von Heeringen says: "The English did not give much quarter, and constantly urged our people to do the like." The Americans are said also to have believed that the Hessians gave no quarter, and to have fought with peculiar desperation, after hope was lost, in consequence. The fact that neither side could understand the other may have tended to diminish the chance of surrender, and have contributed to swell the complaints that some of the Americans had treacherously attacked their captors after yielding. "They were," says Lieutenant Rüffer in his diary,† "so timid that they preferred to be shot rather than to take quarter, because their generals and officers had told them that they would be hanged." Surely the most curious proof of cowardice ever alleged against any soldiers whatsoever.

After the loss of so important a position, and of so many men in proportion to the numbers of his little

* Quoted in Eelking's "Hülfstruppen," vol. i. p. 37 n., from the *Preussisches Militair-Wochenblatt*, 1833, Nrs. 863, 864.

† Quoted in Eelking's "Hülfstruppen," vol. i. p. 45.

army, Washington thought it inexpedient to try to hold the works at Brooklyn, and seeing that the English fleet was preparing to occupy the East River and cut off his retreat, he abandoned Long Island on the night of August 29th–30th, and crossed over to New York, bringing off all his stores and cannon, except a few heavy pieces which stuck in the mud. A myth was current among the Hessians, to the effect that an order of Washington had been found in the deserted camp, stating that, whereas it was impossible to resist such cruel and terrible enemies as the Hessians, one must make the best of one's way off. Thus had the German troops seen their first battle in the New World. It had added to the contempt they had already felt for a rebellious and undisciplined enemy, a contempt which it was to take long years of war and of disaster wholly to eradicate.*

---

* For the Battle of Long Island, see the authorities above quoted and the MS. journals of the Grenadier Battalion von Minnigerode, the Regiment von Lossberg (Heusser), and the same regiment (Piel). For the Evacuation of Long Island, see "Washington's Writings" (Sparks's ed.), vol. iv. p. 69.

CHAPTER VII.

FROM THE OCCUPATION OF NEW YORK TO THE TAKING OF FORT WASHINGTON, SEPTEMBER 15TH TO NOVEMBER 16TH, 1776.

THERE is not much to remind the present inhabitant of New York of the little city that lay at the south end of Manhattan Island a hundred years ago. It was a pretty place, with large, comfortable houses, built mostly of yellow brick. Within were low-studded rooms, with sanded floors, and high, painted wainscots. The sideboards, of solid mahogany, in the better houses, shone with pewter for every-day use; and there was often solid silver, for state occasions. The streets were crooked and had gutters in the middle, but were fairly clean, and bordered with trees. Before the war there had been over twenty thousand inhabitants, but many of these had fled on the approach of the contending armies. There were many Tories, especially among the rich.

At the time when Washington retreated from Brooklyn, New York was defended by a permanent fort, called Fort George, at the west end of the Battery, and by temporary works thrown up at various places along the shore. On the north, or landward, side, a barrier crossed Broadway near the Bowling Green, and there was another near the site of the present Centre Market.

Beyond the fortifications lay the country, "the most beautiful," says a Hessian officer, "that I have ever seen."* Corn-fields, meadows, and orchards covered the charming land, and from the hill-tops the old colonial houses, each surrounded by its piazza and crowned with its balustrade, looked down on the smiling landscape. The Hessian lieutenant, in his enthusiasm, calls them palaces; and truly, there was a dignity in the best domestic architecture of the time that makes that name hardly inappropriate.

In spite of the anxiety of Washington and of Congress to keep possession of New York, the town was clearly indefensible. The British had complete command of the harbor, and a greatly superior force on land. Consequently, when, on the 15th of September, 1776, the royal troops landed on the island, the only care of Washington, who had for several days been removing guns and stores, was to bring off the rear-guard of his army before its retreat should be prevented by the British. The landing was effected under protection of English ships of war at a place called Kip's Bay, near East Thirty-fourth Street. My Hessian lieutenant calls it four miles from New York, but he overstates the distance. The Hessians, with the advanced guard, were, as usual, the chasseurs and grenadiers under Von Donop. These marched immediately on New York, while the English light infantry and Highlanders hastened to occupy the Incleberg, now known as Murray Hill. The Americans, meanwhile, under old Israel Putnam, were making the best of their way up the roads nearest the North River, towards Bloomingdale.

* Lieutenant Hinrichs, in Schlözer's "Briefwechsel," vol. ii. p. 108.

No opposition was made to the landing of the British. The New England militia, who should have delayed that operation, behaved very badly, drawing on themselves the violent indignation of Washington. It is said that a part of the American army would undoubtedly have been cut off in consequence of this panic, had not Mrs. Murray detained Sir William Howe by her hospitable reception, and the attractions of her old Madeira. The worthy lady kept the British general in good humor for two hours, while her ragged and hungry countrymen escaped from his grasp. Never have the hospitalities of Murray Hill answered a better purpose.

On the 16th of September a smart skirmish took place in the neighborhood of Manhattanville. Some British light infantry and two battalions of Highlanders were driven back, and were in a somewhat precarious position, when the omnipresent chasseurs and grenadiers advanced to their assistance, and some other German regiments were also put in motion. Washington, fearing that the enemy were sending a large body to support their party, as was indeed the case, ordered a retreat. Of the English, two hundred and eighty were killed and wounded; of the Americans, about sixty. This action, in which the latter behaved very well, and inflicted a comparatively heavy loss on the British, did much to bring back their confidence after the reverses and retreats of the preceeding days.

The British general had given strict orders to respect personal property, and presently the rich owners of country-houses, who had fled at the approach of the royal forces, leaving their possessions in charge of their servants, began to return. Lieutenant Hinrichs, of the Hessian chasseurs, who had received orders on the 15th of September to prevent depredations, had earned thereby the gratitude of the inhabitants. He was wounded in the skirmish of the 16th, and forced to look for quiet and good nursing. He took shelter with a widow named Oglyby (Ogilvie?) near Hornhook, on the East River, and had the satisfaction of seeing her whole family meet again after the separation caused by the perils of war. Grandfather, mother, and grandchildren, together with the black slaves and their children, met and embraced with so much affection that our good-natured lieutenant was much moved, and passed a feverish night. It is needless to say that his hosts treated him with the greatest kindness. He recovered from his wound, and from others which he afterwards received in the course of the Revolution, and died a Prussian lieutenant-general in 1834.

The city of New York had been but five days in the hands of the British when, on the night of the 20th to the 21st of September, a fire broke out in a low drinking-house near Whitehall Slip. The weather had been dry and hot. A gale was blowing from the southwest. The fire spread with frightful rapidity. The east side of Broadway was burned as far up as Exchange Place. Then, the wind having veered to the southeast, the fire crossed Broadway above Morris Street, and extended to Barclay Street, burning old Trinity Church, but sparing St. Paul's. The fire was at last mastered, mainly by the exertions of soldiers and sailors. Bancroft is positive that this fire was not the work of incendiaries. Such, however, was not the idea of the

British and Hessians at the time, and some modern historians believe their accounts. Sir William Howe states in his report that fire was set in various places. Donop is said by Eelking to have written in his diary that the conflagration was arranged by an American colonel named Scott, who had previously been a lawyer. This man had employed forty desperate fellows, who were provided with all sorts of combustibles, and who set fire to various houses belonging to Tories. According to this story, Scott was arrested, and the whole plan in writing was found upon him. In support of the opinion of those who believe that the fire was set by the Whigs, is the undoubted fact that several leading Americans had advised burning New York, and that the plan had even been proposed by Washington to Congress,* which rejected it. On the other hand, panic and fury, stories of incendiarism, and acts of violence are almost invariable accompaniments of a great conflagration. Statements made at such a time should always be taken with the greatest caution. The story concerning Scott is, I believe, entirely unconfirmed. It is certain that sundry persons were killed by English soldiers during the progress of the fire, and Bancroft says that one poor man, who happened to be a Tory, was hanged by the heels until he died.

On the 10th of October, 1776, General Howe embarked the greater part of his troops with the intention of again trying to cut Washington's line of retreat and shut him up in Manhattan Island. For four days the British were detained in the East River by an adverse wind, and only passed Hell Gate on the afternoon of the

* Washington, vol. iv. p. 74.

14th. The fleet lay at anchor that night and started at six the next morning, but was detained by winds and tides, and did not reach Throg's Neck (or Frog's Point, as Washington calls it), until nightfall. Here Howe had previously landed his advanced guard, but Washington had been beforehand with him, and had occupied the passes leading to the mainland. Howe consequently determined to push on and effect a landing at East Chester. This he succeeded in doing on the 18th of October, after a sharp skirmish. The British army lay on its arms that night, with its left wing protected by a creek near East Chester, and its right near New Rochelle. The Americans, meanwhile, were making the best of their way to White Plains, where they took up a strong position and intrenched it. Just at this juncture the Second Division of Hessians joined the rest of the army. It consisted of three thousand nine hundred and ninety-seven men, commanded by Lieutenant-General Wilhelm von Knyphausen, and had left Cassel early in May. The Waldeck regiment, six hundred and seventy strong, came with this division, as also the second company of chasseurs, under Captain Ewald. Thus the German corps under the command of General von Heister was brought up to about thirteen thousand four hundred men. The new division was left to hold New Rochelle during the British advance on White Plains.

Captain Ewald and his second company of chasseurs had not long to wait before coming into action. On the 23d of October, while attempting a reconnoissance, they were met by a superior force of riflemen, and would have been driven back had not the Highlanders come to their assistance. One lieutenant and six men were wounded, of whom four afterwards died of their wounds. This is the German account in Eelking's book. I will now give that of General Washington's aide-de-camp in his report to the President of Congress: "On Wednesday there was also a smart skirmish between a party of Colonel Hand's riflemen, about two hundred and forty, and nearly the same number of Hessian chasseurs, in which the latter were put to rout. Our men buried ten of them on the field, and took two prisoners, one badly wounded. We sustained no other loss than having one lad wounded, supposed mortally."* This is about as near as such reports usually come to each other.

On the 28th of October, Sir William Howe found Washington's army advantageously posted behind the village of White Plains. It numbered somewhat more than thirteen thousand men, of whom about fifteen hundred occupied Chatterton Hill, on the extreme right of the American position, and were separated from the main body by the river Bronx. Sir William determined to attack this right wing. One English and two Hessian regiments, supported by the Hessian grenadiers, forded the Bronx and scaled the steep and rocky sides of the hill. The regiment Von Lossberg was obliged to charge through a burning wood, and to face the heaviest American fire. Its loss in killed and wounded was not far from fifty men. The result of

* Washington, vol. iv. p. 524. The MS. journal of the Grenadier Battalion von Minnigerode gives Ewald's loss at four killed, three wounded, and two missing. I have not found any mention of this skirmish in Ewald's "Belehrungen."

the contest might have been doubtful, had not Colonel Rall, commanding his own regiment and that named after Knyphausen, also forded the Bronx, outflanked the Americans, and assisted the troops which were making the attack in front. The river was deep, and the Hessian soldiers hesitated to enter it. Lieutenants Wiederhold and Briede dashed in first to set them an example. We shall hear more of the former of these officers.* The second fell a few days later at the taking of Fort Washington.

Some of the Americans fought fairly well on this occasion, against much superior numbers. They had an undoubted advantage of position, and made good use of it, inflicting a loss of about two hundred and eighty killed and wounded on their enemy. Howe mentions in his despatches the good service done by the English and Hessian artillery. Heister's adjutant-general says that the Hessian field-pieces made such a "thunder-storm" that one could neither see nor hear. The Americans had but three small cannon on the hill.†

The American army at this time was largely composed of militiamen, sent by the various states for short periods of service. These militiamen were in great measure ill-armed and in rags, undisciplined, and commanded by officers who had but a few months be-

---

* See Wiederhold's (MS.) diary. Unless Ewald is mistaken, Wiederhold, although still a lieutenant, cannot have been very young at this time. He had already distinguished himself in 1762.—Ewald's "Belehrungen," vol. iii. p. 130.

† For the action at White Plains: Bancroft, vol. ix. pp. 181–183; Eelking's "Hülfstruppen," vol. i. pp. 71–77; Washington, vol. iv. pp. 526–529; MS. journal of the Grenadier Battalion von Minnigerode; of the Regiment von Lossberg (Heuser); Wiederhold's Diary.

fore left the desk or the plough. While some of these improvised officers were persons of character and talent, others possessed no merit but their ability to raise men. The men thus raised would consider and treat such an officer as an equal, "and, in the character of an officer," says Washington, "regard him no more than a broom-stick." * Some of the Americans had distinguished themselves by deeds of valor, but, like all raw recruits, they were subject to panics, often entirely unreasonable. These facts must constantly be borne in mind, or the story of the Revolution becomes incomprehensible. Sir William Howe, on the other hand, commanded a regular, disciplined soldiery, scarcely to be surpassed in Europe, and provided with everything desirable for the conduct of a war.

For three days after the engagement at Chatterton Hill the armies stood facing each other and strengthened their fortifications. On the night of the 31st of October, Washington retreated to a strong position above White Plains, and Howe on the morrow, after harassing the American rear-guard, turned his attention to a new scheme.

On the highest point of New York Island, where a hill rises two hundred and thirty-eight feet above the level of the Hudson, the Americans had built a five-sided earthwork and called it Fort Washington. The fort mounted thirty-four cannon, but without casemates. The ground about it was well suited for defense, and was occupied by smaller works of no great strength. The whole formed a barrier across the upper end of Manhattan Island, preventing the English from

* Washington, vol. iv. p. 113.

making any expedition by land, and rendering winter-quarters in New York neither safe nor comfortable. On the Jersey side of the Hudson, on top of the Palisades, opposite Fort Washington, stood Fort Lee. Between them, Putnam had undertaken to build an impassable barrier, that should close the river against the British. The works were under the immediate command of General Greene. On the morning of October 9th, however, the obstructions had been broken through and the forts passed by two British ships of forty-four guns each, a frigate of twenty guns, and three or four tenders, which had captured or destroyed two American row-galleys on the river.* In view of these facts, Washington wished to abandon the fort named after himself, which was in danger of being surrounded. Greene was of the opposite opinion, and Congress shared the delusion of Greene. The authority of the commander-in-chief was so limited that he did not succeed in making his own views prevail. Instead of being withdrawn, the garrison of Fort Washington was strengthened, until Lieutenant-colonel Magaw, who commanded it, had nearly three thousand men under his orders. The ground to be occupied was two miles and a half long—from a line a little south of the present Trinity Cemetery to the hills above Tubby Hook—and included a redoubt on Laurel Hill.†

It was on the 16th of November, 1776, that this fort was stormed by Sir William Howe's army. The attack was made simultaneously by four columns, advancing

* Bancroft, vol. ix. p. 174; Washington, vol. iv. p. 148.

† Bancroft, vol. ix. p. 189.

against four different points, but that which bore the brunt of the fighting, and to which the glory of the day belonged, was composed of Hessians under Knyphausen. This force crossed over to New York island by Kings Bridge at half-past five in the morning, and was divided into two columns, the right-hand one under Colonel Rall, the left under Major-general Schmidt. In this column Wiederhold was with the advanced guard. For a long time the Germans had to stand quiet, while the English columns got into position and began the attack. Meanwhile Cornwallis had taken the American battery on Laurel Hill. Earl Percy, with two English and one Hessian brigade, had threatened the American works on the south, and Colonel Sterling, with the Highlanders, had crossed Harlem River behind the force opposed to Percy, and threatened to cut off its retreat. In doing this the Highlanders had to charge up a steep bank, and lost about ninety men. Colonel Cadwalader, who commanded the Americans in this neighborhood, had been obliged to retreat, and his men, instead of rallying outside of Fort Washington itself, had rushed into the narrow enclosure, impeding the defensive operations of its proper garrison.

It was between ten and eleven o'clock. The moment for the Hessians to attack had come at last. They waded through a marsh, and climbed the precipitous, rocky hill on which the fort was built. In vain did the riflemen shoot them down. In vain did the artillery rain grape and ball among them. Knyphausen, himself, was continually in the thickest of the fight, "so that it is wonderful," writes Wiederhold, "that he came off without being killed or wounded." The ground was so steep in places that the men had to pull themselves up by the bushes. At last they reached the top, where there was a level space. "Forward, all my grenadiers!" cried Rall. The drums beat, the bugles blew, the men shouted Hurrah! Hessians and Americans were mingled in a mass, all rushing wildly towards the fort.

The outer works were taken, and their defenders driven back to add to the confusion in the main fort. Colonel Rall called one of his captains. "Hohenstein," said he, "you speak English and French; take a drummer with you, tie a white cloth on a gun-barrel, go to the fort and call for a surrender." "I did this at once," writes the captain, "but they kept firing at me and the drummer until we came to the glacis, where the rebels led us off with our eyes bound. They sent me a Colonel,* who was second in command, to whom I made the following proposal: He should immediately march out of the fort with the garrison, and they should lay down their arms before General von Knyphausen. All ammunition, provisions, and whatever belonged to Congress should be faithfully made known. On the other hand, I gave him my word that all, from the commanding officer down, should retain their private property. Finally, a white flag should be immediately hoisted, to put a stop to all hostilities. The commander asked for four hours' time to consider, which, however, I refused, and allowed him only half an hour to speak with his officers. When the half-hour was past the commander came himself, and his fate seemed

* Cadwalader.

hard to him. Thereupon he said: 'The Hessians make impossibilities possible.' I then said to him: 'General von Knyphausen is a hundred paces off. Come with me, on my safe conduct, and see if he will give you better terms.' He was contented with this and went with me."

To Knyphausen Magaw surrendered, in spite of a message from Washington, promising to attempt to bring off the troops, if he could hold out until night. The place, however, was untenable. The Germans lost fifty-six officers and men killed and two hundred and seventy-six wounded * in the attack, the English more than one hundred and twenty. The Americans lost less than one hundred and fifty killed and wounded, but about twenty-eight hundred prisoners, among whom were some of their best soldiers. They also lost a good deal of artillery and many arms and accoutrements.

The quartermaster of the Grenadier Battalion von Minnigerode says, in speaking of this battle, that if it had not been for the prisoners, the loss of the Germans would have been far greater than that of the rebels, and that this is because of the manner in which the latter fight. They lie singly behind trees, bushes, stone walls, and rocks, shoot at long range and with certainty, and run away very fast as soon as they have fired. The Germans cannot shoot a third so far, and can still less catch them running, and the ground here is such that field artillery can seldom be brought up to an attack.

The Hessians are said to have given no quarter,

* MS. journal of the Regiment von Lossberg (Heuser).

during the charge, to the riflemen whom they found in the outworks and the woods. The Americans, many of whom must have seen this, were naturally uneasy at the time of the surrender. The popular imagination had made fiends of the Hessians. Captain von Malsburg relates that when he came into the fortress he found himself surrounded by officers with fear and anxiety in their faces. They invited him into their barracks, pressed punch, wine, and cold cakes upon him, complimented him on his affability, which seemed to astonish them, and told him they had not been led to expect such from a Hessian officer. They begged for his protection, and he, in return, lectured them on the sin of rebellion against their good king.

The garrison marched out between the regiments Rall and Lossberg, laid down their arms, and gave up their banners, which were yellow, white, and light blue. Knyphausen is said to have looked on these "with disdain." The attitude is characteristic of the Hessian feeling of the moment, and the American reader must find consolation in the fact that within six weeks the colors of the regiments Rall and Lossberg were in the hands of Washington's army.

The Hessians gained great credit by this action. Schmidt, Stirn, and Rall, and the troops under their command, were mentioned in general orders, and the captured fort was named Fort Knyphausen. No disgrace can attach to the Americans in the fort, who made a creditable resistance against great odds. The blame lies with those generals who insisted on holding the fort after the abandonment of the island by the main army under Washington, and after the obstructions in the Hudson had been passed by the British ships.*

* For the taking of Fort Washington, see Washington's report; Washington, vol. iv. pp. 178–181; also, Bancroft, vol. ix. pp. 189–193; Eelking's "Hülfstruppen," vol. i. pp. 84–97; MSS. Wiederhold's Diary, Journals of the Grenadier Battalion von Minnigerode, of the Regiment von Lossberg (Heuser), of the same (Piel), of the Regiments von Huyn and von Knoblauch.

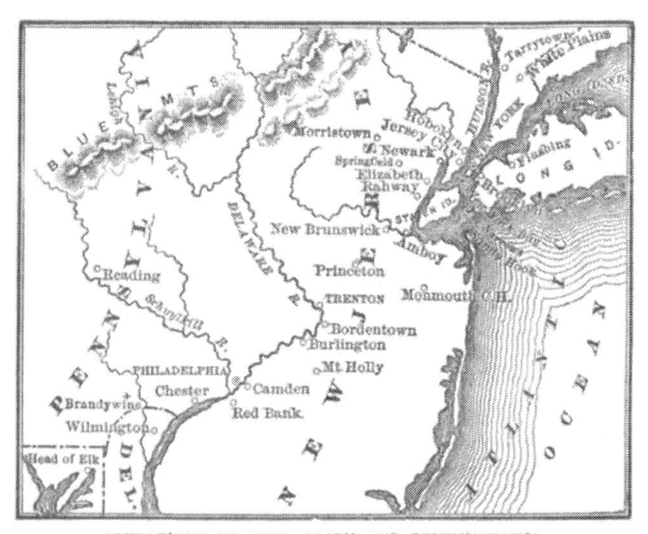

OPERATIONS IN NEW JERSEY AND PENNSYLVANIA.

CHAPTER VIII.

TRENTON, DECEMBER 26, 1776.

AFTER the capture of Fort Washington Sir William Howe showed unusual activity. The fort had fallen on the 16th of November, 1776, and on the 20th the British army crossed the Hudson into New Jersey. Fort Lee had become at once useless and incapable of defence. It was hastily evacuated, and artillery, tents, and provisions were abandoned with it. More than two thousand men, under General Greene, who had formed its garrison, barely escaped across the Hackensack, leaving seventy-three sick behind them. The condition of Washington's army was desperate. The term of service of many of the militia-men expired on the 30th of November. These could by no means be induced to re-enlist, even for a short time, nor would the New Jersey militia turn out to protect their own state, a brigade of them disbanding on the day the British entered New Brunswick. Washington had left a detachment under Lee on the east side of the Hudson, and Lee now disregarded Washington's repeated orders to join him, and grumbled instead of acting. About twenty-four hundred men under Lord Stirling were detached for the protection of Northern New Jersey, and four days afterwards ordered to defend the upper line of the Delaware; and the commander-in-chief had at one time less than thirty-five hundred men with him. The march of the British across New Jersey was hardly opposed, though Washington retreated slowly before them, destroying the bridges. On the 8th of December he retired across the Delaware, removing all the boats for seventy miles to his own side of the river. There was a panic in Philadelphia, and Congress adjourned to Baltimore. Washington felt himself unable, with his small force, to prevent the passage of the British over the river.* Howe was not the man, however, to pursue a winter campaign with vigor. He returned to New York, leaving Cornwallis, and afterwards Grant, in command in New Jersey. Bancroft tells us that the state was given over to plunder and outrage, and that all attempts to restrain the Hessians were abandoned, under the apology that the habit of plunder prevented desertions. "They were led to believe," quotes he, from the official report of a British officer, "before they left Hesse-Cassel, that they were to come to America to establish their private fortunes, and hitherto they have certainly acted with that principle."† Washington, on the other hand, writes, on the 5th of February, 1777: "One thing I must remark in favor of the Hessians, and that is, that our people who have been prisoners generally agree that they received much kinder treatment from them than from the British officers and soldiers."‡

It was the belief of Washington that active operations would speedily be resumed, and that the British

---

* See Washington's writings at the time, *passim*, and especially December 12th.—Washington Writings, vol. iv. p. 211.

† Bancroft, vol. ix. p. 216.

‡ Washington, vol. iv. p. 309.

would march on Philadelphia as soon as the Delaware should be frozen over. A letter intercepted a day or two before Christmas confirmed this opinion.* It became of the utmost importance to strike a blow before the enemy should be ready to move, and before the last day of December, when the term of service of many of his men would expire.

The disposition of troops made by General Grant, the British commander in New Jersey, was as follows: Princeton and New Brunswick were held by English detachments. Von Donop, commanding the Hessian grenadiers and the Forty-second Highlanders, was at Bordentown. Rall, with the brigade which had been for some time under his orders, fifty Hessian chasseurs, twenty English light dragoons, and six field-pieces, was quartered at Trenton. Rall's brigade was composed of three regiments of Hessians, which bore the names of Rall, von Knyphausen, and von Lossberg. It did not differ materially in quality from other Hessian brigades. The regiment von Lossberg had especially distinguished itself at Chatterton Hill. Regiment Rall was made up of bad material, being one of those raised in a hurry to fill the tale of soldiers furnished by the Landgrave,†

* Washington, vol. iv. p. 244: The idea of some such stroke as the surprise of Trenton is first mentioned by Washington on the 14th of December. In a letter to Governor Trumbull he says that the troops who are coming from the north, with his present force, and that under General Lee, may enable him "to attempt a stroke upon the forces of the enemy, who lie a good deal scattered, and to all appearance in a state of security. A lucky blow in this quarter would be fatal to them, and would most certainly rouse the spirits of the people, which are quite sunk by our late misfortunes."—Washington, vol. iv. p. 220.

† Kapp's "Soldatenhandel," p. 63.

but Cornwallis long afterwards told a committee of the House of Commons that Rall's brigade, at Fort Washington, had won the admiration of the whole army.

The town of Trenton, then composed of about a hundred houses, lay on both sides of Assanpink Creek, near where that creek falls into the Delaware, the larger part of the town being on the western side of the creek. This was crossed by a bridge, over which the road led down the Delaware to Bordentown and Burlington. There were roads on both sides of the creek to Princeton. Of these, the one on the western side, passing through Maidenhead, was the shorter. There was also a road to Pennington, in a northwesterly direction, and two roads along the Delaware, going up stream, one near the bank and the other a mile or two from it. The last fell into the Pennington road a little way outside the town.

The regiments Rall and von Lossberg were quartered in the northern part of Trenton, the Knyphausen regiment in the southern part, on both sides of the bridge over the Assanpink. On this bridge a guard of twelve men was stationed. The soldiers in the town were scattered in the various houses, and in fine weather the guns were stacked out of doors, in charge of two or three sentries. Pickets were thrown out on the roads west of the creek. The main guard was composed of an officer and seventy men.

Colonel Rall was a dashing officer of the old school. He was said to have asked to be quartered at Trenton, considering it the post of danger.* He had done very

* MS. Journal of the Grenadier Battalion von Minnigerode.—Wiederhold's Diary.

well at Chatterton Hill, where the American right wing had been turned, and the fate of the day decided, by his brigade. He had taken a leading part in the storming of Fort Washington. The same adventurous spirit which in former years had led him to join the Russians under Orloff as a volunteer to fight against the Turks, served him on those occasions. The ease with which he had seen victories won, since he had come to America, had filled him with an overweening confidence. The ragged wretches who had been driven across New Jersey might capture a patrol or drive in a picket, but were, he thought, quite incapable of a serious attack on a Hessian brigade. "Earthworks!" said he with an oath to Major von Dechow, who came to advise him to fortify the town; "only let them come on! We'll meet them with the bayonet;" and when the same officer requested him to have some shoes sent from New York, he replied that that was all nonsense. He and his brigade would run barefoot over the ice to Philadelphia, and if the major did not want to share the honor, he might stay behind. General Grant, the English general commanding in New Jersey, shared Rall's contempt for the rebels, and when the latter proposed to him to send a detachment to Maidenhead, to keep open the communication between Princeton and Trenton, replied scornfully that he could bridle the Jerseys with a corporal's guard. Von Donop, who commanded at Bordentown, sent a captain of engineers to Trenton to induce Rall to allow the place to be fortified, but the latter was obstinate. Earthworks were unnecessary, he said. The rebels were good-for-nothing fellows. They had landed below the bridge several times already, and had been allowed to get away quietly, but now he (Rall) had taken measures. When they came again he would drive them back in good fashion. He hoped that Washington would come over, too, and then he could take him prisoner. So dangerous did Rall's carelessness seem to his subordinates, that the officers of the Lossberg regiment sent off a letter of remonstrance to General von Heister, but too late.

Rall's contempt for his enemy led him to neglect his most elementary duties. He seldom visited a post, he seldom consulted with an officer. He refused to name a place of safety for the baggage in case of an attack. "Nonsense," said he, when asked to do so, "the rebels will not beat us." Yet the men were constantly fatigued with unnecessary guard duty and countermarching. On the 22d of December, two dragoons, who had been sent to Princeton with a letter, were fired on in a wood. One of them was killed, the other rode back to Trenton and reported the attack. Rall, thereupon, sent three officers and one hundred men, with a cannon, to carry his letter, much to the amusement of the English. The detachment had to sleep on the ground, in bad weather, and march back the next morning. A sergeant and fifteen men would have been amply sufficient for the service.

On the 24th of December, 1776, a reconnoissance was sent out in the direction of Pennington, but was recalled after a march of a few miles. Towards dusk on the 25th an attack was made on the pickets north of the town, by a small reconnoitring party of Americans. The enemy were repulsed, with a loss to the Germans of six men wounded. A patrol of thirty men, under an ensign, was sent one or two miles in pursuit of the retreating Americans, but failed to come up with them. The picket at the junction of the upper river road and the Pennington road was then strengthened by about ten men, under Lieutenant Wiederhold, making it up to a total strength of twenty-five men. Rall made up his mind that all danger was over. He had lately been warned that an attack was imminent, and he took it for granted that the skirmish in which the pickets had been engaged was the attack of which he had been warned. Leslie, who commanded at Princeton, had sent word that Washington was preparing to cross the Delaware, but Rall gave no serious heed. He only ordered his own regiment, which was "of the day," to stay in its quarters. There was, indeed, ground for his feeling of security. It was known to him that no large force of Americans was left in his part of New Jersey. Washington's army lay beyond the Delaware, a ragged, half-armed mob of poor devils, who had lately been driven from state to state and from river to river. Great cakes of ice floated to and fro in the Delaware, drifting with the tide, and making all crossing dangerous. The night was boisterous, even for December, and before morning sleet and snow were driving through the streets. But within all was bright and cheerful. It was Christmas evening. The Germans, comfortably housed in Trenton, could laugh at the storm, and sleep securely.*

* It has frequently been said that Washington surprised the Hessians, still sleepy from the festivities of Christmas. In Germany it is always *Christmas Eve* that is celebrated, and the Hessians would, therefore, have had thirty-six hours to recover from the effects of their potations before

Far differently was the night passed by the American army. The troops under the immediate command of Washington, at his camp on the Pennsylvania side of the Delaware, above Trenton, numbered only twenty-four hundred men in condition to undertake an arduous expedition.* These started at three o'clock on the afternoon of Christmas Day, every man carrying three days' rations and forty rounds. They had with them eighteen field-pieces. This force reached MacKonkey's Ferry at twilight. Here the boats were manned by Glover's sailors, from Marblehead, and between the cakes of floating ice the little army was rowed across the river. So pitiful was their condition that a messenger who had followed them had easily traced their route "by the blood on the snow, from the feet of the men who wore broken shoes."

Meanwhile, Cadwalader was to have crossed the river at Dunk's Ferry, below Trenton, but the ice was packed against the Jersey shore, and, though men on foot could get over, there was no hope for artillery. The eighteen hundred men destined for this part of the expedition waited in vain through the December night. At four in the morning, Cadwalader, sure that Washington, like himself, had been turned back by the difficulties of the expedition, ordered his half-frozen men back to their freezing camp.† "The night," writes

---

eight o'clock on the morning of the 26th. Rall, himself, is said to have been a drinker.

* Bancroft, vol. ix. p. 230. "About twenty-five hundred men."—Diary of Captain Moses Brown of Glover's regiment, kindly communicated by Edward I. Browne, Esq.

† Cadwalader to Washington, Sparks's "Correspondence," vol. i. p. 309.

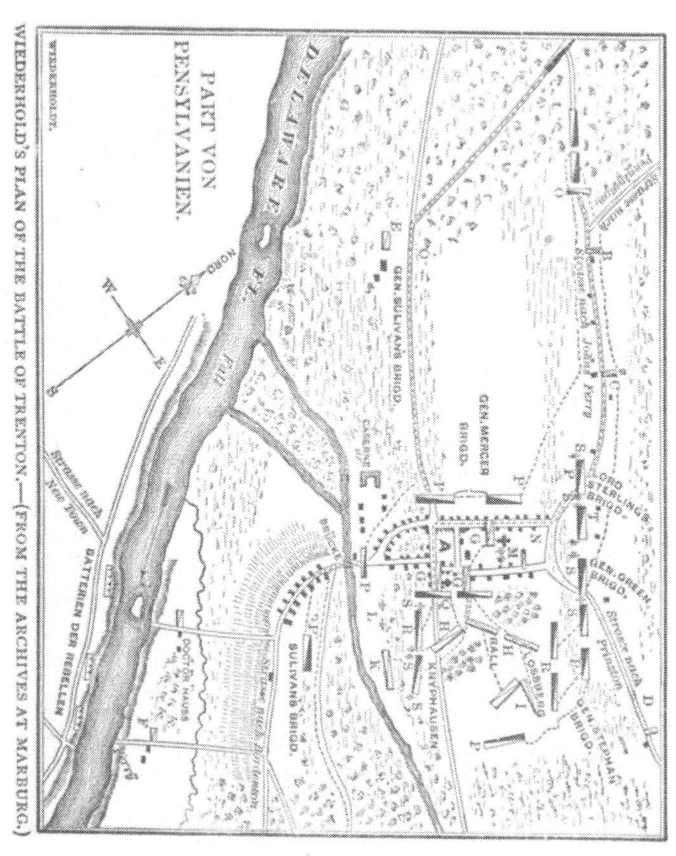

WIEDERHOLD'S PLAN OF THE BATTLE OF TRENTON.—(FROM THE ARCHIVES AT MARBURG.)

PLAN

of the affair which took place on the 26th of December, 1776, at Trenton, between a corps of six thousand rebels, commanded by General Washington, and a brigade of Hessians, commanded by Colonel Rall.

A. Trenton.
B. Picket of an officer and twenty-four men. (Wiederhold.)
C. Captain Altenbocum's company of the Lossberg regiment, which was quartered in the neighborhood, and which formed in front of the captain's quarters, while the picket occupied the enemy.
D. Picket of one captain, one officer, and seventy-five men.
E. One officer and fifty Jägers, who immediately withdrew over the bridge. (Grothausen.)

(*Wiederhold's Plan of the Battle of Trenton—Continued.*)

F. Detachment of one officer and thirty men, which joined Donop's corps.

G. Place where the regiments stopped after leaving the town, and where Colonel Rall attempted to make an attack on the town with his own regiment and that of Lossberg, but was violently driven back to

I. and taken prisoner with the regiments; meanwhile the Regiment von Knyphausen should have covered the flank.

K. Place where the Regiment von Knyphausen had likewise to surrender, after trying to reach the bridge. The cannon of the Lossberg regiment were with the Knyphausen regiment, and unfortunately stuck in the marsh; and while they were being extricated the moment for gaining the bridge was lost, and the bridge strongly occupied by the enemy.

L. Cannon of the Lossberg regiment.

M. Cannon of the Knyphausen regiment, which were not with the regiment during the affair.

N. Cannon of Rall's regiment, dismounted in the beginning.

O. Attack of the enemy from the wood.

P. The enemy advance and surround the town.

Q. Two battalions of the enemy following the Knyphausen regiment.

R. Last manœuvre and attack upon the Knyphausen regiment.

S. Cannon of the rebels.

T. Place where General Washington posted himself and gave his orders.

Thomas Rodney, "was as severe a night as ever I saw." The river was so difficult to cross and so full of ice that it was four o'clock on the morning of the 26th of December before the troops and artillery were all got over and ready to march. They had still nine miles to go before reaching Trenton, and the storm had set in with fearful violence. The shivering soldiers climbed a steep hill and descended into the road, where the trees of the forest might give them a little shelter against the northeasterly storm. At Birmingham the army was divided into two columns. The right, under Sullivan, marched near the river, the left, under Washington, by the upper road. After a while, Sullivan sent word to Washington by one of his aides that the powder of his party was wet. "Then tell your general," answered Washington, "to use the bayonet and penetrate into the town, for the town must be taken, and I am resolved to take it."

It was about an hour after daylight, and Lieutenant Wiederhold had drawn in his outer pickets. It had been a severe night with snow and sleet, but the enemy had not been seen. The little command huddled into a hut that served as a guard-house. Wiederhold happened to step to the door and look out. Suddenly the Americans were before him. He called to arms, and shots were exchanged. "The outguards made but small opposition," says Washington, "though, for their numbers, they behaved very well, keeping up a constant retreating fire from behind houses. We presently saw their main body formed;

This was John Cadwalader, brother to Lambert Cadwalader of the Continental service.—Washington, vol. iv. p. 241, n.

but, from their motions, they seemed undetermined how to act." Drums and bugles sounded in the streets of Trenton. Rall was still in bed, and sleepy in his cups. Lieutenant Biel, acting as Brigade Adjutant, was at first "afraid" to rouse him,* but hastened off to the main guard and despatched another lieutenant and forty men to support the pickets. As he returned to headquarters Rall was hanging out of the window in his night-shirt and crying, "What's the matter?" The adjutant, in reply, asked if he had not heard the firing. Rall said he would be down at once, and presently he was dressed and at the door. A company of the Lossberg regiment, which had quarters on the Pennington road, and acted as an advanced guard, had formed across that road, and received the flying pickets, but had presently fallen back into the town. Washington was pressing in by King and Queen Streets (now Warren and Greene Streets), and Sullivan by the river road into Second Street. A part of Rall's regiment presently succeeded in forming, and after a while Rall himself appeared, on horseback. Lieutenant Wiederhold reported to him, saying that the enemy was in force, and not only above the town but also upon the right and the left. Rall asked how strong the enemy was. Wiederhold answered that he could not say, but that he had seen four or five battalions come out of the woods and that three of them had fired at him before he fell back. Rall called out to advance, but seemed dazed, and unable to form a plan. His forces were still in disorder. Rall struck off to the right into an apple orchard east of the town, and tried

* "Scheut sich" (Marburg Archives).

to obtain command of the Princeton road. He was turned back by Hand's Pennsylvania regiment. He then determined to force his way into the town again with his own and the Lossberg regiments; at least, with as much of them as had been brought together. This he is said to have attempted in order to bring off his baggage, and the plunder of the preceding weeks. He was received, however, by a shower of lead from windows and doorways and from behind trees and walls. The Hessian ammunition was wet by the driving storm. The Americans charged again, and the Hessians were driven farther than they had come. Rall was mortally wounded by a bullet, and the two German regiments, thrown into confusion, laid down their arms.

The Knyphausen regiment fared little better. When Rall left the orchard and turned again towards Trenton, Major von Dechow determined to fight his way back over the Assanpink bridge and strike for Bordentown, where lay Donop's force. It was impossible to accomplish this, for Sullivan had already occupied the bridge. Two cannons stuck fast in a piece of boggy ground, and time was lost in trying to extricate them. Dechow was wounded. A few of the soldiers succeeded in fording the stream, but by far the greater number were surrounded and surrendered to Lord Stirling, reserving their private baggage and the swords of the officers. Those who escaped made their way to Princeton. The chasseurs and English dragoons also escaped and reached Bordentown. Lieutenant Grothausen of the chasseurs was accused of running away too soon. He had been posted with fifty men on the lower river road, and on Sullivan's approach he retreated before him over the Assanpink bridge. According to Bancroft, the whole number who thus got off was one hundred and sixty-two. Washington, in his first report to Congress, gives the number of those who surrendered at twenty-three officers and eight hundred and eighty-six men. A few more afterwards found in Trenton raised this number to about one thousand. "Colonel Rahl [*sic*], the commanding officer, and seven others," he writes, "were found wounded in the town. I do not exactly know how many were killed; but I fancy not above twenty or thirty, as they never made any regular stand. Our loss is very trifling indeed, only two officers and one or two privates wounded."*

Washington's force being inferior in numbers to that of the English and Hessians to the south of him, and a strong battalion of light infantry being at Princeton, he thought it prudent to retire across the Delaware the same evening with the prisoners and artillery he had taken.

The news of the victory of the Americans was received in New York with grief and indignation. Old Heister, already out of favor with Sir William Howe, may have seen in it the omen of his own recall. He wrote on the 5th of January to the Landgrave's minister, Schlieffen, announcing the event. According to his story, Rall's brigade had been surprised by ten thousand men, and the disaster was caused by that colonel's rashness in advancing to meet this superior force, instead of retiring at once behind the Assanpink. Hei-

* Washington, vol. iv. p. 247. Bancroft gives the numbers as seventeen Hessians killed and seventy-eight wounded.

ster acknowledges the loss of fifteen stands of colors.*

The Landgrave of Hesse-Cassel was very angry. He complained that such an event would have been impossible, had not all discipline been relaxed. He ordered an investigation to be made as soon as the officers, who were then prisoners in American hands, should have been exchanged, and threatened to hold those guilty of misconduct to the strictest responsibility. He declared that he would never restore colors to the regiments that had lost them until they should have taken an equal number from the enemy. He wrote to Knyphausen that he hoped that general, like himself, was filled with proper grief and shame; that it was necessary to wipe out the spot on his honor, and that Knyphausen must not rest until his troops had smothered the remembrance of this wretched affair in a crowd of famous deeds.† The Landgrave was indiscriminate in his anger. The true offender against the rules of military duty died in Colonel Rall. It was the opinion of soldiers at the time, and has remained the opinion of those who have studied the matter since, that the defeat and capture of the Hessian brigade at Trenton might have been prevented by common military precautions on the part of its commander. Cornwallis afterwards told a committee of the House of Commons, that in Donop's opinion

* Quoted in Eelking's "Hülfstruppen," vol. i. pp. 375, 376.

† Eelking's "Hülfstruppen," vol. i. p. 377. A letter which has frequently been published, purporting to be written at this time by a Prince of Hesse-Cassel to a Baron Hohendorf, or Hogendorff, commanding Hessian troops in America, is a clumsy forgery.—Kapp's "Soldatenhandel," 2d ed. pp. 199–201 and 255.

Rall could have held out until Donop could have come to his relief from Bordentown, if he had obeyed Sir William Howe's orders and erected redoubts. These Rall was repeatedly urged to build by his subordinate officers. That those under his command should somewhat have participated in the relaxation of discipline wantonly encouraged by their commander was but natural. In the end they all fought bravely, many of them being wounded, though the loss of privates was but small. That an earlier retreat might have enabled the Hessians to escape is possible. But soldiers should not be heavily blamed for trying to hold their ground when surprised, nor is Rall's error, if it were one, in trying to cut his way out towards Princeton, rather than towards Bordentown, to be laid to the score of his subordinates.*

The importance of Trenton to the Americans is not to be reckoned by the mere numerical test of killed, wounded, and prisoners. It was a new proof to the

* The only dissenting voice is that of Ewald, who excuses Rall, and lays the blame on the officer of chasseurs (Grothausen) who should have discovered the enemy. Ewald also blames Donop for having been decoyed from Bordentown to Mount Holly, and out of supporting distance of Trenton, by false reports. Ewald, who was under Donop at the time, says, moreover, that this little affair of Trenton caused such a panic in the English army, hitherto regularly victorious since the opening of the campaign, that they continually thought they saw Washington and his soldiers, and did not get over their fear until they had fought again. Ewald's "Belehrungen," vol. ii. p. 127. Grant, Rall's immediate superior, writes on December 27: "I did not think that all the rebels in America would have taken that brigade prisoners" (Archives at Marburg). The finding of the court-martial blamed Rall and Dechow, both dead (ibid.). For the battle of Trenton see authorities quoted and Eelking's "Hülfstruppen," vol. i. pp. 112, 132; (MSS.) Wiederhold's Diary, journals of the regiment von Lossberg, and Grenadier Battalion von Minnigerode.

unskilled and destitute colonists that they were good for something as soldiers, and that their cause was not hopeless. Coming after a long course of retreat and disaster, it inspired them with fresh courage. Bunker Hill had taught the Americans that British regulars could be resisted. Trenton proved to them in an hour of despondency that the dreaded Hessians could be conquered.

CHAPTER IX.

THE WINTER OF 1777.

THE Hessian officers and soldiers who had been taken prisoners at Trenton had to march on the 26th of December, 1776, over the same cold and snowy road by which the Americans had advanced to the attack. We can fancy them shivering in their uniforms, while their tattered and bare-footed captors marched gayly beside them, and forgot the icy wind in the glow of victory. Again the Delaware was crossed amid the cakes of floating ice, and we may be sure that it was not the ragged Americans whose teeth chattered;* but reaction came after so much labor and excitement, and on the morrow one half of the victorious army was worn out and disabled. For forty consecutive hours the Americans had stood to their arms, and marched and fought in the snow and sleet of a December storm, and nature now claimed a few days of rest and shelter. Only Washington was indefatigable, and although the term of service of a large part of his army was expiring, the great leader prepared to take advantage of his success.

The Hessian officers were treated with great courtesy by the American commanders. Washington expressed

* It was not without danger that they crossed the Delaware. Wiederhold says that he had to wade seventy paces to get to shore, with water and ice up to his breast.

his sympathy with them immediately after their surrender. Stirling, who had but recently been exchanged after his capture on Long Island, told the officers that visited him that Heister had treated him like a brother, and that so would he treat them. He accompanied them on their visit to General Washington, and invited several of them to dinner.* Washington paid the same politeness to some of the others. One of his guests has left in his journal the record of the impression made on him by the most famous of Americans: "This general does not show in his face the greatness with which he is generally credited. His eyes have no fire, but the smiling character of his expression when he speaks inspires affection and respect."

Wiederhold writes: "On the 28th, as I said, I dined, as did several other officers, with General Washington. He did me the honor of talking a great deal with me, about the unlucky affair, and as I freely told him my opinion that our arrangements had been bad, otherwise we should not have fallen into his hands, he asked me if I could have made a better arrangement, and how. Thereupon I said yes; mentioned all the faults that had been committed, and showed what I should have done, and how I would have got out of the scrape with honor. He not only applauded this, but made me a complimentary speech on the subject, as also on my

* Stirling told the Hessian officers that the Americans at Trenton were "not stronger than six thousand men, and had fourteen cannon and two howitzers with them." This expression may have been used to mislead the Germans. The Americans at Trenton, according to Bancroft, numbered but twenty-four hundred men, veterans chiefly of New England, Pennsylvania, and Virginia, and Washington's whole army in Pennsylvania at the time only sixty-two hundred effective men. See also p. 92, note.

watchfulness, and the defence I had made with my few men on the picket line, on the morning of the attack. General Washington is a courteous and elegant man, but seems to be very *polite* and reserved, speaks little, and has a sly physiognomy. He is not very tall and also not short, but of medium height, and has a good figure." It is pleasant to imagine the scene—the farm-house parlor, the fire of big logs, the guttering candles, the bowl of smoking punch, and General Washington discussing the art of war with his captive, who, though but a lieutenant, has seen foreign service, and may be worth listening to.

The prisoners were shortly marched off to Pennsylvania and Virginia. Everywhere the people flocked to see them, and if the alien invaders were sometimes met in their adversity with threats and curses, we must not blame too severely those whose sons and brothers the auxiliaries had been let out to slay. We shall rather find that the balance inclines to favor the American people, who on many occasions met their captive enemies with forgiveness and kindness. The prisoners' escort invariably did its duty, and succeeded in protecting them from anything worse than verbal insult. The Hessian officers and men were separated from each other, and it is needless to follow their wanderings in detail. The officers were in Philadelphia, and called on General Israel Putnam on New Year's Day. "He shook hands with each of us," says one, in his journal, "and we all had to drink a glass of Madeira with him. This old graybeard may be a good, honest man, but nobody but the rebels would have made him a general." *

* Journal of the Regiment von Lossberg (Piel).

After being quartered at Dumfries and in the Valley of Virginia, and suffering many petty annoyances, the officers were brought, in December, 1777, to Fredericksburg, where they were treated with great hospitality and kindness. Wiederhold becomes really pathetic at the idea of parting from his friends there. The prisoners had been much favored by the ladies of the neighborhood, who are, says the lieutenant, "beautiful, courteous, kindly, modest, and withal very natural and easy." Sixteen ladies "of the first rank" organized a surprise party, which visited the captain in his quarters, and of which he had been discreetly informed beforehand. He tells us that they came intending to spend only an hour, but stayed from half-past three to ten o'clock in the evening. General Washington's brother, sister, and niece were among them. The German officers regaled their guests with tea, coffee, chocolate, claret wine, and cakes; and entertained them with music, both instrumental and vocal, in which the ladies sometimes joined. "In Europe we should not have got much honor by our music, but here we passed for masters. Sobbe played the flute, Surgeon Oliva the violin, and I the guitar. We were so overwhelmed with praise that we were really ashamed. Their friendship for us was too great. Some of the American young gentlemen were jealous."

All this kindness had its effect upon the captives. At Dumfries, nine months before, Wiederhold had set down in his journal that he would rather have a small farm in Hesse than the greatest plantation in Virginia, and that America was good for people who were escaping the gallows at home. Now he was quite sad at leaving Fredericksburg, though it was to return to the army at Philadelphia. For this, however, he had personal reasons. "It was surely a great thing to enjoy so much friendship, yes, love, I may say, from people whose enemies we were, and against whom we were soon again to act as enemies. Yet, said a fair one, who was very favorably inclined to me, and whom I shall always respect and honor: 'would God you could stay here, and that I might never be so unhappy as to part from you; as I may have to do to-morrow, and perhaps forever. But go where duty and honor call you, and be ever happy!' This was magnanimity such as does not dwell in all rebels, for she was a good American in her feelings, beautiful and rich." No wonder the lieutenant counted the miles as he marched away from Fredericksburg.

The private soldiers reached Philadelphia a few days later than the officers. Of their reception by the populace one of the corporals writes in his diary: "Big and little, old and young, stood there to see what sort of mortals we might be. When we came directly in front of them they looked sharply at us. The old women howled dreadfully, and wanted to throttle us all, because we had come to America to rob them of their freedom. Some others, in spite of all the scolding, brought brandy and bread, and wanted to give them to us, but the old women would not allow it, and still wished to strangle us. The American guard that had us in charge had received orders from Washington to lead us all about the town, so that everybody should see us; but the people crowded in on us with great fury, and nearly overpowered the guard. So when we were near the barracks our commanding officer said: 'Dear Hessians, let us march into these barracks.' We did so, and the whole American detachment had to check the raging people." Why the American officer addressed his captives in terms of endearment does not appear, but a great degree of confidence seems to have been established between them. Eelking tells a story, hardly to be taken without a grain of salt, that when the party was being moved from Lancaster to Winchester, in the autumn of 1777, and came to the boundaries of Virginia, the Pennsylvania escort refused to march farther, and would not set foot on the sacred soil. In fact, they dispersed, and all went home. The escorting company which should have come to meet them from Winchester had not arrived. The captain who had been in command of the Pennsylvanians was a man of much presence of mind, and of equal confidence in human nature. He told the Hessians, whose affections he had won by his humanity, that they must march on without an escort, as he himself should hurry forward to Winchester. He trusted to the prisoners, promising them good treatment on their arrival. So he departed. The prisoners, if such they can be called, whom none constrained, marched on in an orderly manner. On the third day the old captain came back with an escort of Virginians, and found all the Hessians present at roll-call, though some unprincipled Englishmen had disappeared. The Germans were, thereupon, all treated to brandy, while the English captives had to take up their line of march without that stimulant, and the Hessians received many indulgences forever afterwards.*

Washington is said to have soothed the popular feeling by pointing out that the Hessians had come to America against their will. The lot of the prisoners seems not to have been unnecessarily hard. Many of the privates let themselves out as farm servants, and received food and wages.

So much of Washington's little army as remained fit for service recrossed the Delaware in the last three days of December, and was speedily joined by Cadwalader's and Mifflin's commands. This raised their numbers to about five thousand, of whom three fifths were ignorant of military service. Against this small force Cornwallis advanced with a larger number of British and Hessian veterans. He came with his whole force from Princeton by Maidenhead, in spite of Donop's advice to march in two columns, on both sides of the Assanpink. Some skirmishing took place on the 2d of January, 1777, and Lieutenant Grothausen of the chasseurs, who had escaped from Trenton seven days before, without having done his whole duty, as some people thought, was killed. Eelking relates that he was shot by some riflemen, who decoyed him under pretence of surrendering.

On the afternoon of the second of January the English and American armies stood face to face on opposite sides of the Assanpink River. In vain did several officers urge Cornwallis to attack at once. The sun was sinking, the bridge had been successfully defended, the English army must ford the stream to get

* Eelking's "Hülfstruppen," vol. i. pp. 138–141.

at their enemy, and the event seemed doubtful. The British general determined to delay the attack until the following day. Washington did not venture to stake the fate of America on the resistance of his undisciplined militia. The night was cold and the roads in good condition for the passage of artillery. Wood was piled on the American watch-fires, and a guard left to replenish them. Meanwhile, the American army, passing round Lord Cornwallis's left flank, marched away through the clear January night, and at nine in the morning attacked three English regiments of foot and three companies of horse at Princeton. These the Americans routed, killing and wounding about two hundred men and taking two hundred and thirty prisoners, of whom fourteen were British officers. The American loss of men was small, but of officers heavy, owing to a check at the beginning of the affair. This victory at Princeton was the last engagement of the campaign which deserves the name of a battle. The British abandoned the greater part of New Jersey, retaining only New Brunswick, Amboy, and Paulus Hook. But the outposts of the two armies kept up a skirmishing warfare throughout the winter. Thus, on the 5th of January, 1777, a party of about fifty Waldeckers was attacked by a body of militia, "not superior in numbers," who killed eight or ten and made prisoners of the remainder, including two officers.*

In this skirmishing kind of warfare, the leading part, in so far as the Hessians were concerned, was taken by the jägers, or chasseurs, as the English and Americans called them. These were trained marksmen, recruited

* Washington, vol. iv. p. 264.

among the hunters and gamekeepers of Germany. One company of them had come to America with von Heister, in August, 1776, another, under Captain Ewald, with von Knyphausen in October. They were found so useful that the establishment was raised, by special treaty with the Landgrave, during the winter of 1777, to one thousand and sixty-seven men, in five companies, one of which was mounted. Other companies were procured from Hanau and Anspach. The corps, after the summer of 1777, was under the command of Lieutenant-colonel von Wurmb, but the companies or detached parties very generally acted separately. There were, indeed, few operations of any importance in which the chasseurs did not take part. We can easily believe that they made many a bold and lucky stroke, and yet shrug our shoulders a little when we are informed that the American militia wore broad-brimmed hats, which they used to draw down over their eyes for protection against the wind and snow, so that the chasseurs were able to slip up to them in broad daylight, and strike them down or disarm them before they knew it. Those Yankees are usually such very sleepy fellows.*

Ewald tells us that in the early part of the year 1777 Lord Cornwallis determined to surprise Boundbrook, in New Jersey, which was held by one thousand Ameri-

* Eelking's "Hülfstruppen," vol. i. p. 182.—For the text of the treaties concerning chasseurs with Hesse-Cassel and Hesse-Hanau, see "Parliamentary Register," 1st series, vol. vi. p. 152, and vol. vii. p. 49. It seems probable that the total number of Hessian chasseurs was never reached. When organized in the summer of 1777, the corps numbered six hundred chasseurs, of whom one hundred and five were Anspachers, and thirty grenadiers, with two three-pounders.—Journal of the Jäger Corps.

cans under Colonel Butler. The attack was to be made in three divisions. The first, under General Matthews, was to make a feint on the front of the American works. The second, under Cornwallis, was to pass to the left, by Somerset, round Butler's position, and take it in the rear. The third, marching to the right by Greenbrook, was to cut off the retreat of the enemy to Morristown. Ewald commanded the advanced guard of the First Division. The road from Raritan Landing to Boundbrook, leading up the left side of the Raritan River, and about two and a half miles in length, ended in a causeway over a morass. Through the morass ran a brook, over which was a stone bridge. The Americans had built a redoubt to command the bridge and the causeway.

The division started about two in the morning. Half-way to Boundbrook, Ewald, well ahead as usual, thought he saw something stirring. In the hope of surprising a hostile patrol, he sent back a messenger to order the rest of his men to come up quietly. He was discovered, however, and challenged. Calling in a low voice to his soldiers, he advanced close to the enemy, who turned out to be about thirty strong. They fired a volley and made off, and Ewald after them. Contrary to orders, the chasseurs also fired a few shots. It would have been better, says Ewald, to follow them slowly, as they might have taken the chasseurs for an ordinary patrol, such as was to be met with on that road almost every night. Ewald hoped, however, to make his way over the causeway and into the redoubt with the Americans, but the distance was too great and day was breaking. He had followed his nose, he says, and forgotten to look behind him, until, coming within a hundred yards of the redoûbt, he found himself exposed to a sharp fire, which wounded some of his volunteers. He then looked round and found that his whole force consisted of one lieutenant and seven men. With these he threw himself upon the bridge, hardly forty yards from the redoubt, and dodged behind the stone parapet. He hoped that more of his party would come to the rescue, but it turned out that General Matthews had commanded the column to halt, as he did not wish to sacrifice lives unnecessarily. Ewald's seven chasseurs kept firing at the embrasures of the redoubt, and their fire was hotly answered, but no one on their side was hit. In less than a quarter of an hour they had the pleasure of hearing brisk firing beyond the redoubt, which had been taken in its rear by Cornwallis. The garrison abandoned the work, and Ewald, with his lieutenant and seven men, proceeded to take possession, and captured twelve prisoners into the bargain. "But," says Ewald, "it was through my error that Lord Cornwallis took only one hundred and fifty prisoners and two cannon, instead of a thousand men. For the enemy were awakened by the firing of the redoubt, and got time to escape, together with General Lincoln." *

Here is another of Ewald's anecdotes, concerning this campaign: "When we were posted at New Bruns-

* Ewald's "Belehrungen," vol. ii. p. 122.—The date was April 13th, 1777. Lincoln had about five hundred men in Boundbrook.—Bancroft, vol. ix. p. 346. The Americans lost two lieutenants and about twenty men, and two guns. The British stayed about an hour and a half and then returned to Brunswick, and General Lincoln took his post again.—Washington, vol. iv. p. 391 n.

wick, in Jersey, in the beginning of the year 1777, during the American war, I had charge of the outermost end of the picket line near Raritan Landing, on the Boundbrook road. This post could only be held through great watchfulness, and on account of the love and good-will of the chasseurs to myself. We were daily skirmishing with the Americans, for we were only about a mile apart. One morning towards spring, the Americans, under cover of a thick fog, crept so near to one of my outposts that they reached one of my pickets at the same moment with a patrol I had sent out, and routed it. They rushed in on me so quickly as to get within about two hundred yards of me. Fortunately, there was a sunken road between us, into which I threw myself with sixteen chasseurs, calling to Lieutenant Hinrichs to cover my right flank with the rest of the men until Captain Wreeden could come up with his company. Just as I reached the sunken road I received the brisk fire of a regiment of light infantry, under Colonel Buttlar, whereupon my men, who were usually brave fellows, lost their heads and ran away. Astonished, as you may readily believe, I called after them, 'You may run to the devil, but I'll stay here alone.' At this moment I perceived that one man, Jäger Bauer, had stayed by me. He answered, 'No, you shall not stay alone,' and he called after the chasseurs that were making off: 'Boys! stop! a scoundrel runs away.' After he had shouted out these words a few times they all came back and fought like brave fellows. The Americans, who had kept up a continual fire all this time, had not been aware of this frightful scrape I had been in. Captain Wreeden, and the light infantry of the English guard, under Colonel Osborn, came to our assistance, and the Americans were driven back with great loss and pushed nearly to Boundbrook." * Jäger Bauer, who stood by Ewald on this occasion, was an insignificant-looking fellow from the Anspach district. Ewald had at first refused to take him into the company on account of his appearance, but had been persuaded to enlist him on seeing the excellence of his shooting. Shortly after the affair above mentioned Bauer gave another proof of his daring. On the morning of the 25th of May, Ewald, with a party of eleven chasseurs and thirty dragoons, fell into an ambuscade near Boundbrook. They were surrounded and in danger of being taken, and just at that moment Ewald's horse stumbled, and the captain lay in the road. When the chasseurs, who were a little way off, saw their captain's horse coming towards them riderless, Bauer and two others started out to bring off the injured officer. They carried him back amid a shower of lead, and had got him into a safe place, when Bauer noticed that Ewald's hat was missing. "We must go get it," said he, "or they will carry our captain's hat in triumph into Boundbrook to-morrow." So they ran back again, and actually brought off the hat in spite of the bullets.†

Ewald asserts that Colonel Reed visited Donop twice before the surprise of Trenton, on the pretext of making an exchange of prisoners, but really for the purpose of reconnoitring. He goes on to tell the following story: "In the same way the two colonels, Hamil-

* Ewald's "Belehrungen," vol. i. p. 15.

† Eelking's "Hülfstruppen," vol. i. p. 186.

ton and Schmidt,* came with a trumpeter to the post which I held near New Brunswick, in Jersey, in the beginning of the campaign of 1777, after General Howe had advanced from New Brunswick to Milztown,† and marched back again. They had unimportant letters to General Grant from two English officers of his brigade, who had been taken prisoners the day before, through their own carelessness in riding about for pleasure. I let these two gentlemen, who were very elegant and polite men, understand that I was very well aware of their business, and gave them the well-meant advice to be off as quickly as possible, and not to visit me again in a hurry. At this they seemed very much astonished, but followed my advice with all speed. I would certainly have sent them under arrest to headquarters, with their eyes bound, if I had not known from experience that people would have laughed at such prudent measures against the Americans. The best thing to do, when such gentlemen come at unseasonable times with messages, is to take them about with one for at least half a campaign." ‡

I do not at all believe that Hamilton came to the British outposts with the object here attributed to him, and I am certain that if he did so it was without Washington's knowledge. There is no reason, however, to doubt that Ewald suspected him, and dismissed him as described.

It was in this winter of 1776–77 that negotiations

* Lieutenant-colonel William S. Smith of New York (?).

† Millstone, an American proper name spelled by Ewald, can often be considered no more than a hint.

‡ Ewald's "Belehrungen," vol. iii. p. 339.

began in consequence of which Lieutenant-general von Heister was recalled from the command of the Hessian troops, and Lieutenant-general von Knyphausen succeeded him. The recall was insisted on by Lord Suffolk on the ground that Sir William Howe was not satisfied with Heister. How far Sir William's dislike may have been caused by purely personal reasons, or how far the suspicion may be justified that Heister was too "regardful of the preservation of the troops under his command," it is perhaps now impossible to determine. But we know that Howe was dissatisfied with Heister before the affair at Trenton, at a time when the English losses had been decidedly heavier than the Hessian. Heister had, by the treaty between the King of England and the Landgrave, a right to the immediate command of about one half of Sir William Howe's army. The stipulations of the treaty were sufficiently indefinite to have given rise to many questions. Heister is said to have been unruly. At any rate, he did not get on well with his commanding officer. This should have been a sufficient reason for recalling him.

The English government preferred not to appear openly in the matter, and the recall was made by the Landgrave on the ground of Heister's health and age, and only "for a time." It was well understood, however, that the old general was going off in disgrace. To Knyphausen the Landgrave writes: "Nothing but the entire neglect of all order and discipline can have brought this shame [of Trenton] upon us. I think it very necessary to speak with Lieutenant-general von Heister on the subject, and his health is, moreover, not robust enough for the climate over there. I therefore write to him to come here for a while, and confer the command *ad interim* over my troops in America on yourself." Heister quite understood that he was in disgrace, and died within two months after reaching Cassel, of sorrow and disappointment.*

In the early spring of 1777 the actual possessions of the King of England on the soil of the United States may be summed up as follows: In the State of New York, the islands in the harbor, and perhaps a little piece of Westchester County, near King's Bridge. In New Jersey, Amboy, New Brunswick, and Paulus Hook. In Rhode Island, the actual island. But the importance of these posts was out of all proportion to their extent. Sir William Howe commanded an army, small, indeed, as modern armies are reckoned, but large enough to outnumber that of Washington, and composed of disciplined troops, many of them veterans, while the American force was a shifting mass, principally made up of militia. Congress had voted, on one of the last days of 1776, that Washington be allowed to raise, organize, and officer sixteen battalions of infantry, three thousand light horsemen, three regiments of artillery, and a corps of engineers. But these troops, the first army of the United States, as such, together with the eighty-eight battalions to be furnished at the same time by the several states, as yet existed principally on paper. On the 14th of March, 1777, Washington writes to Con-

* Heister did not actually leave the army until June 22d, 1777. For the negotiations concerning his recall, see Eelking's "Hülfstruppen," vol. i. pp. 388–393.

gress: "From the most accurate estimate that I can form, the whole of our numbers in Jersey, fit for duty at this time, is under three thousand. These, nine hundred and eighty-one excepted, are militia, and stand engaged only till the last of this month. The troops under inoculation, including their attendants, amount to about one thousand." * Sir William Howe's army at this date can hardly have numbered less than twenty-five thousand soldiers.

The handful of men who actively upheld the cause of American freedom were without money, without credit, often without clothing. Against them were pitted the might of a great empire, the loyalty inspired by an ancient monarchy, an unlimited credit, incalculable resources. A second British army was preparing to co-operate from Canada with that under Sir William Howe, and by occupying the line of the Hudson, to cut the country in two. The Americans could not hope for foreign help until they should have shown their ability to help themselves. Their reliance could only be on their own steadfastness, and on the genius and patriotic fortitude of their Great Leader.

---

* Washington, vol. iv. p. 364.

CHAPTER X.

THE BRUNSWICKERS IN CANADA, 1776.

THE Brunswick contingent of the German troops hired by England to suppress the revolt in her North American colonies was commanded by Baron Friedrich Adolph von Riedesel. He was of a noble Hessian family, and was born in 1738. At the age of fifteen he was sent to Marburg to study law, though he hardly knew how to write and had learned but a few scraps of Latin. A battalion of Hessian infantry was quartered at Marburg at the time, and Riedesel liked better to look at the soldiers than to listen to the professors of the school. The major, who had made the boy's acquaintance, saw the chance of a recruit. He advised Riedesel to enter his company in the hope of advancement, and told him, moreover, that he was well acquainted with his father, and would write to him to ask his consent to the scheme. Shortly afterwards the major told Riedesel that he had heard from the latter's father, who had consented to his enlistment. The boy was delighted at the news, and was presently mustered into the service. When he wrote to thank his father, however, he received a disappointing answer. The Baron von Riedesel had never heard of the major, and had never granted permission to his son to leave the profession chosen for him. Now that the young man had entered the service, his honor obliged him to stand by his colors, but he must look for no more assistance from his father. Nothing remained for young Riedesel but to make the best of his circumstances. The whole affair was but an instance of the German recruiting system of the time.

The Landgrave of Hesse-Cassel had let out some of his regiments to England. Riedesel accompanied his battalion to that country with the rank of an ensign. He had not stayed there long enough, however, to learn the language perfectly, before his regiment was ordered back to Germany to take part in the Seven Years' War, in which England and Prussia, with Hanover, Brunswick, and some of the smaller German states, were opposed to France, Austria, Russia, and Sweden. From this time Riedesel's advancement was rapid. He became a favorite of Prince Ferdinand, and exchanged the service of Hesse for that of Brunswick. He had risen to the rank of colonel at the time of the outbreak of the American Revolution, and was appointed major-general on the day when he marched from Brunswick at the head of the contingent for America.

Riedesel saw nothing disgraceful in the work in which he was engaged. He was a soldier of a type common in the eighteenth century, and in military matters knew no duty but his orders. He was, moreover, a tender husband and father, and his wife and children were to follow him to the New World as soon as the health of the former would allow it. "Dearest wife," writes he from his first halting-place, "never have I suffered more than this morning as I came away. My heart was breaking, and if I could have returned, who knows what I might have done. But, my love, God has given me this calling; I must follow it; duty and honor bind me to it, and I must console myself and not complain."*

General Riedesel set out from Brunswick on the 22d of February, 1776, for Stade, on the Elbe, at the head of two thousand two hundred and eighty-two men. The troops were embarked between the 12th and the 17th of March, and got to sea on the 22d of that month. There were seventy-seven soldiers' wives with this division. The remainder of the Brunswick contingent marched to Stade in the month of May. The divisions amounted together to the number of forty-three hundred men. The regiment of Hesse-Hanau, six hundred and sixty-eight strong, joined the expedition at Portsmouth. The Brunswickers were reviewed and mustered into the English service by Colonel Faucitt, who was not pleased with the appearance of the soldiers. Many were too old, many were half-grown boys. The uniforms of the first division were so bad that the English government was obliged to advance £5000 to Riedesel to get his men a new outfit in Portsmouth. He was cheated by the English contractors, and when the cases of shoes were opened at sea, they were found to contain ladies' slippers. For a Canadian campaign no overcoats had been provided. New uniforms for the first division were sent after them in the course of the summer.†

* Baroness Riedesel, p. 1.

† As late as January, 1779, fourteen Brunswick soldiers and two soldiers' wives froze to death on a march in Canada, and about thirty were frost-bitten; and their officer excused himself on the ground that they were insufficiently clad.—Eelking's "Hülfstruppen," vol. ii. p. 187.

The general was well pleased with the spirit of his troops. "I cannot sufficiently describe the contentment of our soldiers," writes he from shipboard, to his old chief, Prince Ferdinand of Brunswick; "all are bright and in good spirits."* Soon, however, sea-sickness came to add to the discomfort of the crowded ships. "The soldiers have almost all been sick, and most of them continue so, as do also my servants," writes Riedesel to his wife from off Dover. "The poor cook is so bad that he can't work at all, nor so much as lift his hand. This is very uncomfortable for us, for Captain Foy and I have to do our own cooking. You would laugh to see us." Before the end of the voyage the drinking-water was foul.†

The fleet of thirty sail weighed anchor at Portsmouth on the 4th of April, and arrived off Cape Gaspé on the 16th of May and before Quebec on the 1st of June. Riedesel here received the command of a separate corps made up of one English and two German battalions, with one hundred and fifty Canadians and three hundred Indians, and posted along the St. Lawrence between Quebec and Montreal. "This country will delight you; it is as beautiful as can be," writes Riedesel to his wife on the 8th of June; and again, on the 28th, he says: "You will find this neighborhood beautiful. It is only a pity that the colonies are still in their childhood, so that vegetables, fruit, and such other things as belong to a good table are very hard to find; but we have meat, poultry, and milk in profusion. The houses are all only of one story, but have many

* Eelking's "Riedesel," vol. ii. p. 18.

† Baroness Riedesel, pp. 13, 22.

rooms in them, and are very clean. The inhabitants are very polite and obliging, and I do not believe that our peasants would behave so well under similar circumstances."

So slowly did news travel at that time, that the defeat of Montgomery and Arnold before Quebec, on the 31st of December, 1775, was not known in England when the fleet sailed thence. It was first learned by Riedesel and his companions on their way up the St. Lawrence River. Shortly after their arrival Canada was cleared of "rebel" troops as far as the northern end of Lake Champlain, on which lake the Americans had improvised a fleet, consisting of four sloops, eight "gondolas," and three row-galleys. The summer was spent by the British in building vessels of war and transports for an advance up the lake. The troops were quartered, or encamped, along the St. Lawrence and Richelieu rivers, and but one considerable skirmish occurred to break the routine of drill, countermarching, and intrenchment while the boat-building was in progress.

On the 23d of June General Riedesel was present at a solemn meeting in the former Jesuits' Church at Montreal, between General Carleton, Governor of Canada, and the chiefs of the Five Nations. All the principal officers of the army were invited, and about three hundred Indians were present. The European officers were provided with chairs in the choir of the church, the governor sitting in the middle with his hat on. The Indians sat on benches in the body of the building, smoking their pipes. After speeches had been made and interpreted, the services of the Indians were accepted by the English general, and posts were assigned to them. The Indians shook hands with the European officers, and rebel scalps were presented to Generals Carleton, Burgoyne, and Phillips. What the English gentlemen did with these charming presents of their humane allies does not appear. At a later conference, held by General Carleton with Indians from farther west, one of them appeared wearing the uniform of General Braddock, whom he himself claimed to have killed.

Of Montreal Riedesel says: "This city is, indeed, somewhat finer than Quebec, and has about sixteen hundred houses. It is surrounded by nothing more than a wall, with loopholes for cannon and musketry, and what is called the citadel is a block-house in very bad condition. These works were begun in 1736. The whole island of Montreal, as well as the city, belongs to the seminary. . . . Near this seminary is the best garden in all Canada, but it is not better laid out than that of a private person at home. They have most sorts of European plants there."

At last, on the 9th of September, the transports were ready for an advance up Lake Champlain. It was necessary, however, to wait a month longer for the war vessels. These, when completed, exceeded those of the Americans more than two to one, both in numbers and in the weight of metal carried. They were manned by picked English sailors, while the sloops and gondolas under Benedict Arnold were mostly sailed and commanded by landsmen. The result was what might have been expected. Arnold chose, on the 10th of October, 1776, a disadvantageous position between Valcour Island and the western shore of the lake.

Here he maintained an unequal fight on the 11th, and hence he escaped on the following night by boldly slipping through the line of the British fleet. On the 13th he was overtaken by Carleton near the Island of the Four Winds. Some of the boats struck; some were run ashore and burned; only five escaped. Arnold and his crews behaved with the greatest courage throughout; but courage alone could not compensate for want of seamanship and for inferior numbers. Some of the Germans took part in the naval engagement of the 11th, and one of the batteaux on which were the Hanau artillery was sunk by the American fire. The soldiers and sailors that manned it, however, were saved by another boat.*

Presently, after this naval battle, Carleton occupied Crown Point without opposition. Scouting parties were pushed out into the neighborhood of Ticonderoga. Riedesel was so near that fortress on the 22d or 23d of October as to see it plainly from a hill. He thought it might easily be taken by the British army in Canada, were the whole of that army to be brought forward, yet he reckoned the numbers of the effective garrison decidedly too high. Sir Guy Carleton chose to think it too late to undertake further conquests that autumn. He even abandoned Crown Point and retired to the northern end of the lake.

The troops were ordered into winter quarters; the Germans along the Richelieu River and in the neighborhood of Lake St. Pierre. Riedesel's headquarters were at Trois Rivières. Pains were taken that the

---

* For a graphic account of the fight of October 11th, see the MS. "Tagebuch vom Capit. Pausch."

presence of the soldiers should not weigh too heavily on the inhabitants, unless on those who had shown sympathy with the rebels. Strict discipline was maintained. The soldiers received rations, and cut their own firewood in the forest. The labor of hauling the wood when cut, and of cooking, seems to have been laid on the inhabitants. The soldiers were provided with long trousers of thick cloth, coming up high on the body, and warm mittens and hoods.

The second division of Brunswickers had arrived in Canada in September, after a long and stormy passage. Officers and men had at last been put on short rations of musty food. When the division, of about two thousand soldiers, arrived in Quebec, nineteen men had died and one hundred and thirty-one were sick of the scurvy.

The long Canadian winter presently set in. It was employed by Riedesel in drilling his troops when the weather would allow it, and especially in practising them in shooting. He had noticed that the Americans were better marksmen than the Germans, and he exerted himself to remedy this deficiency of his soldiers. He travelled over eighteen hundred miles in the course of the winter in a sleigh, visiting his scattered detachments, and waiting on General Carleton in Quebec and Montreal. He was at the former place on the 31st of December, 1776, when a solemn service was held in the cathedral to celebrate the deliverance of the city from Arnold and Montgomery on that day of the preceding year. The service was conducted by the bishop, and eight unfortunate Canadians had to do open penance, with halters round their necks, and beg pardon of God, the Church, and King George for having helped the Americans.*

During the latter part of the winter Riedesel gave a ball at Trois Rivières every week, partly to please the inhabitants and partly to keep his officers out of mischief. The 20th of January, the birthday of the Queen of England, was celebrated with great pomp. Forty guests sat down to dinner. Healths were drunk in champagne, and a small cannon was fired at every toast, after the manner of the first act of "Hamlet." In the afternoon and evening was a ball, at which so many as thirty-seven ladies appeared. To these supper was served in the evening, and they were waited upon by the gentlemen. "The Demoiselle de Tonnencour," writes an eye-witness, "increased her charms by her jewels, but poor Demoiselle R——e, in her shabby cotton gown, was preferred by many of us, on account of her natural and pleasant manners and her beautiful voice. You must know, sir, that the Canadian fair ones sing French and Italian songs at table, and that several songs have already been written and composed in honor of General Riedesel, and that they are often sung at Trois Rivières." So, with duty and pleasure, the months wore away until the beginning of June, 1777, when an eventful campaign was to open for the Brunswickers.†

* Schlözer's "Briefwechsel," vol. iv. p. 306.

† Ibid., vol. iv. pp. 308, 309.

CHAPTER XI.

BARONESS RIEDESEL'S JOURNEY, 1776 AND 1777.

THE Baroness Riedesel had started to join her husband, bringing with her her three little daughters, of whom the oldest was but four years and nine months old, and the youngest an infant of ten weeks. The journey from Germany to Canada in those days was no light matter, nor was it free from imaginary as well as actual perils. "Not only did people tell me of the dangers of the sea," writes Frau von Riedesel, "but they also said that we must take care not to be eaten by the savages, and that people in America lived on horseflesh and cats. But all this frightened me less than the thought of coming to a land where I did not understand the language. However, I had made up my mind to everything, and the idea of following my husband and doing my duty held me up through the whole course of my journey."

The baroness left Wolfenbüttel, near Brunswick, on the 14th of May, 1776, and travelled by Calais to England. "At Maestricht I was warned to be on my guard, because the roads were very unsafe on account of highwaymen. A hundred and thirty of these had been hanged, or otherwise executed, in the course of the last fortnight, but there were more than four times as many still about. When taken they were immediately strung up without further ceremony on the roads and at the places where they plied their trade. This news frightened me very much, and I made up my mind not to travel at night; but, as I got very bad horses, I had to go through a wood about dusk, where something that was hanging struck against me through the open window of the carriage. I took hold of it, and, feeling something rough, asked what it was. It was a hanged man, with woollen stockings. While I was still startled at this, my anxiety was much increased as we drew up before a lonely house in this same wood, and the postilions refused to drive any farther. The place was called Hune. I shall never forget it! A man of rather suspicious appearance received us, and led us into a room in a very retired part of the house, where I found only one bed.

"It was cold, so I had a fire made in a great fireplace. Our whole supper was composed of tea and very coarse bread. My faithful Rockel [her old servant] came to me with a very anxious face and said: 'Things aren't right here! There's a big room full of fire-arms. I think the other people are out. They are certainly rogues. But I'll sit up all night in front of your chamber with my gun, and will sell my life dearly. The other servant shall sit in the carriage, also with his gun.' All this, naturally, did not make my sleep peaceful. I sat on a chair and laid my head on the bed. Yet, at last I fell asleep, and how great was my joy on waking, at about four in the morning, to have them come and tell me that all was ready for us to travel on. I then put my head out of the window, and listened to a number of nightingales in the wood in which we were, whose pleasant song made me forget my past anxiety."

Such were the discomforts of travelling on the Continent a hundred years ago. We shall see presently what disagreeable adventures awaited foreigners in England. The baroness crossed safely from Calais to Dover, and posted to London. The innkeeper in Calais had told her that it would not be safe for her to travel alone, and, after a great pretence of seeking, had introduced a man to her, whom he represented to be a gentleman, who had consented to act as her escort. This man accompanied her to London, where she was lodged in the fourth story of an inn, though she had asked for good rooms. In her narrative she says: "The next day the innkeeper came to me with a shamefaced expression, and asked me very respectfully if I knew the person with whom I had come, and of whom I had told him to take such good care (for I had considered it improper to let him eat with me in London). I told him it was a gentleman who, at the request of Mr. Guilhaudin, mine host in Calais, had been so considerate as to accompany me on my journey. 'Ha!' answered he, 'it is one of his tricks. It's a hired servant, an arrant swindler, whom he employs to carry on his business, and when I saw you sitting in the carriage with this fellow, as you arrived, I must acknowledge that I did not believe you were the person that you gave yourself out for, and therefore thought these rooms would be good enough for you. As I now see, from the people that come to visit you, that I made a mistake, I humbly beg your pardon, and entreat you to take other rooms, for which you shall pay me no more than for these, so much do I wish to make good my error.' I thanked him, and begged him to get rid of the person for me as soon as possible; yet the man demanded four or six guineas (I don't remember now exactly how much) for his company."

Baroness Riedesel had found acquaintances in London, and among others Schlieffen, the Minister of the Landgrave of Hesse-Cassel, the man who had made the largest bargain for the sale of German troops to England. She went somewhat into society, but was much kept at home by the care of her infant daughter. "One day," she writes, "I had an unpleasant adventure in London. I had been advised to buy a little cloak and a hat, without which I could not go out. I was dining at the house of Herr von Hinüber, the Hanoverian Minister. His wife proposed to me to take a walk to St. James's, but omitted to tell me what in our dress was contrary to the English fashion. Little Augusta was dressed in French style, and wore a little hoop and a pretty little round hat. I noticed that people were almost pointing their fingers at us, and asked the cause. She [Frau von Hinüber] told me that I had a fan, which ought not to be carried with a hat, and that my little girl was overdressed, so that we were taken for French people, who were not in favor here.

"The next day I went there again, and we were all dressed in the English fashion, so I thought that no one would notice us; but I was mistaken, for I heard them again calling out, 'Frenchwomen! Pretty girl!' I asked the servant why we were taken for French people, and was told it was because I had put ribbons on the children. I tore them off and put them in my pocket, but people still stared at me, and I heard that it was on account of the hats, which children in England wore of another shape. I saw from this how necessary it was to conform to the fashion of the country in order to be comfortable there, for the mob collects at once, and if you let yourself be drawn into bandying words with it, you are insulted."

A few days later the baroness went to Bristol. She writes: "The day after I arrived my hostess called me to see a pretty sight (as she expressed it). When I stepped to the window I saw two naked men who were boxing with great fury. I saw their blood flow, and the rage in their eyes. Unaccustomed to so ugly a spectacle, I drew back as quickly as possible to the most retired corner of the house, so as not to hear the cries of joy which the spectators gave when one of the men received a blow. I had an unpleasant adventure during my stay in Bristol. I wore a chintz dress trimmed with green taffetas. This must have appeared too foreign to the Bristol people, for when I went out one day to walk with Mrs. Foy, more than a hundred sailors, gathered together, pointed their fingers at me and called out 'French ——!' I flew as quickly as I could into the house of a shopkeeper and made a pretext of buying something there; meanwhile the crowd dispersed. But this disgusted me with my dress, and when I got home again I gave it to my cook, although it was quite new."

Frau von Riedesel spent ten months in England. Her husband had told her not to travel without the company of a lady, and had recommended Mrs. Foy, above mentioned, who was also to join her husband in Canada. This lady kept the baroness waiting all through the summer of 1776, and at last absolutely refused to go. It was late in the autumn, and Baroness Riedesel was advised not to attempt the passage, as she might find the St. Lawrence blocked with ice. She therefore returned to London, where she found good lodgings among kind people, and spent the following winter. The care of her children forced her to lead a quiet life. She was presented at court, however, of which ceremony she gives the following account: "I was advised to go to court, as the queen had expressed a wish to see me. So I had a court dress made, and Lady George Germaine presented me. It was on New Year's Day, 1777. I thought the palace very ugly and very old-fashioned in its furniture. The ladies and gentlemen all took their places in the audience chamber; then the king, who had three gentlemen walking in front of him, came into the room. The queen followed, with one lady holding her train, and a gentleman in waiting. The king went round to the right and the queen to the left. Neither of them passes any one without speaking to him. At the end of the chamber they meet, make each other a low bow and courtesy, and each goes where the other has come from. I asked Lady Germaine what I should do, and whether the king kissed all the ladies, as I had heard he did. 'No,' answered she, 'only the Englishwomen and the marchionesses,' and there was nothing to do but to stand still in your place. Now, when the king came up to me I was much astonished to have him kiss me, and I blushed scarlet, because I was not expecting it. He immediately asked me whether I had received letters from my husband. I answered, 'Yes, of the 22d of November.' 'He is well,' answered he; 'I have inquired expressly about him; every one is pleased with him, and I hope the cold will do him no harm.' I answered that I hoped and believed that he would not feel the cold so much, as he was born in a cold climate. 'I hope so too,' said he, 'but I can assure you of this, that the air there is very healthy and clear.' Thereupon he made me a pleasant bow and went on. When he was gone I said to Lady Germaine that I was now naturalized, since the king had kissed me.

"Afterwards came the queen, who was also very kind to me, and asked if I had been long in London. I said, two months. 'I thought it was longer,' answered she. I answered, in London only so long, but in England already seven months. She asked whether I liked it here. I said yes, but that I much wished to be in Canada.—'Are you, then, not afraid of the sea?' she then asked; 'I don't like it at all.'—'Nor I either,' I replied, 'only there is no other way to see my husband again, and I shall travel with friends.'—'I admire your courage,' said she, 'for it is a great undertaking and very difficult, particularly with three children.'

"I saw, from this conversation, that she had already heard of me, and I was therefore glad that I had gone to court. After the ceremony I saw all the royal children, but one who was sick. There were ten of them, and I thought them all beautiful.

"I went again several times, as I had been so well received. When I took leave of the queen in the spring, before going to Portsmouth to embark, she asked me again if I were not afraid of so terrible a journey, and when I answered that, as my husband wanted me to follow him, I did so with courage and pleasure, because I thought I was doing my duty, and I was sure that she, in my place, would do the same, she said to me: 'Yes, but as I am told, you are making the journey without your husband's knowledge.'— I answered, that as she was a German princess she must know that without my husband's consent I could not have undertaken this, because I should not have had the money. 'You are right,' said she; 'I approve of your determination, and wish you all imaginable good-fortune. What is the name of your ship? I shall often inquire after you, and hope that you will visit me on your return.'—She kept her word, and often inquired after me, and often sent me polite messages."

Baroness Riedesel embarked on a packet-ship on the 15th of April, 1777, in company with a fleet of thirty transports, under convoy of two ships of war. She arrived in Quebec on the 11th of June, after an uneventful voyage. Spending only half a day in Quebec, the indomitable woman, with her three little daughters, pressed on over rough roads and stormy rivers to Chambly, where, at last, on the 14th of June, she met her husband. They could spend but two happy days together, for the army was in motion, and the baroness was obliged to return to Trois Rivières. On the 14th of August, however, she again joined the army, whose subsequent fate she shared. I will give but one more of her adventures before returning to the consideration of the military operations of the Brunswick contingent.

The baroness had set out from Trois Rivières to join her husband at Fort Edward, on the Hudson. The party travelled in two boats, one of which carried the baggage. She writes: "Night overtook us and we saw ourselves obliged to land on an island. The other boat, which was heavier laden and not so well manned, had not been able to keep up with us; so we had neither beds nor light, and, worst of all, nothing to eat; for we had brought no more in our boat than we had expected to use during the day, and found nothing on this island but the four bare walls of a deserted and, indeed, never finished house, full of boughs, on which we made our camp. I covered them with our cloaks and took the cushions from the boat to help us out, so that we slept very well.

"I could not persuade Captain Willoe to come into the hut with us, and saw that he was very uneasy, which I could not understand. Meanwhile, I noticed a soldier who was setting a pot on the fire. I asked him what he had in it. 'Potatoes, which I brought with me.' I looked wistfully at him; he had so few that I thought it cruel to rob him of them, particularly as he looked so happy over them. At last the desire to give my children some conquered my modesty, so I asked and got half, which may have been, at most, a dozen. Thereupon he pulled two or three candle-ends out of his pocket, which made me very happy, because the children were afraid to stay in the dark. I gave him a big thaler for it all, which made him as happy as I was. Meanwhile, I heard Captain Willoe give orders to make fires around the building and to keep guard all night about it. I also heard them making noises all through the night, which interfered a little with my sleep. Next morning, at breakfast (which I took on a broad rock which served us for a table), I asked the captain the cause of the noise. He informed me that we had been in great danger, inasmuch as this island was the *Ile aux Sonnettes*, so called from the number of rattlesnakes on it; that he had not known of this, and had been very much alarmed when he heard it, but had not dared to venture going farther in the night on account of the current. He had, therefore, nothing to do but to build large fires and make a great deal of noise in order to frighten the snakes away. But he had not been able to close his eyes the whole night from anxiety on our account. I was much alarmed at this story, and remarked to him that our danger had been greatly increased by lying on the boughs in which the snakes like to hide. He agreed with me, and said that if he had known sooner where we were, he would have had all the boughs taken away, or have begged us rather to stay in the bark. He had first learned it, however, from one of the people in our other boat, which had followed us later. In the morning we found skins and slime of these nasty beasts all about, and hurried through our breakfast as quickly as possible."*

---

* Baroness Riedesel's "Berufs Reise nach America."

CHAPTER XII.

TICONDEROGA AND BENNINGTON, JULY AND AUGUST, 1777.

THE operations in Canada and on Lake Champlain, during the summer and autumn of 1776, had been conducted by Sir Guy Carleton, the British governor of the province. Generals Burgoyne and Phillips and General Riedesel had served under his orders. For the campaign of 1777, however, a new arrangement was made by the English ministry. Carleton retained the governorship and the command of the army in Canada, but the expedition which was to pass beyond the boundaries of the province, and to oppose the rebels in New York and New England, was intrusted to Burgoyne.

Lieutenant-general John Burgoyne was at this time fifty-five years of age. Lord Macaulay describes him as "a man of wit, fashion, and honor, an agreeable dramatic writer, an officer whose courage was never questioned, and whose skill was at that time highly esteemed."* The time spoken of was but shortly previous to the American war.

Burgoyne was a favorite with the British ministry. He was not a favorite with General Riedesel, nor with that general's wife. Riedesel got on very well with Carleton, but had no faith in Burgoyne, who was prob-

* Essay on Lord Clive.

ably too much a man of pleasure and of wit to win the confidence of the seriously-minded German officer. Riedesel complains that he was never consulted, and that Burgoyne's plans were not confided to him. It is plain that there was jealousy between the English and German troops, and that Riedesel felt that injustice was being done to himself and to his command.

The plan of operations, of which the main features were made out by Burgoyne himself, was very simple. The main body of the army was to advance from Canada up Lake Champlain to Ticonderoga. When that fort should have been taken, the army was to push still southward to Albany, where it was to meet the army of Sir William Howe, or a part thereof, coming up from New York. A body of light troops, under Colonel St. Leger, was to co-operate with Burgoyne, marching by Oswego to the Mohawk River, which it was to follow to its junction with the Hudson, above Albany, at which point this expedition was to unite with the main army.

The Brunswickers under General Riedesel's orders on the 1st of June, 1777, numbered four thousand three hundred and one officers and men on the rolls, with an effective strength of three thousand nine hundred and fifty-eight.* The Hesse-Hanau regiment had sailed in the previous year, six hundred and sixty-eight strong, and had probably not fallen below six hundred men fit for service. This would make the total number of Germans in Canada at the opening of the campaign four thousand five hundred and fifty-

* Eelking's Life of Riedesel, vol. ii. p. 90, n.

eight men, of whom six hundred and sixty-seven were left under the command of Sir Guy Carleton, and three thousand eight hundred and ninety-one accompanied the expedition under Burgoyne. This estimate does not include the Hanau chasseurs who were attached to St. Leger's expedition. The total number of white men under Burgoyne was greater than eight thousand, about two hundred and fifty of these being Provincials.

Some five hundred Indians accompanied the army, and at first did good service as scouts, and exhibited to their humane employers the scalps of American soldiers. The sight found favor in the eyes of the fashionable gentleman who commanded his majesty's army. He issued an order that deserters from his own force should be caught and scalped likewise. The savages were thought to have carried their amiable customs too far when they killed Jane McCrea, a young woman betrothed to a Tory with the British army, who had been intrusted to the protection and guidance of two of them. Burgoyne, however, did not venture to execute the murderer, for fear of "the total defection of the Indians."

Before the establishment of railways had changed the lines of travel, the principal highway between Canada, on the one hand, and New England and the more southern colonies, on the other, was the great water route, which, leaving the St. Lawrence at Lake St. Pierre, led up the Richelieu River, past Fort St. John, to Lake Champlain, and up Lake Champlain, past Crown Point, to Ticonderoga. At Ticonderoga a choice of two ways lay before the traveller, or the invader. He might cross the short portage to Lake George, pass up that beautiful lake to its head, and make a portage of twelve miles to Fort Edward, on the Hudson. This was the usual and the easier way. Or he might follow the narrow upper end of Lake Champlain to the site of the modern Whitehall, in the old district called Skenesborough, and make a longer portage to Fort Edward by Fort Anne. From Fort Edward the way lay down the Hudson to Albany and New York. The general direction of the route is north and south, and remarkably straight, considering that it follows the great natural features of the country. The whole distance from Lake St. Pierre to New York is a little more than three hundred and fifty miles. Whitehall lies about midway between them, and Ticonderoga some twenty miles north of Whitehall.

No point between the St. Lawrence and New York was considered more important from a military point of view than Fort Ticonderoga. This was so placed as to protect the portage from Lake Champlain to Lake George, and to command the passage to the southern extremity of the former lake. The fort was built by the French in 1755, and called by them Fort Carillon. It was improved by Montcalm in the following year, and in 1758 withstood the attack of an English army of fifteen thousand men, the largest body of Europeans which had yet been assembled under arms in America. General Abercrombie, who commanded the English army, so mismanaged his attack that his force was repulsed with great slaughter.

In 1759 the French abandoned Fort Carillon on the

approach of General Amherst, who repaired the works. These were now held for nearly sixteen years by the British, unmolested, until the small garrison was surprised, and the fort seized, on the 10th of May, 1776, by a party of Americans under Ethan Allen, "in the name of the Great Jehovah and the Continental Congress." During the two years that the fort had been in American hands, great pains had been taken to strengthen it, and it was most liberally supplied with guns, ammunition, and provisions. A new fort had also been constructed on the east side of the lake, at Mount Independence. The Americans would seem to have overshot the mark in the greatness of their preparations. The works, two miles and a half in length, were much too large for the garrison. Moreover, the fort could be completely commanded by artillery on Mount Defiance, a hill which was not included in the lines.

The result of these errors was disastrous. On the 1st of July, 1777, Burgoyne's army appeared before the fortress. Riedesel, with the Germans, was on the east shore of the lake operating against Mount Independence. But little fighting took place. St. Clair, the American commander, seeing himself in danger of being surrounded, retreated, with the garrison of about thirty-three hundred men, leaving the forts with more than seventy cannon, two hundred head of cattle, and a great store of ammunition and provisions, to fall into the hands of the British army. The remnants of the American fleet, which fled in the direction of Whitehall, were presently followed by the British, who had only been delayed by the necessity of breaking through the bridge and boom which had been built across the lake. Two of the five vessels were captured, and three burned by the retreating Americans, who thus lost all the material they had endeavored to save.

The main body of St. Clair's force retreated by the road to Hubbardton. It was closely followed by General Fraser with twenty companies of Englishmen, supported by Riedesel with three Brunswick battalions. Fraser came up with the rear-guard of the Americans, under Colonel Warner, at Hubbardton, on the 7th of July, was sharply attacked, and outflanked. He was in danger of being driven back when Riedesel came to his assistance. The Americans were repulsed. Their loss is not exactly known, but about two hundred stragglers and wounded men were that day made prisoners. The Brunswickers had twenty-two men killed or wounded, the British one hundred and fifty-five. This was the first engagement in the open field which Riedesel saw in America.

On the 8th of July a British regiment was driven back from Fort Anne, but the Americans promptly abandoned that fort also, leaving it in ruins.

On the 22d of July General von Riedesel issued an order against marauding, and threatened all soldiers who should be guilty of it with a beating for the first offense and with running the gantlet four times for the second offense. Officers were to decide what was lawful booty. Riedesel issued this order at the request of Burgoyne, who wished to encourage the Tory colonists of the neighborhood. The days when it would be possible for the Brunswickers to plunder in America were, however, almost past.

So rough was the country between Lake Champlain and the Hudson that it took Burgoyne a month to bring his army the twenty-five miles which lay between Whitehall and Fort Edward. "The toil of the march was great, but supported with the utmost alacrity," writes Burgoÿne to Lord George Germaine on the 30th of July, 1777. "The country being a wilderness, in almost every part of the passage the enemy took the means of cutting large timber trees on both sides the roads so as to fall across and lengthways with the branches interwoven. The troops had not only layers of them to remove in places where it was impossible to take any other direction, but also they had above forty bridges to construct and others to repair, one of which was of logwood, over a morass two miles in extent."* We find a letter from Burgoyne to Riedesel, on the 18th of July, exhorting the latter to make his officers cut down the amount of their baggage. Many English officers, says Burgoyne, are reduced to a small tent and a knapsack.†

The army met with little serious opposition on the way, though scarcely a day passed without firing. The Americans had retreated to Saratoga. Yet it was not until the 9th of August that Brigadier-general Fraser led the advanced guard to Fort Miller, seven miles beyond Fort Edward. He was followed by Lieutenant-colonel Baum, with the Brunswick dismounted dragoons and light infantry, some Canadian volunteers, and two small cannon. It had at first been proposed by Riedesel, and agreed to by Burgoyne, that Baum's

* De Fonblanque's "Burgoyne," p. 268.

† Eelking's "Riedesel," vol. iii. p. 259.

force should make an expedition into the Connecticut Valley in search of horses and draught cattle. The Duke of Brunswick's regiment of dragoons was thus to be mounted at the expense of the Americans, and the British army was to be provided with pack-horses. To understand the pressing need of beasts of burden we must remember that the army was then eating bread made of English flour, and beef salted in England, and that these provisions had to be brought from Lake Champlain, or Lake George, to the Hudson on men's backs. The plan was, however, changed before the column had passed Fort Miller, and instead of marching on Manchester, the expedition was sent to Bennington, where the Americans were supposed to have a large supply of stores. Riedesel took the liberty of remonstrating against this change of destination, but Burgoyne held to it on the following grounds: First, it would be of the greatest benefit to the army to live for ten or twelve days on the stores they might capture at Bennington. Second, he (Burgoyne) meant to advance on Stillwater with the main army, so that Arnold would not be able to send a strong detachment to oppose Baum. Third, he had heard that St. Leger was besieging Fort Stanwix, on the upper waters of the Mohawk River, and it was important to prevent Arnold from detaching a strong corps for the relief of that place. So Lieutenant-colonel Baum started off on the 11th of August, 1777, on his march towards Bennington, in command of about five hundred and fifty white men, of whom three hundred and seventy-four were Germans. About one hundred and fifty Indians accompanied the expedition. This did not satisfy the Tory who served as guide. He told Burgoyne that at least three thousand men would be necessary to insure success, but Burgoyne would not, and, indeed, could not, spare so many.*

On the 12th Baum captured some stores and cattle at Cambridge.

On the morning of the 14th he found some stores at Sancoik and took five prisoners. He reported to Burgoyne that there were fifteen or eighteen hundred men at Bennington, but that they would probably leave it on his approach. He would proceed so far as to fall on the enemy early the next day, and make such disposition as he should think necessary, from the intelligence which he should receive. People were flocking in hourly and wanted to be armed. The Indians could not be controlled, and ruined and took everything they pleased.† Baum, who could not talk English, apparently relied on the assurances of the Tory governor, Skene, who would seem to have been a very credulous personage. Burgoyne would appear not to have entirely shared in the delusions of his subordinate, for he sent back orders not to advance should Baum find the enemy too strongly posted, and

* It is impossible to determine the exact numbers of Englishmen and Provincials. They were "the select corps of British marksmen, a party of French Canadians, a more numerous party of Provincial loyalists."—Bancroft, vol. ix. p. 383. Compare also Eelking's "Riedesel," vol. ii. pp. 127, 132; Schlözer's "Briefwechsel," vol. iii. p. 36; Eelking's "Hülfstruppen," vol. i. p. 279, where the whole force, including Indians, is set at only five hundred and fifty-one. Notice that the composition of the corps was modified between August 9th and 11th.

† Coburn's "Centennial History of the Battle of Bennington," where the letter is given (probably a translation). It is dated "Sancoik, Aug. 14, 1777, 9 o'clock" (presumably nine A.M.).

maintaining such a countenance as to make a *coup de main* hazardous.* Later in the same day Baum sent another report, stating that he had been attacked by a rebel force of seven hundred men, and had driven them back with a few cannon-shots, but that there were eighteen hundred men in a well-placed, fortified camp near Bennington, and that he would wait for re-inforcements. This report reached Burgoyne during the night, and at eight in the morning of the 15th he ordered Lieutenant-colonel Breymann, with six hundred and forty-two German soldiers, to march to Baum's support. Breymann started off without tents or baggage or sufficient ammunition, and only two small field-pieces. He had only twenty-four miles to go, yet he made but little more than half the distance before he encamped for the night. The day was rainy and the road was bad, yet such slowness in a party of soldiers in light marching order going to the relief of their brothers in arms seems incredible. I have found no complete description of the uniform of the Brunswick infantry. Riedesel had introduced some modifications in it, to adapt it to the service and the climate, but it was still far too heavy. A large part of Baum's men were dismounted dragoons. They were armed with short, thick rifles and big sabres. It was said in the army that the hat and sword alone weighed more than the whole equipment of an English soldier. A man thus armed might be formidable on horseback on a level parade-ground, but afoot, in August, in a cart-track through the thick woods, he was hardly a match for an American farmer and hunter in his shirt-sleeves.

* Sparks, "Correspondence of the American Revolution," vol. ii. p. 518.

It is clear that no one, not even Baum himself, had realized the seriousness of that officer's situation. In the middle of the morning of the 15th Burgoyne wrote that if a retreat were necessary it must be so conducted as to give the enemy no opportunity for triumph, otherwise the Indians might be discouraged. Therefore, all captured cattle and wagons must be brought off, and any flour and corn that could not be carried away must be destroyed.* It was not until afterwards that Burgoyne suggested that Breymann might have pushed on without his artillery.

Lieutenant-colonel Baum spent the 15th of August, 1777, in intrenching himself on a hill about four miles north of Bennington. About nine o'clock on the morning of the 16th he noticed small bodies of men, mostly in their shirt-sleeves and with fowling-pieces on their shoulders, passing quickly and quietly behind his intrenched camp. The good officer took these shirt-sleeved fellows for Tories seeking his protection. It is said that many people in that part of the country had taken the oath to the king. In the course of the morning an attack was made and easily repulsed. At last, about three in the afternoon, the Germans were completely surrounded, and the battle began in good earnest. Most of the Indians, Canadians, and Tories made good their escape. The Brunswickers held out for an hour or two, until their ammunition began to fail. The Americans fought with desperation. They rushed to within eight paces of the cannon that were loaded with grape-shot, and discharged their rifles at the artillerymen. Stark, who commanded

* Eelking, "Riedesel" vol. iii. p. 261.

them, had inspired them with his own spirit. "Come on, my lads," he is reported to have said before the battle, "we shall either beat the British, or Molly Stark will be a widow this night." At last the fire of the Germans slackened. The Yankees rushed again on the intrenchments. It was gunstock against sabre. Baum fell, mortally wounded, and the Brunswickers were taken.

The battle with Baum's soldiers was over when Breymann arrived in the neighborhood of the field. He says that he drove the Americans before him, and only stopped pursuing them for want of powder and shot; but certain it is that he presently fell back, and made off in the night without his cannon, having lost more than one third of his men. General Burgoyne, who received word of these misfortunes early in the morning of the 17th, started at six o'clock, with the whole army, to save Breymann. The main body advanced, however, no farther than the Battenkill, while Burgoyne himself, at the head of an English regiment, pushed on until he met the retreating Germans.

Nearly seven hundred prisoners, of whom about four hundred were Germans, fell into the hands of the Americans. Of Baum's command, three hundred and sixty-five Germans did not return to camp; of Breymann's two hundred and thirty-one were killed, wounded, and missing.

This battle was the beginning of the end for Burgoyne, though he did not know it at the time. It proved the impossibility of living on the country, and sent him back to his English beef and flour, and his dependence on the provisions he could carry with him.*

The failure of St. Leger's expedition to the Mohawk occurred about this time. Colonel St. Leger had left Montreal in the early part of July, in command of about seven hundred and fifty white men and one thousand Indians. Among the former was a company of chasseurs from Hesse-Hanau. This force made its way by the St. Lawrence and Lake Ontario to Oswego, and then by Oneida Lake to Fort Stanwix, on the upper waters of the Mohawk River. This fort was a well-constructed earthwork, manned by some six or seven hundred militia, under Colonel Gansevoort. St. Leger was to take the fort and then follow the Mohawk towards its junction with the Hudson, thus threatening the flank of Gates's army. But the fort would not be taken. About eight hundred inhabitants of the Mohawk Valley, mostly of German extraction, under General Herkimer,† were advancing to its relief. These were surprised on the 6th of August, 1777, in the woods, by an overwhelming force of Provincials and Indians. After the first panic a desperate fight took place. The militia well knew that from their savage foes they could expect no quarter. It was better to fall beneath the arrow, or the tomahawk, than to be reserved for the torturing knife.

* For German accounts of the Battle of Bennington and the events that led thereto, see Riedesel's report to the Duke of Brunswick and subsequent justification of his own part in the misfortune; Breymann's report to Burgoyne, lists of losses, with many other interesting documents in Eelking's "Riedesel," vol. iii. pp. 184–197, 210–214 and 261. See also Schlözer's "Briefwechsel," vol. iii. pp. 35–42.

† In German Nikolaus Herckheimer.

Herkimer, who had been wounded in the leg, was propped against the trunk of a tree, and directed the defense, puffing meanwhile at his pipe. The men were set in pairs behind the trees, that each might defend the other while he was loading. This plan worked well, and the militia began to get the advantage. A party of Tories from the valley itself came to the assistance of the Indians. This inflamed still more the wrath of the Americans, for these new enemies were their neighbors and had been their friends. The desperate battle continued. It had lasted more than an hour and a half, and one hundred and sixty of the militia had been killed, wounded, or taken, when firing was heard in the direction of Fort Stanwix. Colonel Gansevoort, informed of Herkimer's approach, had sent two hundred and fifty men from the fort to effect a diversion. These fell upon the English camp and pillaged a part of it. Five flags and much baggage fell into the hands of the party from the fort. On hearing the cannon behind them, the Tories and Indians feared lest they should be taken between two fires. They made off, taking some prisoners with them to undergo the horrors of Indian torture, but leaving many dead upon the field. What remained of the militia retreated to Fort Schuyler, where now the city of Utica stands. This sanguinary affair is called the Battle of Oriskany. It settled the fate of St. Leger's expedition, and contributed, with Bennington, to determine that of Burgoyne and of the Brunswickers. These two small engagements form a turning-point in American history.*

* A company of Hessian (Hanau) chasseurs accompanied St. Leger to

The brave Herkimer died of his wounds ten days after the battle. But less than a week after that time, Benedict Arnold, bringing with him a small force, and again assembling the militia of the valley, raised the siege of Fort Stanwix, and St. Leger, abandoned by many of his Indians, made off with the remnant of his force to Oswego, leaving his tents and "a considerable baggage."*

Burgoyne was somewhat discouraged at the failures of Baum and St. Leger, but he still relied on help to come from the southward, and felt bound by the orders he had received from England.

Fort Stanwix. I have not found any journal of this company. A second company arrived at Oswego, August 26th, 1777, only in time to hear that St. Leger had retreated. The report of the officer commanding this company is in the Archives at Marburg. From it we learn that the first company lost most of its tents and baggage. For the Battle of Oriskany, see Kapp's "Deutschen im Staate New York."

* Arnold to Gates, August 23d, 1777; Sparks, "Correspondence of the American Revolution," vol. ii. p. 519.

CHAPTER XIII.

STILLWATER, SEPTEMBER 19TH AND OCTOBER 7TH, 1777.

FOR nearly a month after his defeat at Bennington Burgoyne remained in the neighborhood of Fort Edward and behind the line of the Battenkill. The time was employed in bringing up stores and in transporting boats from Lake Champlain and Lake George. On the 13th of September, 1777, the army crossed the Hudson at Schuylerville, and abandoned its line of communications to make a bold stroke for Albany and a junction with Sir William Howe. One hundred and eighty boats, which had been hauled across the carries, attended the march of the army, whose left flank rested on the Hudson. These boats carried one month's provisions. "Now we went to work again at our dear salt pork and flour," writes a German officer. "Dear friends, do not despise these royal dishes, which really cost a royal price then and there, for the transportation from England must have been not a little expensive. Pork at noon, pork at night, pork cold, pork warm. Friends! although with your green peas and crabs' tails you would have looked with loathing at our pork, yet pork was to us a lordly dish, without which we should have starved; and had we afterwards had pork enough, our ill-luck might not have brought

7*

us to Boston."* Meanwhile, the Americans, encouraged by their victory at Bennington, and by their successes in the Mohawk Valley, were pouring into Gates's camp at Stillwater. They were without uniforms, but were for the most part well armed with the rifles and fowling-pieces they had constantly used since boyhood. It was reported to Burgoyne on the 7th of September that there were fourteen or fifteen thousand of them. There was no alternative, however, but to attack them or to abandon the campaign.

The army set out on its southward march in three columns. The right was under Brigadier-general Fraser, the dashing commander of the light troops. The centre was commanded by Burgoyne himself, and the left, near the Hudson, by Riedesel. The British army advanced slowly, repairing roads and bridges. The rate of march barely averaged two miles a day. On the afternoon of the 19th of September Burgoyne's central division was sharply attacked on Freeman's Farm, north of Stillwater. The English, with a few guns, occupied a clearing. The Americans had no artillery. The fight lasted all the afternoon, and was conducted on both sides with great valor. Towards nightfall, Riedesel, with seven companies of German infantry and two cannon, advanced to Burgoyne's assistance, and attacked the right flank of the Americans, pouring in grape-shot. The English rallied and charged, and the Americans fell back, carrying off their wounded, and about one hundred prisoners. They had lost about three hundred and twenty men in the battle, and the British not far from twice that

* Schlözer's "Briefwechsel," vol. iv. p. 346.

number. The latter retained possession of the ground, and may, therefore, fairly claim a victory; but it was a barren victory, which they were never able to follow up. On the 20th, Burgoyne began to intrench his position. His chance of success henceforth lay in cooperation from the southward—a help which never came.

The Germans rendered most important services to Burgoyne in the course of this day. Breymann, with the grenadiers and light infantry, distinguished himself early in the afternoon, by coming to the relief of an English regiment which was falling back. Captain Pausch of the Hanau artillery, with his two six-pounders, and Riedesel with his seven companies, finally turned the tide of battle. Both Breymann and Pausch were publicly thanked by Burgoyne.

Meanwhile the rear of the army had been seriously threatened. Colonel Brown, acting under the orders of General Lincoln, had taken some of the outer works of Ticonderoga, with nearly three hundred prisoners, but had been repulsed from the main fortress.

Baroness Riedesel had accompanied the army on its march. She had been encouraged, she says, when they crossed the Hudson, at hearing General Burgoyne say that Englishmen never retreat. Her distrust had been excited, however, by finding that the officers' wives with the army knew of all expeditions which were planned, and she remembered that in Prince Ferdinand's army, in the Seven Years' War, everything was kept very secret. But now the Americans knew all plans beforehand, and expected the English wherever they went.

Frau von Riedesel was an eye-witness of the battle of the 19th of September, trembling at every shot for the safety of her husband. Three wounded officers were brought into the house where she lodged, and one of them, the nephew of people who had been kind to her in England, died, a few days later, in the next room to hers, while undergoing an operation. The baroness could hear his last sighs through the thin partition.*

The condition of the army was fast becoming serious. Provisions were scarce, wine and coffee terribly dear. Uniforms and clothing were torn on the bushes, and soaked with camping on the damp ground, and new ones were not to be had at any price.† The American camp, supposed to contain twelve thousand men, was so near that the drums and the shouts of the soldiers could be distinctly heard. The woods were so thick, however, that it could not be seen. The English had constructed a bridge of boats across the Hudson, and scouts were sent out to try to see the American camp from the other side of the river, but in this they were not successful.‡

A letter written in cipher arrived from Sir Henry Clinton on the 21st of September, dated on the 10th of that month. Clinton announced his intention of attacking Fort Montgomery, on the Hudson, in ten days.§ Burgoyne immediately sent back the messenger with a letter enclosed in a silver bullet, which was

* Baroness Riedesel, pp. 164–166.

† Schlözer' "Briefwechsel," vol. iv. p. 350.

‡ Pausch's narrative.

§ Burgoyne's Report, given in Eelking's "Riedesel," vol. ii. p. 197.

to be delivered into Sir Henry's own hands. The letter urged Clinton to hasten his advance and create a diversion in Burgoyne's favor. The messenger made his way through the hostile country to Fort Montgomery, but here his presence of mind would seem to have deserted him. He is said to have mistaken American troops for English, to have inquired for General Clinton, and not to have discovered his blunder until he was brought into the presence, not of Sir Henry, but of the American General Clinton. The man then swallowed the bullet, but an emetic was administered, the despatch was found, and the messenger hanged as a spy.*

On the 6th of October, Forts Clinton and Montgomery were stormed by Sir Henry Clinton. One Anspach regiment, one Hessian regiment, and two companies of Hessian chasseurs, which last had lately arrived from Europe, took part in this feat. The Hudson was thrown open to the British. This would have been the time to push on to Burgoyne's relief, but Sir William Howe had led the larger part of his army to Philadelphia, and only a small expedition, under General Vaughan, came burning and plundering up the Hudson.

Burgoyne's situation was becoming daily more critical. On the 4th of October one third was cut off from the soldiers' rations. Desertions had become frequent, in spite of severe punishments; even the

---

* There were two American generals named Clinton—George, governor of New York, and James, his brother. The former was at this time stationed at Fort Clinton, the latter at Fort Montgomery. These forts were taken on the 6th of October by Sir Henry Clinton.

death penalty did not prevent them. Skirmishes were of frequent occurrence. The weather was frightfully hot, and the army was wasting away in inaction.

On the day on which the men were put on short rations, General Burgoyne called a council of war. Generals Phillips, Riedesel, and Fraser were present. Burgoyne proposed to them to leave the neighborhood of the river and try to turn the American left flank. Eight hundred men were to be left to guard the boats and stores; the rest of the army was to take part in the expedition. It was objected that the roads and the position of the Americans were both unknown, that three or four days would be necessary to turn the American flank, and that during all this time the stores must be left under a feeble guard. No conclusion was reached on the 4th, and a second council was called for the evening of the 5th. At this council Riedesel declared his opinion, that the army was in such a condition that unless the enemy could be reached and forced to fight a decisive action in one day, it would be better to fall back across the Hudson and wait behind the Battenkill for General Clinton's approach. Here the army could not be cut off from Fort George. Fraser agreed with Riedesel. Phillips would give no decided opinion, and Burgoyne, loath to retreat, declared he would make a reconnoissance on the 7th, and that if this should show that the enemy was not to be successfully attacked, he would fall back.

On the 6th of October, 1777, four days' rations were served out, and on the 7th, about ten in the morning, fifteen hundred men, of whom about five hundred were Germans, marched out for the reconnoissance, with eight brass cannon and two howitzers. The four generals were with the party, which was made up from all the regiments in the army. They advanced into a clearing about three quarters of a mile from the American left flank—a wretched position, according to Riedesel, where they could see nothing of the enemy.* Brigadier-general Fraser commanded on the right of the line, the German detachments were in the centre,† Major Ackland, with the English grenadiers, on the left. It was determined to await an attack, and Brigadier-general Fraser undertook to carry off the forage from two barns in the neighborhood. Small detachments of the enemy appeared from time to time, and the party "amused themselves" by firing cannon at them, until suddenly a heavy fire of musketry was heard on the left, and presently Ackland's grenadiers came running in, leaving their commander wounded behind them.

The German left flank was thus uncovered and thrown back in confusion, and the Hessian cannon exposed. These continued for some time in action, but were finally taken. The British right seems to have held out longer than the rest of the line, but after a while General Fraser was mortally wounded and his men were driven back, though in better order than the left flank had preserved. The Germans also

---

* Riedesel's comments of Burgoyne's report; Eelking's "Riedesel," vol. ii. p. 206.

† Under Lieutenant-colonel von Speth or Colonel Specht. There is curious confusion in the authorities about this name.

retreated, in some confusion, and all the cannon with the reconnoissance were left behind.

The retreating party threw themselves into a redoubt and maintained their position for the rest of the afternoon, in spite of the repeated and desperate attacks of the Americans.

Lieutenant-colonel Breymann held a small redoubt on the extreme right of the position of the army. His corps had been reduced by the losses sustained at Bennington and on the 19th of September to about five hundred men, and three hundred of these had made part of the reconnoissance, and were now driven back with the rest of the soldiers of that party into the large redoubt of the right wing. The part of the British line which connected Breymann's redoubt with the main position was also cleared of men. The Americans made their way through this gap in the line, Breymann and his two hundred men were attacked in flank and rear, the lieutenant-colonel was shot dead, and the men were put to flight or taken prisoners.

When news of this reached the main body, some of the Englishmen grumbled at the conduct of their German allies. Angry at this, Lieutenant-colonel von Speth got together four officers and about fifty men, and started off through the dark woods to retake Breymann's redoubt. He lost his way and was led by a treacherous guide into the hands of the Americans.*

The Americans fought on this day with great valor,

* Riedesel's comments on Burgoyne's report; Eelking's "Riedesel," vol. ii. p. 208. Burgoyne says that he gave orders to retake Breymann's redoubt, but mentions no further particulars.

and had the advantage of superior numbers, but were without a competent general. Neither Gates nor Lincoln appeared on the field. Benedict Arnold, who had no proper command, fought with his usual reckless courage, but had not the talent of a strategist. He was severely wounded in the capture of Breymann's redoubt. It would have been fortunate for him had the wound proved mortal.

Nothing was left for Burgoyne's army but to retreat. Promptitude might, perhaps, still have secured its escape, but on every side were disorder and delay. Early in the morning of the 8th of October, 1777, the British and Germans were drawn together on the heights that overlook the Hudson. Here, on the evening of that day, General Fraser was buried, in a spot which he had himself chosen as his last resting-place. He had been brought, mortally wounded, into the house occupied by Baroness Riedesel, with whose husband he had served in the Seven Years' War. The Baroness had expected to give a little dinner-party on the 7th. "General Fraser," she says, "and, I believe, also Generals Burgoyne and Phillips, were to have dined with me on that day. I saw a great deal of movement among the troops. My husband told me that a reconnoissance was to be made, which did not astonish me, as this had often occurred. On my way home I met a great many Indians, in their war dress and carrying guns. I asked where they were going, and they shouted 'War! War!' which meant that they were going to battle; and this quite overcame me. I had hardly recovered when I heard skirmishing, and then the firing became heavier and heavier, until at last the noise was frightful. It was a terrible cannonade, and I was more dead than alive. About three in the afternoon, instead of my guests coming to dinner, they brought me one of them, poor General Fraser, on a stretcher, mortally wounded. Our dinner-table, which had already been set, was taken away, and a bed for the general put in its place. I sat in a corner of the room, trembling. The noise kept growing louder. The thought that they might bring me my husband in the same condition was horrible to me, and tormented me incessantly. The general said to the surgeon, 'Conceal nothing from me! Must I die?' . . . I often heard him exclaim, with a sigh. 'Oh, bad ambition! poor General Burgoyne! poor Mistress Fraser!'" *

The general lingered through the night and died on the following morning. So crowded was the house that the baroness had to remove her children into the passageway that they might not cry out and disturb the dying man. His corpse lay all day in her room. As his staff and the general officers of the army gathered about his grave, the Americans, ignorant of their purpose, directed artillery against them. Thus, with the hostile cannon firing his last salute, the gallant leader of the light troops was laid to rest.

At ten o'clock on the night of the 8th the army set out northward. Riedesel commanded the head of the column. The hospital, with its eight hundred inmates, was left behind. The boats, with what remained of stores, made their way slowly up stream. The watch-

* (*Sic.*) The Baroness gives these last words in English; Baroness Riedesel, p. 169.

fires were left burning to deceive the vigilance of the Americans.

General Burgoyne's army made but a short march that night, and then halted until the following afternoon. On the evening of the 9th the British occupied the village of Saratoga. During the night they forded the Fishkill and encamped on rising ground in the angle between that stream and the Hudson. Thus, from the evening of the 7th to the morning of the 10th, Burgoyne, to whom time was of capital importance, had retreated but a little over eight miles.

CHAPTER XIV.

SARATOGA, OCTOBER 11TH TO 16TH, 1777.

AT the camp north of the Fishkill Burgoyne halted, and never resumed his march. Lieutenant-colonel Southerland was sent forward to build a bridge across the Hudson near Fort Edward, but was presently recalled. At daybreak on the 11th a brigade of Americans made a dash across the Fishkill, seized all the boats and much of the stores, took a few prisoners, and retreated before a brisk fire of grape-shot. All day long the English army was cannonaded from front and rear.

In the evening General Burgoyne summoned Generals Riedesel and Phillips to consult with him on the situation of the army. Burgoyne himself held it impossible to attack the enemy, or to maintain his own position if attacked in the centre or on the right wing. General Riedesel thereupon proposed to retreat in the night, abandoning the baggage, fording the Hudson four miles below Fort Edward, and making through the woods for Fort George. No decision was reached, however.

Another council was held on the following afternoon, two brigadier-generals being admitted to it. General Riedesel insisted on his plan of the day before, "very emphatically, and with hard words," and

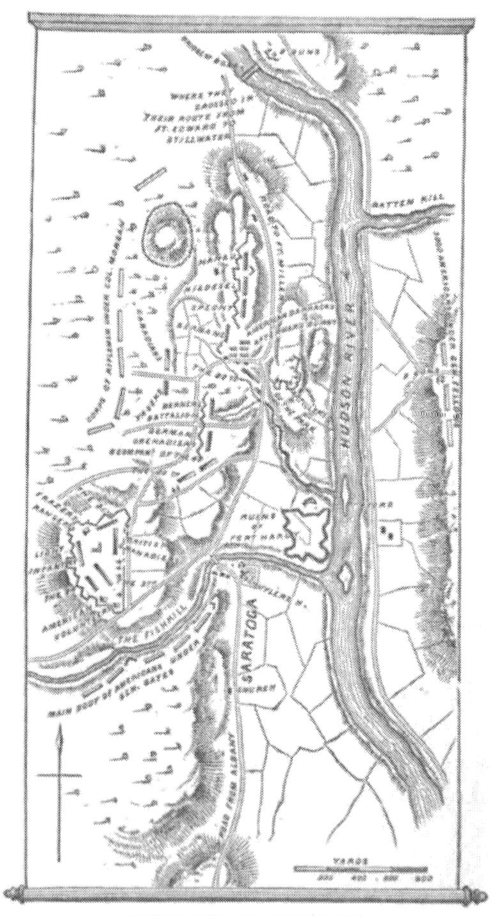

SURRENDER OF BURGOYNE.

the plan was agreed to. As it appeared that rations had not been given out to the troops, the movement was postponed until late in the evening. At ten o'clock Riedesel sent word to Burgoyne that all was ready, but was answered that it was too late to undertake anything. Thus was the last chance thrown away, for on the next morning the army was completely surrounded.

On the 13th of October a third council of war was called, including the regimental commanders. General Burgoyne explained the hopelessness of the situation. Only five days' provisions were left. The whole of the British camp could be reached by the American grape-shot and rifle bullets. Gates's army was drawn up behind a marshy ravine, so far from the Hudson that if Burgoyne were to move out to attack it the Americans could cross the river and take him in the rear. Even should the enemy be successfully attacked and defeated there were not enough provisions remaining for the march to Fort George. The position in which the army now stood could not be defended in the centre or on the right wing. (This was the part of the ground principally occupied by the Germans.)

Burgoyne declared that no one but himself was responsible for the situation of the army, as he had asked no advice and only expected obedience. Riedesel thanked Burgoyne for his declaration, which made it clear to all that he (Riedesel) had had no share in planning the movements of the army, and he called on the English officers present to bear witness to this, if ever he were called to account.

Burgoyne then laid the following questions before the council:

1st. Whether there were examples in the history of war that an army in this condition had capitulated.

2d. Whether in such a condition a capitulation were dishonorable.

3d. If this army were really in a condition where it must capitulate.

To the first question all answered that the condition of the Saxon army near Pirna, of General Fink near Maxen, and of Prince Maurice of Saxony, had not been so bad nor so helpless as that in which this army now was; and that nobody had been able to blame the generals who had capitulated under such circumstances, in order to save their armies; only that the King of Prussia had cashiered General Fink; but that was done from personal disfavor.

To the second question all answered that for the reasons above given the capitulation could not be dishonorable. And as to the third question, all were agreed that if General Burgoyne saw the possibility of attacking the enemy they were ready to sacrifice their blood and their lives; but if this were not feasible they held it better to save the troops for the king, by an honorable capitulation, than to hold out longer and run the danger of having to surrender at discretion after exhausting all their provisions, or to be attacked in their bad position and scattered, and then destroyed in detail.

General Burgoyne thereupon produced the draft of a capitulation, the terms of which seemed favorable, and were unanimously approved of by his officers.

A drummer was then sent over to the American camp to announce that on the next day a staff officer would be sent to discuss matters of importance with General Gates; and to ask for a truce in the meanwhile. This General Gates granted.

About ten o'clock in the morning of the 14th of October Colonel Kingston was sent over to the American camp with Burgoyne's proposals, which were in substance that his army should yield themselves prisoners of war, but under condition that they should be taken to Boston and thence shipped to England, agreeing not to serve against the Americans during the war, unless previously exchanged.

General Gates did not accept these proposals, but drew up another form of capitulation, in six articles, setting forth that "General Burgoyne's army being reduced by repeated defeats, by desertion, sickness, etc., their provisions exhausted, their military horses, tents, and baggage taken or destroyed, their retreat cut off, and their camp invested, they can only be allowed to surrender as prisoners of war."

The sixth article provided that "these terms being agreed to and signed, the troops under his Excellency's, General Burgoyne's command, may be drawn up in their encampments, where they will be ordered to ground their arms, and may thereupon be marched to the river side on their way to Bennington."*

General Burgoyne hereupon called the council of war together and read them the above proposals. The officers declared unanimously that they would rather die of hunger than accept such dishonorable terms.

* De Fonblanque's "Burgoyne," pp. 306, 307.

Colonel Kingston was sent back to tell General Gates that if he did not mean to recede from the sixth article, the negotiations must end at once; the army would to a man proceed to any act of desperation sooner than submit to that article. Hereupon the truce came to a close.

Every one in the army was astonished when new proposals were received from General Gates on the following morning (October 15th, 1777). The terms asked for by Burgoyne were substantially granted, but it was stipulated that the conquered army should leave its position by two o'clock on the same day.*

This sudden change excited the suspicion of the English and German officers. The council of war determined to accept Gates's proposal, but to try to gain time. Commissioners were appointed on both sides, and the discussion of details continued until eleven o'clock at night. The Americans granted all that was demanded of them. The Englishmen on their side promised that General Burgoyne should sign the articles and send them to General Gates in the morning. The truce was to continue.

On the same night a deserter came in and announced that there was a rumor that Sir Henry Clinton had not only taken the forts in the Highlands, but had advanced a week ago to Esopus, and was probably at Albany by this time. Burgoyne and some of his officers were so much encouraged by this news that they were strongly tempted to refuse to surrender. The council of war was called together to answer the following questions:

* Gates was undoubtedly influenced by news of Vaughan's expedition up the Hudson.

1st. Whether a treaty finally arranged by commissioners with full powers, which the general had promised to sign as soon as commissioners should have removed all difficulties, could honorably be broken?

2d. Whether the news received was sufficiently certain to be a motive for breaking off an agreement which, considering the position, was so favorable? and

3d. Whether the army was in sufficiently good spirits to defend its present position to the last man?

On the first of these questions fourteen officers, against eight, were of opinion that the agreement could not honorably be broken off. As to the second, opinions were divided. Those who answered in the negative argued that the deserter was speaking only from hearsay, and that even if Sir Henry Clinton were at Esopus, the distance thence was so great that his approach could not help the army in its present condition. To the third question all officers from the left wing answered in the affirmative, but those from the centre and right said that although their soldiers would fight with great valor if led against the enemy, yet they were so well aware of the weakness of their position, that they might not do as well if attacked. As the Brunswick troops principally occupied the centre and right of the line, it is to this declaration of their officers that Burgoyne probably refers when he speaks in a private letter of "the Germans dispirited, and ready to club their arms at the first fire." *

Still hoping to gain time, Burgoyne tried one pretext more. He wrote on the morning of the 16th to General Gates, saying that he had heard from deserters

* De Fonblanque's "Burgoyne," p. 315.

that that general had sent off a considerable part of his army to Albany during the negotiations; that this was contrary to good faith, and that he, Burgoyne, would not sign the capitulation until an officer of his staff should have inspected the American army to assure himself that it was three or four times as large as the English. Gates seems at last to have grown tired of this fooling. He sent back word that his army was quite as strong as it had been, and had moreover received reinforcements; that he held it neither politic nor for his honor, to show his army to one of General Burgoyne's officers; and that that general had better think twice what he did, before breaking his word, as he would be held responsible for the consequences. Gates added that he was ready to show General Burgoyne his whole army as soon as the articles of capitulation should be signed, and he assured him that it was four times as large as the British, without counting that part of it which was beyond the Hudson. He was unwilling, however, to wait more than an hour for an answer, and at the end of that time should be forced to take the most severe measures.

The council was summoned for the last time, and no one was found to advise the general to break his word. Burgoyne called Phillips and Riedesel aside and begged for their friendly counsel. Both were silent for a time, and then Riedesel explained that if Burgoyne were held responsible in England, it could only be for the movements that had brought the army into such a position, and perhaps for first undertaking a capitulation, and because he had not retreated in time to be master of the line of communications with Fort George. But now, after all the steps that had been taken, Riedesel held it much more dangerous to break the agreement, on the strength of an uncertain and untrustworthy rumor.

Brigadier-general Hamilton, who came up and was asked his opinion, agreed with Riedesel. General Phillips only said that things had come to such a pass that he had no advice nor help to give. Burgoyne, after much vacillation, determined to sign, and the articles in due form were sent to General Gates.*

In the surrender five thousand seven hundred and ninety-one men were included. It is stated by Riedesel that not more than four thousand of these were fit for duty. The number of Germans surrendering is set down by Eelking at two thousand four hundred and thirty-one men, and of Germans killed, wounded, and missing down to October 6, at one thousand one hundred and twenty-two.† The total loss of the British and their mercenaries, in killed, wounded, prisoners, and deserters, during the campaign, including those lost in St. Leger's expedition to the Mohawk and those who surrendered on terms at Saratoga, was not far from nine thousand.

The days that preceded the surrender had been days

---

* The above description of the negotiations for the surrender is taken principally from Baroness Riedesel's book, in which is given an extract from a military memoir dated Stillwater, October 18th, 1777, and signed by several of the principal German officers. See also, concerning this memoir, Eelking's "Riedesel," vol. ii. pp. 210, 211.

† It will be noticed that the time from October 6th to October 16th, during which there was a good deal of fighting, is omitted from the above estimate. See Eelking's "Hülfstruppen," vol. i. pp. 321, 322; "Riedesel," vol. ii. p. 188.

of confusion. Baroness Riedesel says that on the evening of the 9th of October, in Saratoga, when they had marched but half an hour during the day, she asked Major-general Phillips why they were not moving on while it was yet time. The general admired her resolution and wished she were in command of the army. The same lady relates that Burgoyne spent half of that critical night in drinking and making merry with his mistress.

The army was given over to misery and disorder. On the 10th the baroness fed more than thirty officers from her private stores, "for we had a cook," says she, "who, although a great scoundrel, was equal to every emergency, and would often cross little rivers in the night and steal mutton, chickens, or pigs from the country people, which he afterwards made us pay roundly for, as we subsequently learned."* These supplies were at last exhausted, and the lady, in her indignation, called on the adjutant-general, who happened to come in her way, to report to Burgoyne the destitution of officers wounded in the service. The commander-in-chief took this in good part, came to her in person, thanked her for reminding him of his duty, and gave orders that provisions should be distributed. The baroness believed that Burgoyne never in his heart forgave her interference. It seems to me, from the writings of both, that spite lay rather in her bosom and her husband's than in that of Burgoyne. The memorandum which General Riedesel wrote and caused to be signed by his officers immediately after the surrender is a long impeachment of Burgoyne, and sets

* Baroness Riedesel, p. 178.

forth the evil consequences of his not consulting the writer, or of not executing the latter's plans promptly. It is clear that Riedesel held Burgoyne responsible for the misfortunes of the army, misfortunes which he himself took so deeply to heart that his health and spirits were for a long time seriously affected. Before leaving America, in the spring of 1778, Burgoyne wrote to the Duke of Brunswick, praising Riedesel's intelligence and the manner in which he had executed the orders of his superior officer.* Upon this Riedesel wrote a most friendly letter to Burgoyne, thanking him in his own name and that of his officers for the kindness which the commanding general had shown to them. "If good fortune did not crown your labors," he continues, "we know well that it was not your fault, and that this army was the victim of the reverses of war." This solitary expression of confidence is not to be reconciled with what Riedesel says at other times and in other places. The military memorandum above-mentioned, published in the baroness's book, is sufficient proof of this. In the same spirit are conceived Riedesel's comments on Burgoyne's report of the campaign. These comments, which were addressed to the Duke of Brunswick and his countrymen, are dated Cambridge, April 8th, 1778, a little more than a month later than the letter above quoted. They complain explicitly that General Burgoyne, while speaking highly of Riedesel himself, passes lightly over the services of his troops. The German general's complaints in this

* De Fonblanque's "Burgoyne," p. 331. See also Riedesel's order to the German troops expressing Burgoyne's satisfaction with them.—Eelking's "Hülfstruppen," vol. i. p. 341.

respect are but slightly justified by Burgoyne's report.*

But we must return to the baroness. On the afternoon of the 10th of October the Americans began to fire again on the British army. "My husband sent me word," she writes, "to go at once to a house which was not far off. I got into the carriage with my children. We were just coming up to the house when I saw five or six men with guns on the other side of the Hudson River, aiming at us. Almost involuntarily I threw the children into the bottom of the carriage, and myself over them. At the same moment the fellows fired and shattered the arm of a poor English soldier behind me, who was already wounded, and was also retiring into the house. No sooner had we arrived than a terrible cannonade began, which was principally directed against the house where we had sought shelter; probably because the enemy had seen a great many people go in and thought the generals must be there. Alas! it was only women and wounded men. We were at last compelled to take refuge in a cellar, where I placed myself in a corner near the door. My children lay on the ground with their heads in my lap. Thus we spent the whole night. A horrible smell, the crying of the children, and, more than all these, my anxiety, prevented my closing my eyes.

"Next morning the cannonade began again, but from another side. I advised everybody to go out of the cellar, and undertook to have it cleaned, as other-

* Eelking's "Riedesel," vol. ii. pp. 193–210. I do not make out whether these comments were actually sent to the Duke of Brunswick or were found by Eelking among Riedesel's private papers.

wise we should all be sick. My advice was followed, and I set many hands to work, which was very necessary, as there was much to do. . . . When everything had been cleared out, I considered our place of refuge; there were three fine cellars, well vaulted. I proposed that the most dangerously wounded officers should be put into one, the women in the second, and all other persons in the third, which was nearest the door.

"I had had the place well swept out and disinfected with vinegar, and we were all beginning to get into our proper places, when the firing began again terribly, and created great alarm. Several people who had no right to come in threw themselves towards the door. My children had already gone down the cellar stairs, and we might all have been smothered, had not God given me strength to place myself before the door and bar the entrance with outstretched arms; otherwise some of us would certainly have been injured. Eleven cannon balls went through the house, and we could clearly hear them rolling away above our heads. One poor soldier had been laid on the table to have his leg taken off, when a cannon ball came and carried away the other. His comrades had all run away, and when they came back to him they found him in a corner of the room, whither he had rolled himself in his fear, and hardly breathing. I was more dead than alive, but not so much on account of our own danger as for that in which my husband was, who yet often sent to ask how we were getting on, and sent me word that he was well.

"Major Harnich and his wife, a Madame Rennels, who had already lost her husband, the wife of the good lieutenant who had shared his broth so kindly with me

8*

the day before, the wife of the commissary, and I were the only ladies with the army.* We were sitting together and bewailing our sad fate, when some one came in, and people whispered in each other's ears and looked sadly at each other. I noticed this, and that they were glancing at me, without saying anything more to me. This gave me a frightful idea that my husband had fallen. I screamed; but they assured me that this was not the case, and made signs to me that it was the poor lieutenant's wife whose husband had met with this misfortune. She was called out a moment later. Her husband was not yet dead, but a cannon ball had taken off his arm at the shoulder. We heard his moans all night, echoing horribly through the vaults of the cellar, and the poor man died towards morning. Otherwise this night was like the last. Meanwhile my husband came to see me, which soothed my trouble and gave me back my courage.

"The next morning we began to get into a little better order. Major Harnich and his wife and Madame Rennels made themselves a little room, shut off with curtains, in one corner. It was proposed to me to have another corner arranged in the same way, but I preferred to remain near the door, so that I could get out quicker in case of fire. I had a heap of straw brought, laid my beds on it, and slept there with my children. My women slept near us. Opposite were the quarters of three English officers, who were

* *Sic.* This list is intended to include the *ladies*, not the *women*, whose numbers I have no data for ascertaining. The Baroness had two female servants. A soldier's wife is spoken of later. The proper names above should be Harnage and Reynell, but all German writers during this war are very careless as to the spelling of proper names.

wounded, but yet were resolved not to stay behind in case of a retreat. One of them was a Captain Green, aid to General Phillips, a very estimable and well-bred man. All three swore to me that in case of a hasty retreat they would not abandon me, and that each of them would take one of my children on his horse. One of my husband's horses always stood ready saddled for me. My husband was often minded to send me to the Americans, in order to get me out of danger. I represented to him that it would be worse than all that I now had to suffer, to be with people whom I should have to meet with forbearance while my husband was fighting against them. He, therefore, promised me that I should continue to follow the army. Yet I often became anxious in the night lest he might have marched away, and crept out of my cellar to look, and when I had seen the soldiers lying about the fires in the cold night, I could sleep more quietly.

"The things that had been intrusted to me caused me great anxiety.* I had them all in the front of my corsets, because I was so afraid of losing some of them, and I made up my mind not to meddle with such things in future. On the third day I got the first opportunity to change my linen, for they had the kindness to clear a corner for me for the purpose; meanwhile my three officers above mentioned stood sentinel not far off. One of these gentlemen could imitate the lowing of a cow and the bleating of a calf very naturally; and when my little daughter Fritzchen cried in the night, he made the noises for her, which quieted her and made us laugh.

* Money and valuables belonging to various officers.

"Our cook procured us food, but we had no water, and I was often obliged to drink wine to quench my thirst, and also to give it to the children. It was almost the only thing that my husband took; which at last made our faithful chasseur Rockel anxious, so that he said to me one day: 'I fear that the general is disgusted with life, from apprehension of becoming a prisoner; he drinks so much wine.' The continual danger to which my husband was exposed kept me in constant anxiety. I was the only one of all the women whose husband had not been killed or met with some misfortune; and so I often said to myself: 'Shall I be the only fortunate one?' especially as my husband was exposed to so much danger, day and night. He never passed the night in a tent, but always lay in the open air by a watch-fire. That alone might have caused his death, as the nights were so cold and damp.

"Our need of water was so great that at last we found a soldier's wife who had the courage to bring some from the river; which no man was willing any longer to undertake, because the enemy shot all those that went to the river through the head. They let the woman alone, out of respect to the sex, as they afterwards told us.

"I tried to distract my thoughts by busying myself with our wounded. I made them tea and coffee, for which I received a thousand blessings. I often shared my dinner with them. One day a Canadian officer came into our cellar hardly able to stand. We at last got it out of him that he was almost dying of hunger. I was very happy to be able to offer him my food, which brought back his strength and won me his friendship. When we afterwards returned to Canada, I made the acquaintance of his family. One of our greatest troubles was the smell of the wounds when they began to fester.

"Once I undertook the cure of Major Plumfield, aide-de-camp to General Phillips. A small musket-ball had gone through both his cheeks, shattered his teeth and grazed his tongue. He could not keep anything in his mouth; the matter almost choked him, and he could take no nourishment but a little broth, or something fluid. We had Rhine wine. I gave him a bottle, in hopes that the acid of the wine would cleanse his wound. He constantly took a little in his mouth, and that alone did such good service that he was healed, by which I gained another friend. And thus, in the midst of my hours of trouble and sorrow, I had moments of pleasure that made me very happy.

"On one of these sad days General Phillips wished to visit me and accompanied my husband, who used to come once or twice every day at the peril of his life. He saw our situation, and heard me entreat my husband not to leave me behind, in case of a hasty retreat. He, himself, supported my cause, when he saw my great repugnance to being in the hands of the Americans. On going away he said to my husband: 'No! I would not come here again for ten thousand guineas; for my heart is quite, quite broken.'

"Meanwhile, all who were with us did not deserve pity. There were also cowards among them, who stayed in the cellar for nothing, and afterwards, when we were prisoners, could take their places in the ranks and go on parade. We stayed six days in this horrible place. At last they spoke of surrender, for they had delayed too long, and our retreat was cut off. A truce was made, and my husband, who was quite worn out, could come into the house, and go to bed again, for the first time in a long while. Not to disturb his sleep, I had had a good bed made for him in a little room, and I lay down to sleep with my children and my two women in a hall near by. But about one o'clock in the night somebody came and wanted to speak to him. Greatly against my will, I was obliged to wake him up. I noticed that the message was not pleasant to him; that he immediately sent off the man to headquarters, and then lay sullenly down again. Presently afterwards, General Burgoyne had all the other generals and staff officers called to a council of war, to be held early in the morning. In this council he proposed, on the strength of false news which he had received, to break the capitulation which had already been made with the enemy. It was at last decided, however, that this was neither feasible nor advisable; and this was lucky for us, for the Americans told us later that if we had broken the capitulation we should all have been massacred, which they could easily have done, as we were not over four or five thousand strong, and had given them time to bring together more than twenty thousand men.

"On the morning of the 16th of October my husband had to go to his post again, and I into my cellar.

"On this day the officers, who had hitherto received only salt meat, which was very bad for the wounds of those who were hurt, had a great deal of fresh meat divided among them. The good woman who had always brought us water made an excellent soup of it. I had lost all my appetite, and during the whole time had taken nothing but a crust of bread soaked in wine. The wounded officers, my companions in misfortune, cut off the best piece of beef, and presented it to me with a plate of soup. I told them that I was unable to eat anything; but as they saw that it was necessary for me to take some nourishment, they declared that they would not touch a morsel themselves, until I had given them the pleasure of seeing me take some. I could no longer withstand their kind entreaties; whereupon they assured me that it made them very happy to be able to offer me the first good thing they had had.

"On the 17th of October the capitulation was effected. The generals went over to the American General Gates, and the troops laid down their arms and surrendered themselves prisoners of war. And now the good woman who, with danger to her life, had brought us water, received the reward of her services. Every one threw whole handfuls of money into her apron, and altogether she received more than twenty guineas. At such moments the heart seems open to feelings of gratitude." *

---

* Baroness Riedesel, pp. 180–191.

CHAPTER XV.

THE BRUNSWICKERS IN CAPTIVITY.

THE terms on which Burgoyne's army had surrendered at Saratoga were never fulfilled. The soldiers were held substantially as prisoners of war. This led to violent complaints on their own part at the time, and on that of German and English writers down to our own day. It is reported by Bancroft that the convention had been broken by the British at the time of the surrender, by the concealment of the public chest and other public property, of which the United States were thus defrauded. In November, 1777, Burgoyne wrote a rash and groundless complaint of its violation by the Americans, and raised the implication that he might use the pretended breach to disengage himself and his government from all its obligations. Burgoyne also refused to give the necessary lists of all persons comprehended in the surrender. Congress thereupon refused to let his army be embarked until the capitulation should be expressly confirmed by the court of Great Britain.

It seems to me that in adopting this course Congress did not regard its own honor, nor that of the country. It was true that Gates had made a bad bargain. But the bargain had been made deliberately, and Burgoyne's soldiers had performed the most important of the conditions imposed upon them when they laid down their arms. It now devolved on the Americans to fulfil their side of the agreement, and nothing less than a very flagrant violation of the minor articles of the capitulation, or very distinct evidence of an intention on the part of the British to break their parole, should have induced the victorious party to refuse to perform its promises.*

While Congress was minded to keep the German prisoners in America, their own prince was in no haste to see them in Europe. On receiving the news of the capitulation of Saratoga, the minister of the Duke of Brunswick wrote to the English commissioner that those men who had surrendered ought not to be allowed to return to Germany, lest they should be discontented and discourage others from enlisting. "Send these remnants to one of your islands in America, place them in Europe in one of your islands, like the Isle of Wight." On no account were the poor devils to be allowed to come home.†

On the 17th of October, 1777, General Burgoyne's soldiers laid down their arms at Saratoga. This they were allowed to do without the presence of any American detachment. General Riedesel had given orders that the flags of the Brunswick regiments should not be given up. He had the staffs burned, and concealed the colors themselves, giving out to the Americans

* Bancroft, vol. ix. p. 466; vol. x. p. 126; Hildreth's "History of the United States," vol. iii. pp. 237, 255, 256; Lecky, vol. iv. p. 96. Lafayette believed that the British intended to break the convention. "Mémoires," vol. i. p. 21.

† Letter from Féronce to Faucitt, in French, dated Brunswick, December 23d, 1777, and quoted by Kapp ("Soldatenhandel," 1st ed. p. 262), from State Paper Office, German States, vol. 109.

that they were burned also. He concealed them until the prisoners had been for some time in Cambridge, when the baroness was taken into the secret. Frau von Riedesel, with the help of a "very honorable tailor," sewed the colors up in a mattress, and an officer was sent to New York through the lines, on some pretence, who took the mattress with him as part of his bedding. The Brunswick colors were thus saved.* Burgoyne had given his word of honor that the officers should not carry off any of the king's property in their private baggage. Perhaps the standards were thought to belong to the Duke of Brunswick, and not to the king, who had only hired them along with their defenders; or, perhaps, Riedesel was not careful of Burgoyne's honor.

After laying down their arms, the Brunswickers passed through the American camp, where the conquering army was drawn up to receive them. Not a regiment was properly uniformed, but every man was in the clothes he wore in the fields, at church, or at the ale-house. But they stood like soldiers, in good order, and with a military appearance very striking to the German officers. "The men stood so still that we were filled with astonishment," writes one; "not a man made a motion to speak with his neighbor. Moreover, kindly nature had made all the men standing in the ranks so slender, so handsome, so sinewy, that it was a pleasure to look at them, and we all wondered at the sight of so well-made a people. . . . In truth, English America surpasses most parts of Europe in the size and beauty of its men."

* Baroness Riedesel, pp. 160, 207.

But few of the officers in Gates's army wore uniforms, and those few wore them according to their own fancy, of any sort of cloth that came to hand. Wigs large and small, wigs black, white, and gray, adorned or deformed their heads. Some of them looked as if they had a whole sheep on their shoulders. For these great wigs, according to our Brunswicker, the common people felt a deep reverence, such being worn by the gentlemen of the committee. Among the wearers of these wigs were many men fifty or sixty years old, now brought for the first time into the ranks, and somewhat awkward in appearance, but thoroughly in earnest, and not to be made light of, especially in the woods. "In serious earnest," says the German officer, "this whole nation has much natural talent for war and for a soldier's life.*

As the troops that had surrendered passed between the ranks of the Americans, not a man of the victorious army showed them any disrespect or insulted their misfortunes. It is the common testimony of the Germans that officers and soldiers treated them with courtesy and kindness. General Gates invited all the superior officers into his tent, and retained the generals to dinner. Schuyler showed especial courtesy to Frau von Riedesel. He met her as she came into the camp, lifted the children from her carriage, kissed them, and helped her to alight. After a few reassuring words he led her to General Gates, with whom she found Burgoyne, apparently on the most friendly footing. He told her to be without anxiety, for her troubles were at an end. "I answered," writes the baroness, "that

* Schlözer's "Briefwechsel," vol. iv. pp. 357-359.

I should be indeed wrong to be anxious any longer, when our chief was not so, and when I saw him on such good terms with General Gates."

Schuyler had dinner served to Frau von Riedesel and her children in his own tent ("smoked tongue, beefsteaks, potatoes, good bread-and-butter"), and she spent three days with his family at Albany, treated with the greatest kindness. Burgoyne, also, was Schuyler's guest at Albany. He apologized to the latter for burning his house and barns at Saratoga. "It is the fortune of war," answered Schuyler; "say no more about it." *

The prisoners, or "conventionists," as they called themselves, now set out on their march across Massachusetts. The weather was cold, and the roads bad. The march lasted from the 17th of October to the 7th of November. In some places the inhabitants refused to take the prisoners into their houses, and in other places, where it was necessary to halt, there were not houses enough to hold them. The inhabitants, on their side, complained that the passing prisoners burned their fences, destroyed their fodder, and stole clothes and furniture from their houses.† From all sides the country people flocked to see the prisoners, and pressed into the houses where they were quartered, until the officers began to think that their landlords took money for the show.

In this way the Germans saw a great many of the women of the country, and the same officer who gave

* Baroness Riedesel, p. 195.

† General Glover to General Washington. Sparks's "Correspondence," vol. ii. p. 72.

the above description of the American soldiers has left us his first impressions of New England women.

"The women of all this district as far as Boston and New York are slender and straight, and are plump without being stout. They have pretty little feet, good strong hands and arms, a very white skin, and a healthy color in their faces, without having to paint. Hardly any of those I have seen were pitted with smallpox; but then inoculation has been common here for many years. Their teeth are very white, their lips beautiful, and their eyes lively and laughing. Moreover, they have a natural, unconstrained manner, a free and cheerful countenance, a natural assurance. They care much for cleanliness and for being well shod. They dress very becomingly, but all their clothes must fit them very closely. . . . They curl their hair every day, make it up behind into a chignon, and in front over a cushion of moderate height. They generally go about bareheaded, and at most set a little heart-shaped thing, or some such trifle, on their heads. Here and there a country nymph lets her hair fly and braids it with a ribbon. However poor may be the hut in which they live, they put on a silken mantle and gloves when they go out. They know how to wrap themselves in the mantle very prettily, so that one little white elbow peeps out. Then they put on some kind of well-made shade-hat, from under which they peep coquettishly with their roguish eyes. In the English colonies the fair ones have taken a fancy to mantles of red silk or wool. Dressed in this way a girl runs, jumps, and dances about, wishes you a pleasant good-day, or gives, according to the question, a saucy answer. So they stood by dozens all along our road, passed us in review, laughed mockingly at us, or from time to time dropped us a mischievous courtesy and handed us an apple. We thought at first that they were girls from the towns, or, at least, from class number two, standing by the roadside; but, lo and behold! they were the daughters of poor peasants, whom you could recognize as poor peasants by their clothing.

"But in spite of all the fine things I have said of the fair sex here, I must confess, to the honor of my dear countrywomen, that the soft, languishing, and tender manners, which often give the latter such an amiable charm, are seldom to be found in the beauties of this country; and that, consequently, the bliss that comes from them may be very rare here. Here you see perfectly beautiful nymphs, but seldom a true grace. And if you look for the estimable qualities which should be joined to natural beauty—but where am I going? It is high time to stop writing about girls."

The officer goes on with his social observations. It seems that all over America the men are entirely subject to the women. The latter use their authority in Canada for the good of the men, but in New England to their ruin. The women are extravagant. How they manage to tax the men so heavily is a mystery to our good German, seeing that they do not bite, nor scratch, nor go into fainting fits. There is hope in all this for the British crown. The women are now wearing their Sunday finery on week-days. When it wears out peace will have to be made with Great Britain in order to get a new supply.

Next we come to the negroes. These are to be

found on most farms west of Springfield. The black family lives in a little outhouse. "The negroes here are very prolific, like the rest of the cattle. The young ones are well fed, especially while they are still calves. Moreover, the slavery is very bearable. The negro is to be looked on as the servant of a peasant; the negress does all the coarse house-work; and the black children wait on the white children. The negro can take the field in the place of his master, and so you do not see a regiment in which there are not a large number of blacks; and there are well-grown, strong, and sturdy fellows among them. There are, also, many families of free blacks here, who occupy good houses, have means, and live entirely in the style of the other inhabitants. It looks funny enough when Miss Negress pulls up her woolly hair over a cushion, puts a little shade-hat on her head, wraps herself in her mantle, and shuffles along the road in this finery, with a slave negress waddling behind her."*

Baroness Riedesel was making her first observations of the American people. She relates that one night her husband was ill, and that the guard were drinking and making a noise before his door. He sent word to them to stop, whereupon they only redoubled their clamor. Frau von Riedesel then went out, told them that her husband was sick, and begged them to make less noise. They were quiet immediately, "a proof," says the baroness, "that this nation also has respect for our sex." The citizen officers of America were a continual puzzle to the Germans. No story was too extravagant for the latter to believe. "Their generals,

* Schlözer's "Briefwechsel," vol. iv. pp. 363-366.

who accompanied us, were some of them shoemakers," writes Frau von Riedesel, "and on the days we halted made boots for our officers, or even mended the shoes of our soldiers. They set a great value on coined money, which was very scarce among them. The boots of one of our officers were badly torn. He saw that an American general had on a good pair, and said to him, for a joke: 'I would give you a guinea for them.' The general immediately got off his horse, gave up his boots, took the guinea, and mounted again in the officer's torn pair."* General von Riedesel's temper was at this time imbittered by ill-health and misfortune. It is to this that we must attribute the judgment he passes on the Americans. Indeed, he is quoted as saying that he had met but one American officer in Cambridge whom he respected. Of the members of the General Court of Massachusetts he gives an extraordinary description. "One can see in these men exactly the national character of the natives of New England. Especially are they distinguished by the fashion of their clothing. They all present the appearance of respectable magistrates, with their very thick, round, yellowish wigs. Their clothes are of the very old English fashion, and they wear, winter and summer, a blue cloak with sleeves, which they fasten round their bodies with a leathern strap. You seldom see one without a whip. They are mostly thick-set

---

* Baroness Riedesel, p. 198. We get a side light on this story from the writer in Schlözer's "Briefwechsel" above quoted. He mentions one *Tielemann* whom he calls *marschcommissaire* (commissary *general?*), a native of Mannheim, innkeeper at Albany, *shoemaker* by trade, and major in the militia.

and of medium height, so that it is difficult to tell one from another, when they are summoned by the consul of Boston as delegates of their townships, or have to appear on militia business. Not one in ten of them can read writing. Still less can they write. This art is only known to the knights of the pen and to the female sex. The latter are well brought up, and therefore succeed in obtaining mastery over the men more than in any nation in the world. The New-Englanders all want to be politicians, and, therefore, love the tavern and grog-bowl, over which they do their business, and drink from morning till night. They are all extremely curious, credulous, and madly in love with freedom, but at the same time so blind that they have not yet become at all aware of the heavy yoke of slavery laid on them by Congress, under which they are, in fact, already beginning to sink." *

On the other hand, if we may believe the Brunswick officer above quoted, the Americans could not understand the social condition of their captives. "It was hard to make the inhabitants understand," says he, "that our officers had no professions. They had believed that it was from caprice that they would not work at their trades." †

The German "conventionists" were put into barracks on Winter Hill, near Cambridge, Massachusetts, while the English occupied the neighboring Prospect Hill. These barracks had been erected by the Americans for their own use during the siege of Boston, and were of the lightest description. The wind whistled through

* Eelking's "Life of Riedesel," vol. ii. p. 230, 231.

† Schlözer's "Briefwechsel," vol. iv. p. 378.

the thin walls, the rain came through the roofs, the snow lay in drifts on the floor. Wood and straw were but scantily furnished,* and the uniforms that had been worn through a hard campaign in the wilderness hung in rags on the freezing soldiers. They cut off the tails of their coats to make patches for the rest of their clothes. Even in the hospital it was freezing cold. Hope and disappointment followed each other in the breasts of the prisoners as the negotiations for their return to England were renewed or broken off. Once, during the year of their stay, came the hope of a rescue, and preparations were made by the Germans to welcome the friendly fleet, and by the Americans to march off their captives to quarters farther inland. But the greatest suffering, perhaps, of the prisoners was the monotony of their confinement. There was nothing to do, for a little drilling without guns can hardly be called an occupation. We recognize in the journals and letters of the officers the petulance of inactivity. There were quarrels with the American guard. In this respect, however, the Germans fared somewhat better than the English. The care of Riedesel to preserve discipline among his men was recognized, and

* Wood was very scarce that winter. In October, before the arrival of the prisoners, General Heath had written to Washington: "Wood is now twelve or fourteen dollars per cord, on the wharves, and the inhabitants cannot obtain a supply at that price. So many of the coasters are taken by the enemy's cruisers, that they are become very unwilling to run the risk of falling into their hands. I submit to your Excellency the propriety and expediency of obtaining a protection from Lord Howe for such a number of vessels as may be thought necessary to supply the prisoners, from the eastern country. If some such method cannot be devised, I do not at present see how it can be obtained."—Sparks's "Correspondence," vol. ii. p. 17.

the Americans took up the habit of turning delinquent Germans over to their own officers for punishment.

The condition of the soldiers not included in Burgoyne's surrender, the prisoners of Bennington, and of the battles north of Stillwater, was in some respects more fortunate. These, for the most part, let out their services to the New England farmers. Many of them were allowed to visit the camp on Winter Hill—in order to induce the "conventionists" to desert, say the Germans. In the spring, as the temptation to get away into the country became strong, Riedesel thought it wise to open the door somewhat, and gave permission to some soldiers to go off to work on the farms, on condition of returning to camp once a week. The German officers were mostly quartered in the uncomfortable houses near the hill, or in the barracks themselves. The generals, however, had good houses in Cambridge. No man, of whatever rank, was allowed to go to Boston. Baroness Riedesel went there occasionally. She says that the town was very pretty, but inhabited by violent patriots, and full of bad people. The women would spit before her in the streets. The principal errand of the baroness was to visit Mrs. Carter, a daughter of General Schuyler. This lady was kindly and good, like her parents, but her husband Frau von Riedesel believed to be wicked and deceitful. "They often came to visit us, and dined with us, in company with the other generals. We tried to show them our gratitude in every way. They seemed to have a great friendship for us, and yet it was at this same time, that, as General Howe had set fire to a great many villages and small towns, this nasty Carter made the horrible proposal to the Americans, to cut off the heads of our generals, pickle them in firkins, and send one to the English for every village or small town that was set fire to; which inhuman proposal was fortunately not adopted." *

"On the 3d of June, 1778, I gave a ball and supper in honor of my husband's birthday. I had invited all the generals and other officers. The Carters were there, too. General Burgoyne sent an excuse, after keeping us waiting until eight o'clock in the evening. He was always excusing himself, on different pretexts, from coming to us, until his departure for England, when he came and made me many excuses, to which I only answered, that I should have been sorry if he had put himself to inconvenience on our account.

"We danced a great deal, and our cook prepared us a splendid supper for more than eighty persons. Moreover, our courtyard and garden were illuminated. As the birthday of the King of England fell on the 4th, we decided not to separate until we should have drunk his health, which was carried out with the most hearty attachment to his person and to his interests.

"Never, I think, was 'God save the King' sung with more enthusiasm, or more genuine feeling. Even my two oldest daughters were with us, having been brought down to see the illumination. All eyes were full of tears, and it seemed as if every one were proud to have the courage to do this in the midst of the enemy. Even the Carters had not the heart to separate themselves from us. As the company was leaving us, we saw that the house was entirely surrounded by Ameri-

* Baroness Riedesel, p. 202.

cans, who, when they saw so many people go in, and noticed the illumination, suspected that we were contemplating an insurrection; and if the least disturbance had taken place, it might have cost us dear.

"The Americans, when they wish to call their troops together, set burning beacons on the hills, and all men hasten to come at the signal. We were once witnesses of this, when General Howe wished to try to land at Boston, to free the captive troops. This was known, as usual, long beforehand, and tar-barrels were lighted; whereupon, for three or four days in succession, we saw a crowd of people without shoes or stockings, and with guns on their backs, hastening in. So many people came together in this way that it would have been too difficult to effect a landing." *

In November, 1778, the Brunswickers were obliged to leave the neighborhood of Boston, where they were beginning to feel somewhat at home, and undertake the long march to Virginia. Frau von Riedesel still accompanied her husband, having found a comfortable English carriage in which to make the journey. At one of the stopping-places on the road she met General Lafayette, whom she asked to dinner. Lafayette told her of the civility which he had received from the King of England, and how everything had been shown him. The baroness asked him how he could have the heart to receive so many favors from the king, when he was on the point of going off to fight against him. The marquis seemed somewhat ashamed, and an-

* Baroness Riedesel, pp. 204–206. This was probably at the end of August, 1778, when an English fleet followed d'Estaing to the neighborhood of Boston, after his unsuccessful attempt on Newport.

swered: "It is true. The idea passed through my mind, so that one day when the king offered to have his fleet shown to me, I answered that I hoped to see it some day, and then went away secretly, to avoid the embarrassment of having to refuse again." *

Frau von Riedesel was able, while travelling, to observe something of the feeling of the inhabitants towards the mercenaries. At one house where they stopped for the night she noticed a great deal of meat, and asked the hostess to let her have some. "I have many kinds," was the answer, "beef, veal, and mutton." The baroness's mouth watered. "Give me some," said she, "I will pay you well." The woman snapped her fingers. "You shall have none," cried she. "Why did you come out of your own country to kill us and devour our property? Now you are our prisoners, and it is our turn to plague you." "See these poor children," answered the baroness, "they are almost dying of hunger." The woman would not be persuaded until Frau von Riedesel's little daughter, only eighteen months old, seized her hand and said to her: "Good woman, I am very hungry." Thereupon the woman took the child into the next room and gave her an egg. "No," said the child, "I have two sisters." The woman was moved, gave the child three eggs, and bread and milk to the mother. Frau von Riedesel saw her opportunity, brought out her stock of tea, then a great rarity, and offered some to the countrywoman. The baroness presently went into the kitchen, where the woman's husband was eating a pig's tail. This he

* Baroness Riedesel, p. 211; see also Lafayette's "Mémoires," vol. i. pp. 13, 14.

handed to his wife, who ate a little of it and gave it back to him. Seeing the baroness staring at them, they passed the stump to her, and she felt obliged to pretend to take a few bites, and then threw it into the fire. Peace was now entirely made, and Baroness Riedesel obtained some potatoes, and made a pot of soup.

This was not the only occasion on which food was refused or lodging begrudged to the baroness and her children. The people with whom she lodged were generally ardent revolutionists. On one occasion she spent the night at the house of a Colonel Howe, whom she thought to compliment by asking him if he were related to the British general of that name. "God forbid!" answered the colonel, "he is not worthy of me." "This same colonel had a pretty daughter, fourteen years old, but of a bad disposition," says Frau von Riedesel. "I was sitting with her before a bright, open fire; she looked at the coals, and cried out 'Oh, if I only had the King of England here! With what pleasure I would cut open his body, tear out his heart, cut it in pieces, lay it on these coals, and then eat it.' I looked at her with abhorrence, and said to her: 'I am almost ashamed to be of the same sex with one who could have such a desire.'"*

In the middle of January, 1779, the Germans reached Charlottesville, in Virginia. Here they found no barracks ready for them, and were obliged to build for themselves. Soon a village was raised, and here, and in various other parts of Virginia, the remainder of their captivity was passed. For many of them this lasted until the end of the war. The soldiers made

* Baroness Riedesel, p. 220.

themselves gardens and poultry yards. The officers bought good riding horses. In one settlement a small theatre was erected by the English soldiers, and satirical pieces were played, in which the captives made fun of their captors, until it was found necessary to forbid the American militia forming part of the audience.* General von Riedesel returned to New York on parole in the autumn of 1779, and was shortly afterwards exchanged. His health had suffered much from exposure, low spirits, and a slight sunstroke received in Virginia. After he was exchanged he returned to Canada, where he remained in the service of the King of England until the end of the war, but he never again met the Americans in the field.

* About thirty English miles from Staunton (Schlözer's "Briefwechsel," vol. v. p. 404-408). In May, 1780, there were still one thousand five hundred and three German "conventioners" in Virginia (Sparks's "Correspondence," vol. iii. p. 143).

CHAPTER XVI.

BRANDYWINE, GERMANTOWN, AND REDBANK, SEPTEMBER AND OCTOBER, 1777.

IN the summer of 1777 Sir William Howe, instead of co-operating with Burgoyne, turned his attention to the capture of Philadelphia. He advanced a few miles from New Brunswick, failed to draw Washington into a general engagement, and fell back to Amboy. Then, hoping that Washington had left his favorable position, Howe returned to the attack. He was in so far successful that his right-hand column had a skirmish with an advanced body of Americans under Stirling, drove them back, and took three cannon and eighty prisoners. After this the British army returned to Amboy, and went over to Staten Island. Here it was embarked, and on the 23d of July cleared Sandy Hook. The force consisted of about eighteen thousand men, of whom less than a quarter were Germans. The fleet of two hundred and thirty-four sail arrived off Cape May on the 30th of July, but the frigates that had been sent to reconnoitre reported that the Delaware was strongly defended, and Sir William determined to approach Philadelphia by Chesapeake Bay. On the 22d of August the fleet reached the mouth of the Elk River, and the troops were landed on the 25th and 26th in good order and without opposition.

On the 3d of September the chasseurs forming the

advanced guard had a sharp skirmish with the American rear-guard, losing about twenty men killed and wounded. Between thirty and forty Americans were buried on the field. From this time the chasseurs were continually at the front, and slept on their arms.

On the 11th of September Washington's army was drawn up on the north side of Brandywine Creek. The main force was posted at Chad's Ford, while General Sullivan, with the right wing, was to watch the upper passes. At daybreak the British started from Kennet's Square, seven miles from Chad's Ford, in two columns. The right-hand column, under General Knyphausen, marched straight on the American front, which it approached at about ten in the morning. Here Knyphausen remained throughout the larger part of the day, keeping up a cannonade, but making no serious attack on the enemy.

The second column, under Howe and Cornwallis, made a long circuit to the left, and met with little opposition until it had reached and safely passed the forks of the Brandywine, where a small force could perhaps have stopped it. The Americans, however, had neglected this spot. Meanwhile Washington, deceived by contradictory reports, had not ventured to cross the creek and attack Knyphausen's division.

On learning that Howe had passed the Brandywine, Sullivan hastened to meet him. He had not time, however, fully to form his division. He seems, also, to have blundered in his arrangements. About half-past three the Hessian chasseurs, on the extreme left of the British line, came upon the American advanced guard and drove it back upon the main body. About this

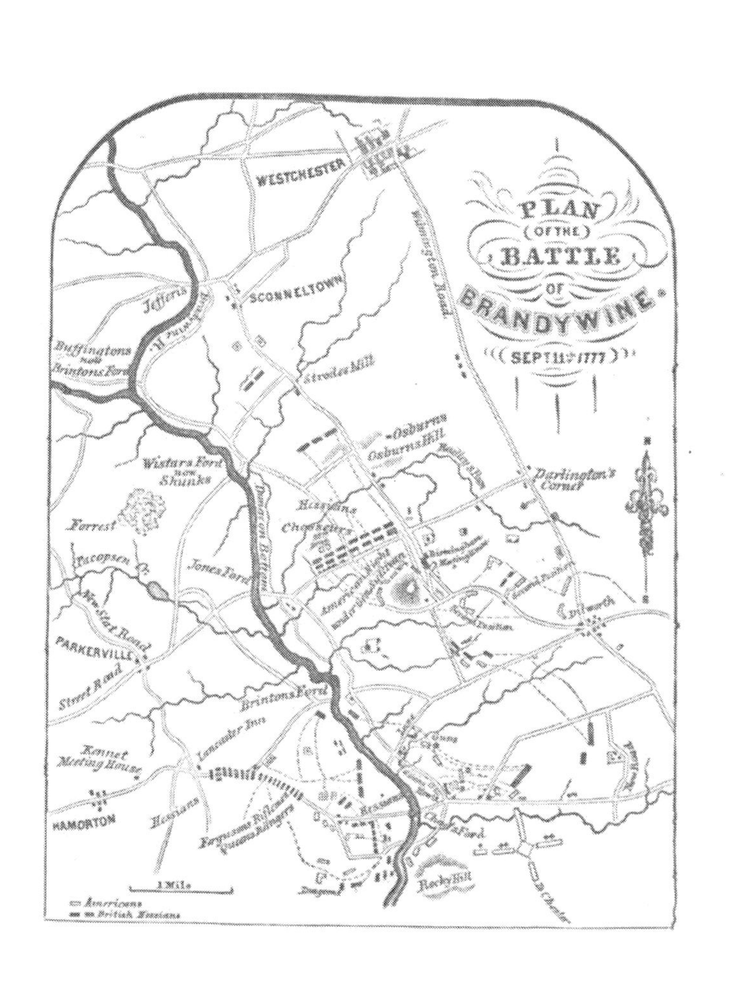
PLAN
OF THE
BATTLE
OF
BRANDYWINE
SEPT 11th 1777
WESTCHESTER
SCONNELTOWN
Jefferis
Buffingtons now Brintons Ford
Strodes Mill
Wilmington Road
Osburns
Osburns Hill
Darlington's Corner
Wistars Ford now Shunks
Farrest
Hessians
Jones Ford
New Street Road
PARKERVILLE
Street Road
Dilworth
Brintons Ford
Lancaster Inn
Kennet Meeting House
HAMORTON
Hessians
Chadds Ford
Rocky Hill
1 Mile
Americans
British Hessians

time the action became general. Sullivan's division was driven back. Lafayette, serving as a volunteer, was wounded in the leg. Washington brought up Greene's division and two more brigades, and covered Sullivan's retreat.

On hearing the cannon of Cornwallis, Knyphausen crossed the Brandywine at Chad's Ford and attacked the American intrenchments. These were defended for a time by Wayne, but the British were already in his rear, and late in the afternoon he abandoned his position, and fell back towards Chester.

There were Hessian soldiers on this day in both columns of the British army. The chasseurs were with the advanced guard of Cornwallis's division, and had forty-six men killed and wounded. Captains Ewald and Wreden received the Hessian order *pour la vertu militaire* for their conduct on this occasion. This was a great honor, as they were the first officers of the rank of captain to be thus distinguished. The whole loss of the British army at the battle of the Brandywine was six hundred and twenty-two,* and the American loss was about a thousand men. Among the ten or fifteen cannon taken from the Americans were two which had been captured at Trenton with Rall's brigade.†

The Americans were supposed to be in full retreat, and the autumn day was drawing to a close. Two battalions of British grenadiers were sent to occupy a little village on a hill beyond Dilworth. The battalions advanced carelessly, tired by a long day's march and

* Knyphausen's Report.

† MS. Journal of the Grenadier Battalion von Minnigerode.

elated by recent victory. The officers had not drawn their swords. Captain Ewald, who had commanded the foremost detachment of Cornwallis's column all day, had left his men to rest, and, having nothing in particular to do, had ridden out with the grenadiers to have a look at the country. Suddenly, at fifty paces from the village, they were received by a brisk fire of musketry. General Maxwell and the American rear-guard had thrown themselves into the village to cover Washington's retreat. A party of Americans were seen at the same time coming round the hill to take the English on their left flank. Ewald galloped back for assistance, and brought up two English regiments under General Agnew, which immediately attacked the Americans, and saved the grenadiers, who had been almost surrounded. Night presently put an end to the fighting. The English loss in this little affair was heavy; nearly half of the two battalions and the greater part of their officers fell, according to Ewald.*

After the British army had been disembarked at Head of Elk, the English fleet had left Chesapeake Bay. Meanwhile seven English frigates and fourteen transport ships, with provisions from New York, had entered the Delaware and gone up to Wilmington. Two days after the battle of the Brandywine, Cornwallis entered that town, thus securing a new base of supplies for the army.

The English advanced without meeting serious opposition, though there was continual skirmishing, and a party under General Wayne was surprised and beaten. On the morning of the 26th of September, 1777, Lord

* Ewald's "Belehrungen," vol. ii. p. 337; vol. iii. p. 463.

Cornwallis entered Philadelphia at the head of two English and two Hessian battalions of grenadiers, and proceeded to fortify the town. The main army encamped at Germantown. The Hessians here formed the left wing, with the chasseurs in advance on the Lancaster road.

On the 3d of October, 1777, about noon, Captain Ewald was visited by a man ("by no means a Tory," says he), whose property he had, on a previous occasion, protected from pillage. On going away the American said to him: "My friend, be on your guard to-night and to-morrow." Ewald took the hint, and reported the remark to his colonel, who passed it on to headquarters. The generals took no notice of it; but we shall see from the following account that the chasseurs were ready for the attack.*

"*October 4th.* It was probably the fact that General Howe had sent many detachments to Philadelphia and into Jersey, to besiege Mud Island and occupy the city, and especially the fact that he had himself received reinforcements, which moved General Washington to attack the royal army. With this intention he

* Knyphausen does not mention Ewald's warning in his report to the landgrave, but says: "We knew nothing of all these movements of the enemy, on account of the thick fog, until after daybreak, when a patrol of Hessian chasseurs, on the left wing, a mile beyond the outposts, which stood on the other side of the bridge over the Wissahickon, fell in with about three hundred of the enemy's troops; and at the same time the outposts of the second battalion of light infantry, which stood in front of Germantown on the road to Beggarstown, were driven in."—Knyphausen to the Landgrave, Oct. 17th, 1777. See, however, Stedman's "History of the American War," vol. i. p. 300. Ewald says that patrols were sent out, by orders of Colonel von Wurmb, in consequence of the warning above mentioned.—"Belehrungen," vol. ii. p. 32.

had left his camp at Skibback Creek, and about two o'clock this morning we received news of his approach. Lieutenant-colonel von Wurmb immediately started with the Jäger Corps, reported what was going on to General Knyphausen, and occupied the bridge leading over the Visihigging (Wissahickon) Creek, near Van Doeren's house. We presently heard firing on the right wing, and about half-past three the Jäger Corps was attacked by four thousand men, with four six-pounders. So the corps was forced to leave the bridge, but took position on the hill opposite, and defended this post with its rifles, against the repeated attempts of the enemy to force it. The enemy's four cannon played constantly on the chasseurs, while our three-pounders could not reach the enemy. Meanwhile the firing became general, and very strong on the right wing; until about nine o'clock Lieutenant-general von Knyphausen sent us word that the enemy's left wing was beaten. Hereupon Lieutenant-colonel von Wurmb attacked the bridge again, and drove back the enemy both from there and from the opposite height, under a heavy fire. As the attack had to be made through a long defile, the enemy had time to retire. We, therefore, found only twenty dead, and as the chasseurs were already much fatigued, and were not supported, and as they only numbered three hundred men, no further pursuit was made.

"In the centre of the army the enemy had fallen on the light infantry and driven it back. Lieutenant-colonel Musgrave, with the Fortieth regiment, threw himself into a stone house, where the enemy stopped to attack him. They might otherwise have fallen upon our army much sooner, and before it was entirely under arms. But, as it was, our army attacked them, beat them out of the town, and put them to flight. They, thereupon, retired to their former camp, on Skibback Creek, leaving three hundred dead, six hundred wounded, and four hundred prisoners behind them. Our loss is, also, about four hundred killed and wounded; among the former General Agnew. Lord Cornwallis, hearing the firing at Philadelphia, immediately ordered three battalions of grenadiers to start. He, personally, arrived in time to take part in the end of the action, but the battalions came too late." *

It now became of the first importance to Sir William Howe to open the Delaware River, between Wilmington and Philadelphia, to his ships of war and his transports. On these he must in great measure rely for his provisions and communications. The river was barred some ten miles below Philadelphia by *chevaux de frise*, which were protected by Fort Mercer at Redbank, on the New Jersey shore, and by Fort Mifflin, on an island, near the opposite shore of Pennsylvania. Between the forts obstructions had been sunk in the channel, and these again were defended by galleys. Some boats with provisions had succeeded in slipping

* MS. Journal of the Jäger Corps. Ewald says that the attack on the chasseurs was evidently a feint, and that, therefore, Knyphausen did not support them, but hastened to the assistance of the right wing.—"Belehrungen," *ubi supra*. The Americans opposed to the chasseurs were Pennsylvania militia under General Armstrong.—Bancroft, vol. ix. p. 424. The chasseurs were the only Hessians heavily engaged, but the Leib Regiment and Regiment von Donop were also under fire. The former had four men wounded.

by all these obstacles, but the free navigation of the river was essential to the British.

Colonel Karl Emil Kurt von Donop was one of the most distinguished of the Hessian colonels, and had been a personal aide-de-camp of the Landgrave, with whom he was a favorite. He had, in the previous year, held a separate command of some importance at Bordentown, and had now expressed a wish to be again detached. Sir William Howe consented to gratify him. He was sent to take Fort Mercer. Donop started on the 21st of October, 1777, with three battalions of grenadiers, a regiment of infantry, four companies of chasseurs, and twelve mounted chasseurs, all Hessians, eight field-pieces belonging to the regiments, and two English howitzers. He is said to have asked for more artillery, and to have been told in reply that if he could not trust himself to attack the fort, the English would take it. "Tell your general," replied Donop to the officer that brought him the message, "that Germans are not afraid to face death." The colonel then declared to those about him: "Either the fort will soon be called Fort Donop, or I shall have fallen." He went on with his expedition, crossed the Delaware in boats, and spent the night at Haddonfield. At about noon on the 22d of October he arrived at Redbank, and rode forward to reconnoitre the ground. The fort was a five-sided earthwork, with a ditch and abatis. It had at first been constructed on too large a scale by the Americans, but Monsieur du Plessis de Mauduit, a young French officer, who had been sent by Washington to assist Colonel Christopher Greene in its defence, had reduced the size of the works which, in their modified shape, formed a somewhat irregular pentagon. A part of the old lines had been left standing, but were not defended. On three sides of the fort the woods afforded shelter to the besieging party to within a distance of four hundred yards. On the south side was the Delaware River. The garrison numbered three hundred men with fourteen cannon.

On arriving before the fort, Donop sent an aide-de-camp to summon the garrison. "The King of England commands his rebellious subjects to lay down their arms," ran the message, "and they are warned that if they wait until the battle, no quarter will be granted." Colonel Greene answered, that he accepted the terms, and that no quarter would be given on either side.* The aide-de-camp reported that he had seen but few men in the fort.

Colonel von Donop drew up his little army. His right flank rested on the river, near which he had placed his eight three-pounders and two howitzers. These were supported by a battalion of grenadiers and by chasseurs, who were to defend the flank and rear against troops disembarking from the shipping in the Delaware. The Hessian line extended the larger part of the way round the fort on the land side, the attack being made simultaneously from north and south. In front of every battalion stood an officer commanding sappers and one hundred men with fascines, hastily made in the woods.

---

* Ewald's "Belehrungen," vol. ii. p. 15-17; Chastellux, vol. i. p. 219. The journal of the Grenadier Battalion von Minnigerode says that Donop sent to summon the fort twice, once on first arriving, and once just before the attack.

About four o'clock all was ready. Donop then spoke a few words to his officers, calling on them to behave with valor. They all dismounted and drew their swords, took their places in front of their battalions, and the attack began. The Hessians charged at double-quick, passed the old disused lines, with a cheer, carried the abatis, but found themselves embarrassed by pitfalls and by the ditch, which they had not fascines enough to fill. Three American galleys, lying in the river, kept up a warm fire on the Hessian right flank. Some of the Hessians climbed the ramparts of the main fort. They were presently beaten back. Donop was struck in the hip by a musket-ball, and fell, mortally wounded. Twenty-two officers were killed or hurt, including the commanders of all the battalions. The Hessians turned and fled, leaving many of their wounded on the field.* Lieutenant-colonel von Linsingen gathered what remained of the brigade, and on the next day brought it back to Philadelphia unmolested. Two English ships of war, which had attempted to take part in the action, ran aground. One of them was blown up next day by hot shot from the American galleys and floating batteries; the other was set on fire and abandoned.†

The Hessians had fled, night had fallen, and a part of the garrison came out of the fort to repair the abatis and care for the wounded. Several Hessian grenadiers

* The journal of the Jäger Corps says that Donop refused to be carried off the field.

† The journal of the Grenadier Battalion von Minnigerode asserts that Donop had received orders not to attack the fort until the 23d, in order to give the English frigates an opportunity to engage the American galleys.

were found crouching close under the parapet, where the balls would go over their heads. The poor fellows could not fight without support, and feared to run away. They were taken into the fort. Among the party that came out to repair the abatis was Captain du Plessis. To him the wounded Donop called out: "Whoever you may be, take me from here." Du Plessis had the colonel carried into the fort. As he was brought in, some of the American soldiers, "either not knowing that his wound was mortal, or heated with the battle, and still irritated by the threats made to them a few hours before, could not help saying aloud: 'Well! is it settled that no quarter is to be given?' 'I am in your hands,' answered the colonel, 'you can avenge yourselves?'" Du Plessis had no difficulty in silencing the soldiers, and then gave all his attention to the wounded man. "Sir," said the latter, "you appear to be a stranger; who are you?" "A French officer," answered du Plessis. "I am content," said Donop, in French, "I die in the arms of honor."

The Hessian colonel lived three days after the attack, and often conversed with du Plessis. He begged the latter to warn him when death should be near. Du Plessis complied with his request. "It is an early end to a fair career," said Donop, "but I die the victim of my ambition and of the avarice of my sovereign." *

The number of Hessians killed, wounded, and taken

* Chastellux, vol. i. p. 223: Eelking denies the authenticity of the last part of the dying words attributed to Donop, on the authority of his inner consciousness. They are taken from the narrative of Chastellux, who visited Redbank with du Plessis, three or four years after the attack.

at Redbank was three hundred and seventy-one, including twenty-two officers. The Americans had thirty-seven killed and wounded.*

This brilliant defence did not permanently secure the control of the river to the victors. On the 9th of November the British batteries opened fire on Fort Mifflin. For six days and nights the bombardment continued. More than twelve thousand shots are said to have been fired. On the 15th the English fleet also came to take part in the action. A ship of war, mounting sixteen twenty-four-pounders, and a large Indiaman, with three guns of the same calibre, were brought so near the fort that hand-grenades could be thrown from their rigging into the works. Five large ships were within range on the other side. The land batteries mounted thirty guns. The block-houses of the fort, which had done good service, were knocked to pieces. Many of the cannon were silenced. On the night of the 15th the garrison retreated to Fort Mercer. Cornwallis was sent to invest this place, and Washington was unable to reinforce it. The fort was abandoned, the barracks burned, and the magazines blown up on the night of the 20th of November, 1777. The American ships in the river were also burned. Cornwallis completed the destruction of the fort, whose ramparts were razed.

---

* Knyphausen's official report in the archives at Marburg; and the American official report, Washington, vol. v. p. 112 note.

CHAPTER XVII.

THE BRITISH RETREAT ACROSS NEW JERSEY, JANUARY TO JULY, 1778.

THE Hessians would appear not to have liked Philadelphia. Wiederhold, returning from captivity, and from his sentimental parting at Fredericksburg, calls the Quaker City "a meeting-place of all religions and nations, and consequently a mishmash of all sects and beliefs, and not less a *confluens canaillorum*," and believes "that it does not yield to Sodom or Gomorrah in respect to all the vices."*

Another officer complains of the climate, and says that the forests make the neighborhood unhealthy. Plants and animals do not acquire their proper size in Pennsylvania, according to this observer, and the people are sickly and prone to madness, "a craziness of the senses, coming rather from poor than from overheated blood. . . . Not one person in a hundred has a healthy color." It is probable that the difficulty of getting fresh provisions in the half-blockaded town was not without influence on these judgments.

Philadelphia has probably changed less in appearance since 1778 than any other large city in the Northern States. The Hessian officer praises the straight streets, the sidewalks of broad stones, the gutters, and the awnings. He laughs at the provinciality of the

* Wiederhold's Journal.

shopkeepers, who advertise "Tobacco, as good as the best imported," and represents the arts and manufactures as being in a very backward state. No sort of work is done in ivory, steel, stucco, bone, embroidery, or silk. "The English send them all that, and all that they send is welcome. And, moreover, the American, and particularly the Philadelphian, is so conceited as to think that no country on earth is more beautiful, happier, richer, or more flourishing than his hardly budding state." Such, however, is not the feeling of the writer of the letter. "If the honorable Count Pen," says he, "would give me the whole country in exchange for my commission, with the condition that I should live here all my life, I would hardly take it."*

In the early part of December, Sir William Howe marched out from Philadelphia to bring on a general engagement. The armies were opposite each other in the neighborhood of Chestnut Hill, about eleven miles from the town, for three days, apparently preparing for a battle—marching, countermarching, and skirmishing; and then the English general, thinking Washington's position too strong to be attacked, slipped very quietly back to Philadelphia.

Two foraging expeditions were made during this month, at the end of which the British army went into winter quarters. Eleven redoubts were built between the Delaware and the Schuylkill, the line running over Morris's Heights, and each of them was occupied by a captain and fifty men, who were relieved every twenty-four hours. The picket line was intrusted to Provincials near the Schuylkill, and to the Hessian chasseurs

* Schlözer's "Briefwechsel," vol. iii. p. 149–153; vol. iv. p. 115–117.

near the Delaware, the latter being posted at Holland Ferry and Greenwich Point.*

While Washington's army at Valley Forge was suffering from want of almost all the necessaries of life, the British in Philadelphia had what they needed, and spent the winter in rest, health, and gayety. They were not crowded; many houses of absent rebels being used for barracks, and some of the soldiers being quartered on the inhabitants that remained in town. The service was light. Sir William Howe, who had already asked to be recalled, was gay and easy-going. The city did not seem very full of soldiers. The Americans only so far succeeded in cutting off provisions as to make them very dear.†

I pass over the skirmishes of the winter and spring, which were unimportant, whether Englishmen, Hessians, or Tories were engaged. The last, indeed, were principally interested in plunder.‡

On the 18th of May, 1778, a farewell festival was given to Sir William Howe, and on the 19th and 20th that general made a fruitless attempt to capture a corps of twenty-five hundred men under General Lafayette, who had ventured near to Philadelphia. On the 24th Howe handed over the command of the army to Sir Henry Clinton. Before leaving America he sent a complimentary letter to Captains Ewald and Wreden of the chasseurs.§

---

* MS. journal of the Jäger Corps.

† MS. journals of the Jäger Corps, the Grenadier Battalion von Minnigerode, the Regiment von Alt-Lossberg (Heuser).

‡ MS. journal of the Jäger Corps.

§ Eelking's "Hülfstruppen," vol. ii. p. 8.

Meanwhile it had become known in Philadelphia that the King of France had concluded an alliance with the rebellious colonies, and that a French fleet might soon threaten the entrance of Delaware Bay, and cut off the communication by water with New York. In other words, as the good Germans put it to themselves, "a strong French fleet, with many thousand land troops and cavalry, had run out of Brest, and was coming to North America, under pretence of being allies to Congress, but really with the intention of acquiring a firm footing on that continent." *

It was the approach of the French fleet, together with orders received from England, that induced Sir Henry Clinton to abandon Philadelphia and retreat to New York. A part of the baggage of the army was put on board the English ships, and about three thousand of the Tory inhabitants prepared to follow their protectors and abandon their native land. The streets, which had been like those of a German town in fair time, were now deserted. In front of many houses stood piles of furniture, to be sold at auction. The inhabitants went about with sad faces, but some of them rejoiced in secret.†

During the month of November the Anspach regiments had been brought from New York to Philadelphia. They were now shipped again to New York, instead of sharing in the march across New Jersey. It was said among the Americans that the British commander could not trust these two regiments. By the Germans it was said that they had shown their in-

* MS. journal of the Grenadier Battalion von Minnigerode.

† Dinklage's Diary, quoted Eelking's "Hülfstruppen," vol. ii. p. 9.

ability to march.* They were the regiments that had mutinied at Ochsenfurth.

From the 14th to the 18th of June, 1778, the English and Hessians were evacuating Philadelphia. In spite of the fact that much baggage had been sent off by sea, the train numbered about fifteen hundred wagons.† Ships at the wharves and on the stocks were burned. The Americans did not interfere with these preparations, nor seriously harass the departing troops. On the 18th of June the march of the army began. The way lay by Haddonfield, Mount Holly, Monmouth Court House, and the Neversink Hills to Sandy Hook. Parties of Americans destroyed the bridges in front of the British, and hung on the flanks and rear. The heat was terrible; many men were killed by sunstroke. The New Jersey mosquitoes did their work so thoroughly that the soldiers' faces were swollen past recognition.‡ On the 25th of June nearly a third of the Hessians were overcome by the heat, and lay by the roadside.§ There were many desertions.‖

It seems extraordinary, in view of all these difficulties, that the Americans did not succeed in embarrassing the retreat very seriously. Many of Washington's subordinates considered it unwise to attack the retreating enemy. This opinion was principally enforced by Charles Lee, who, as senior major-general, was able

* Compare Washington, vol. v. p. 433, and MS. journal of the Regiment von Lossberg (Heuser), June 9th, 1778.

† Knyphausen to the Landgrave, July 6th, 1778.

‡ Ewald's "Belehrungen," vol. ii. p. 352.

§ MS. journal of the Regiment von Lossberg (Heuser).

‖ Two hundred and thirty-six Hessians deserted during the march across New Jersey.—Knyphausen to the Landgrave, July 6th, 1778.

greatly to hinder the execution of Washington's plans. The battle of Monmouth Court House was not quite a victory for either side. The Americans were driven back by Clinton's rear-guard, and almost put to rout, owing to Lee's incompetence or indifference. It is true that Washington rallied his men and repulsed an attack, but the true object of the day was not accomplished. Clinton continued his march, with hardly the loss of a baggage wagon. In the first week of July the British army reached Sandy Hook, whence it was transferred by water to New York.

CHAPTER XVIII.

NEWPORT, NOVEMBER, 1776, TO OCTOBER, 1779.

IN November, 1776, when Sir William Howe seemed to be carrying everything before him, he detached some seven thousand men, of whom about one half were Hessians, to occupy Newport. This corps landed without opposition, and spent three years in Rhode Island, lying, during the larger part of the time, inactive, and suffering during the last years from scarcity of flour and of wood. There is little doubt that the men could have been better employed elsewhere. With six thousand, or even with four thousand more soldiers at his command, Clinton might have acted more promptly and efficiently than he did for the assistance of Burgoyne. We may well suppose, however, that Sir William Howe, having taken possession of Newport when he thought he had no better use for his troops, was afraid of losing prestige if he abandoned the town. He drew some regiments from the garrison in the summer of 1777, before the opening of the campaign.

On the whole, I do not think that the service in Rhode Island could have been very trying to the soldiers. If flour was scarce, meat was plenty. The inhabitants were shy at first, and shut up their families. On Shelter Island, when the strangers approached, the country people ran away; believing, says one, that the

Hessians ate up little children. "But in time," writes an officer, "they became more familiar with us, learned to understand our broken English, showed us their families, and let their fear of us disappear."

When this easy footing had been established, there was substantial comfort to be found in the hospitable houses of Newport. The inhabitants entertained entirely in the English fashion. All dishes were placed on the table at once. Every guest ate and drank at his pleasure, without urging. Soup was seldom given, but there were four or five kinds of vegetables on the table, and boiled potatoes with every dish. The list of drinks given in the journal before me includes punch, cider, strong beer, porter, grog, madeira, port, claret, sherry, toddy, sangaree, and syllabub. People pledged each other during the meal, and regular toasts were given after the cloth was removed. The toasts went round to the right, the bottle to the left.*

Sir Henry Clinton was the first commander of the expedition, and was succeeded by Lord Percy. The latter laid down the command in May, 1777, to return to England. The hopes which had brought him to America had been disappointed, for it is said that on leaving home he had sworn not to come back unless with the olive branch of peace. He was popular at Newport, and the Tory inhabitants sent him a complimentary address on his departure, wishing him a safe and pleasant passage and a long continuance of perfect health. "Your excellency's illustrious rank and character," they add, "render it unnecessary to wish you any other blessing of life." In return, his lordship

* MS. journal of the Regiment von Huyn.

assured them that it was the duty and the wish of every British and Hessian soldier to protect all peaceable and innocent inhabitants.

The people of Newport were less satisfied with Major-general Prescott, Lord Percy's successor. They were not long obliged to suffer from him. The general had chosen for his headquarters a lonely house about four miles from Newport, and as much as a mile from the nearest troops. He relied for safety on a small guard and on a ship anchored not far from the house. On the night of the 10th of July, 1777, about midnight, a party of Americans under Colonel Barton landed from two whaleboats at Redwood Creek, crept across the fields to Prescott's headquarters, overpowered the guard, broke into the house, pulled the general and his aide-de-camp out of their beds, and made off with them without giving them time to dress. The boats safely ran the gantlet of the British shipping, and carried the captives to Providence.

The command now devolved on Major-general Pigot, and things went on in their old course. Constant expeditions were made to the neighboring islands, or to the mainland, for provisions or wood. At the end of July a party of women and children were sent to Providence, on account of the scarcity of food in Newport. I do not think, however, that the soldiers suffered severe privations. On the whole, the year 1777, and the first half of 1778, passed quietly away, though the Americans sometimes made as if they would attack the island. Meanwhile Burgoyne had taken Ticonderoga, had advanced on Albany, and had surrendered at Saratoga; Howe had taken Philadelphia, and Clinton had abandoned it; the King of France had declared war, and an anxious hour for the little army at Newport was approaching.

On the 15th of July, 1778, General Prescott, who had been exchanged since his capture, arrived from New York with reinforcements. Among these were the two regiments of Anspach. He announced that the French fleet was coming to America, and on the 29th that fleet appeared off Newport. It was commanded by Count d'Estaing, and consisted of five ships of seventy-four guns, six of sixty-four, and three of twenty-six. At eleven o'clock in the morning these vessels were lying at anchor before the harbor. The island of Connanicut was immediately evacuated by the Germans and occupied by the French, who took some provisions which there had not been time to remove. The English and Hessian soldiers expected an immediate landing of the enemy on Rhode Island. The town was in confusion, and the Tories in despair.

The French admiral, however, did not immediately follow up his advantage. It was not until the 8th of August that he forced his way into the harbor, past batteries at Brenton's Neck, King's Fort, Goat Island, and North Point. The cannonade lasted an hour and a half, at the end of which time the fleet anchored near Connanicut. Not a man was wounded in the town, but the ships had suffered some damage.

The regiments that had been outside of Newport were now called back within the lines. General Sullivan had landed on Rhode Island with a rebel army. The British and German soldiers were crowded like sheep in the town. They were worn out with continual toil, for ever since the appearance of the French fleet every available man had been busy in the intrenchments. Four frigates and two smaller vessels were burned, and one frigate and another vessel sunk, to keep them from falling into the hands of the enemy. There was great anxiety in Newport, but on the 9th of August came relief. An English fleet of thirty-six sail, under Lord Howe, appeared off Point Judith. Count d'Estaing sailed out the next morning to meet it, undergoing a brisk cannonade from the shore batteries. The English fleet fell back, pursued by the French. The 10th was a day of suspense. On the 11th a violent storm arose, and both fleets were scattered before it.

It was the French fleet that reappeared first. "Now all our hopes were vain," writes the Hessian quartermaster; "we already, in our thoughts, saw ourselves in the hands of our enemies, for our force was too small to withstand so strong a corps, from the side of the land and of the sea." Suddenly, to the joy and surprise of the garrison, the fleet sailed away.

For a week longer Sullivan remained in front of the intrenchments of Newport, while his army of militia melted away. On the evening of the 28th he fell back to the northern end of the island, and was followed by the English on the morning of the 29th. The Americans turned, however, inflicted a check on their pursuers, and on the night of the 30th left the island without being further molested. The expedition had been grossly mismanaged. The losses on each side, in the affair of the 29th, were between two and three hundred men. Of these, one hundred and twenty-eight were Germans. It was well for the Americans that they made off when they did, for on the 1st of September Sir Henry Clinton arrived in Newport harbor with a fleet and reinforcements.

For more than a year longer the British and Germans remained on Rhode Island, useless and inactive. At last, in October, 1779, a fleet was again seen in the offing, but, as it came along the Sound, it was recognized as friendly. It turned out to be composed of transports, come to take away the garrison. Immediately the baggage was put on board, the store of fuel given away. The sad spectacle of Tory families flying from their native land was repeated. There were more who wished to go than could be taken in the ships, and some were forced to stay and face the wrath of their neighbors.

Cordial feelings had grown up in the course of three years between the Hessians and the inhabitants of Newport. General Prescott feared that some of his soldiers might wish to stay behind, and gave orders that on the day when the troops were to embark all the houses should be closed and no one, especially no woman, should be seen at a window. With bands playing and flying colors the regiments marched through the empty streets and took their places in the boats which carried them to the ships. The hostile occupation of Rhode Island was ended.*

* For the occupation of Rhode Island, cf. Bancroft, vol. ix. pp. 200, 357, 358; vol. x. p. 146 *et seq.*; Eelking's "Hülfstruppen," vol. i. p. 105 *et seq.*; vol. ii. pp. 14, 15, 30 *et seq.*; Ewald's "Belehrungen," vol. ii. p. 249 *et seq.*; MS. journal of the Regiment von Huyn.

CHAPTER XIX.

THE NEIGHBORHOOD OF NEW YORK, 1777 TO 1779.

THE history of the Revolutionary War is principally the history of a series of important expeditions, conducted with varied success, against various parts of North America. The contending armies appeared, fought, and disappeared again. But the city of New York was occupied from the summer of 1776 to the autumn of 1783 by the British troops. In the country, within a short march of Manhattan Island, hostilities were ever recurring. At no time during the first five years could the inhabitants of the villages of central New Jersey or southwestern Connecticut feel themselves safe. The forts on the Hudson were taken and retaken.

It may not be uninteresting, in this connection, to look at a description of New York as seen by Hessian eyes at the time of the British occupation. The following extract is taken from a letter written by an officer who came over with reinforcements in the summer of 1777, and gives his first impressions:

"Now to give you an idea of America, or rather, of the little piece of America that we have become acquainted with. I cannot help saying that it is a beautiful, pleasant, and level country, and New York, although the part nearest the sea is burned down, one of the finest and most pleasing seaports that I have yet seen. For the houses are not only all built in English fashion, regular and handsome, and most of them like palaces, but are also all papered and very expensively furnished. It is, therefore, a pity that this country, which is also very fruitful, is inhabited by such wretches, who in their luxury and wantonness have not known what to do with themselves, and who have only their pride to thank for their fall. Every one at home who takes their side, and thinks they had a reasonable ground for rebellion, should, for a punishment, live awhile among them, and so understand the condition of things here (for the worst man here, if he will only do something, can live like the richest at home). Whoever would do this would soon change his tone, and understand that not poverty, but crime and luxury, are the cause of the whole rebellion. For although most of them are descended from runaway vagabonds who were driven out from other places, yet they are so arrogant, and live in such state in all parts of the country, and especially in New York, as I hardly believe to be practised anywhere else in the world. For instance, the women, who are almost all handsome, be they the wives of shoemakers, tailors, or day-laborers (which last, however, are but few, for almost every soul here has a few black slaves to wait on him), go daily in mantles of silk or muslin. This luxury increases daily, for they receive much money from the troops, and do not have to give so much as a grain of salt for nothing. Nothing is, indeed, more annoying than that people who after all are no more than rebels, must, by express order of the king, be treated by the soldiers with the greatest politeness; and, as I said above, not a grain of salt can be demanded of them gratis. So the poor soldiers would have to die of hunger if they did not receive threepence worth of ships' provisions every day, consisting of a pound of biscuit, salt pork hardly fit to eat, a few mouldy beans, a little oat-meal, and a little rum; on which they must live, though many of them lose their health." *

In the skirmishes and smaller expeditions about New York the Hessians generally took part; and it may be worth while to glance at a few of these events before turning to the more important operations in the Southern States, by which the fate of the country was finally decided.

In the latter part of August, 1778, the Jäger Corps was posted on the Spyt den Duyvel Hills, near Courtland's Plantation. Early in the morning of the 31st, a captain with one hundred and fifteen chasseurs, of whom fifteen were mounted, was sent out on a scouting expedition towards the Phillips House. They had marched less than half an hour when they were surprised by a party of Americans and Indians under the Chevalier Armand, who had been in ambush in a ravine on the right hand side of the road. Sixteen chasseurs were killed, wounded, or taken, and the others ran away. Colonel von Wurmb, who commanded the Jäger Corps, hastened to the assistance of his detachment as soon as he heard the firing, but the Chevalier Armand retired with his prisoners, and crossed the Phillips Manor towards East Chester, where Lieutenant-colonels Cathcart, Simcoe, and Emmerich were posted with their light troops.

---

* Schlözer's "Briefwechsel," vol. iii. pp. 32, 33.

The lieutenant-colonels heard of Armand's approach, and immediately prepared an ambuscade. Simcoe and Cathcart drew off their infantry into the woods, on the right and left, and so placed themselves as to command a defile through which the Americans and Indians had to pass. Emmerich's infantry was drawn up to await the attack, with orders to fall back before the enemy. Emmerich posted himself with the cavalry behind a hill, ready to charge on the attacking party as soon as it should have been drawn into the open. Captain Ewald, with two companies of chasseurs, was sent by Lieutenant-colonel von Wurmb to the support of Emmerich's infantry.

The plan of the lieutenant-colonels was successfully carried out. About four in the afternoon the Americans and Indians appeared on the field of battle. Emmerich's skirmishers retreated before them, and drew them into a field of Indian corn, where they were suddenly attacked in front and rear and upon both flanks. All the Indians were killed except one, who was left to tell the tale. They belonged to the Stockbridge tribe, and were led by Sachem Neham. About fifty Americans were taken prisoners, but Armand and some others escaped through the bushes.

Eelking remarks on this story that it is a proof that the Americans did not disdain to use Indian allies in this war, as well as the British. A distinction is surely to be drawn between leading Indians against British and German soldiers, as was here done by the Americans, and sending them against the inmates of lonely farm-houses and unprotected hamlets, as was constantly done by the king's servants. The Stockbridge tribe are said to have been in so far destroyed and so completely discouraged in this expedition that they took no further part in the war.*

Ewald does not confine himself to stories that tell to the glory of his own side. Besides accounts of Trenton, Redbank, and other important actions in which Hessians or Englishmen were defeated, he has a chapter on the bold and lucky strokes made by small parties of Americans. Thus, he tells how, in the spring of 1777, the British had collected a large quantity of forage at Sag Harbor, on Long Island, and how Colonel Meigs started from Guilford, in Connecticut, with less than two hundred men, in whale-boats. They crossed the Sound on a stormy night, dragged their boats over the land, launched them again, landed near Sag Harbor, surprised the guard, destroyed the provisions, burned several vessels, took a number of English prisoners, got into their boats again, and reached Guilford safely. A similar descent was made at Cow Bay in broad daylight in November, 1780. In 1781 a Brunswick major was kidnapped from his quarters on the north side of Long Island. Indeed, it was the custom for small bands of Americans to land on the island, dodge the English and German soldiers, and plunder the Tories. These expeditions were conducted with great boldness, and are a complete answer, according to Ewald,

* Eelking's "Hülfstruppen," vol. ii. p. 17 and note; Ewald's "Belehrungen," vol. ii. pp. 312–318. I can find no other account of this skirmish either in German journals or in Washington's correspondence, which at this time is almost entirely devoted to events on Rhode Island. Ewald was an eye-witness, however, and he is very trustworthy as to the main facts of his stories, though they generally lose nothing in his telling.

to the accusations of want of courage sometimes made against the Americans in this war. "He who has served against this nation," says he, "will be convinced of the contrary, and will not be able to speak of them with contempt." *

Ewald relates, with great admiration, the gallant taking of Stony Point by the Americans, under Anthony Wayne, on the 16th of July, 1779. "Do not these men deserve to be admired?" cries he, "who, but a few years before, had been lawyers, doctors, ministers, or farmers, and who, in so short a time, made themselves excellent officers, putting to shame so many of our profession who have grown gray under arms, but who would have been in a frightful state of mind if they had been commissioned to carry out such a plan. I shall perhaps be told that these men were endowed by nature with a great talent for war. This may be the case with one or another of them, but, on the whole, nature is not so extravagant with her favors. Allow me to say it, these people did not choose military service as a refuge, as the nobility generally does, nor as a house of correction for an ill-bred son who would not learn anything at the academies, as is often the case among the middle classes, but they chose this profession with the firm resolution of being zealous in every way, of serving their country usefully, and of pushing themselves forward by their merits. I was sometimes astonished when American baggage fell into our hands during that war to see how every wretched knapsack, in which were only a few shirts and a pair of torn breeches, would be filled

* Ewald's "Belehrungen," vol. ii. pp. 247, 248.

up with military books. For instance, the 'Instructions of the King of Prussia to his Generals,' Thielke's 'Field Engineer,' the partisans 'Jenny' and 'Grandmaison,' and other similar books, which had all been translated into English, came into my hands a hundred times through our soldiers. This was a true indication that the officers of this army studied the art of war while in camp, which was not the case with the opponents of the Americans, whose portmanteaus were rather filled with bags of hair-powder, boxes of sweet-smelling pomatum, cards (instead of maps), and then often, on top of all, some novels or stage plays."*

The British kept permanent possession of two or three places on the western side of the Hudson. One of these places was Paulus Hook, now Jersey City. The Hook was a peninsula made up of steep, rocky hills, and surrounded in part by the Hudson and in part by a marsh intersected by creeks and ditches. The position, strong in itself, was fortified with palisades, block-houses, and redoubts. It was occupied by a battalion of New Jersey Tories, under Lieutenant-colonel Bushkirk.

On the 18th of August, 1779, a party of forty Hessians, with two officers, were brought over to reinforce the garrison of Paulus Hook, and at nine in the evening of that day Bushkirk started on an expedition towards the new bridge over the Hackensack, some fourteen miles distant. Meanwhile, Major Henry Lee, of Virginia, with about three hundred men, supported by Lord Stirling with about five hundred more, ap-

* Ewald's "Belehrungen," vol. ii. pp. 284–293.

proached the new bridge in the opposite direction, under pretence of foraging. Here Stirling halted, but Lee during the night came near Paulus Hook, having passed Bushkirk unperceived. On approaching the fort, Lee sent an officer, with a small party, forward to reconnoitre. The officer reported that the garrison were not on the alert. Lee then advanced with his command. They forded the ditches, entered the fort, and surprised a number of Provincials, sleeping in a block-house. They then approached a second block-house, occupied by a small party of Hessians. "Wer da?" cried the sentry. "Stony Point!" answered the Americans. The sentry fired, and thus gave the alarm, but the under-officer in command of the block-house surrendered with ten or fifteen men. Lee next surprised and took possession of the principal redoubt, and the whole of Paulus Hook seemed his. Fortunately for themselves, however, some twenty-five Hessians had their wits about them. They threw themselves into a small redoubt, where they were joined by their captain and by Major Sutherland, commanding the post, and refused to yield. Lee, who had not known that any Hessians were in the fort, and who probably overrated their numbers, made off before morning without even spiking the cannon or destroying the war material. He took with him about one hundred and fifty prisoners. Lee had received orders not to attempt to hold the place, and a rapid retreat was necessary to prevent his being cut off; but the twenty-five Hessians, by their gallant conduct, had probably prevented the capture or destruction of the stores and buildings in the fort, and had certainly

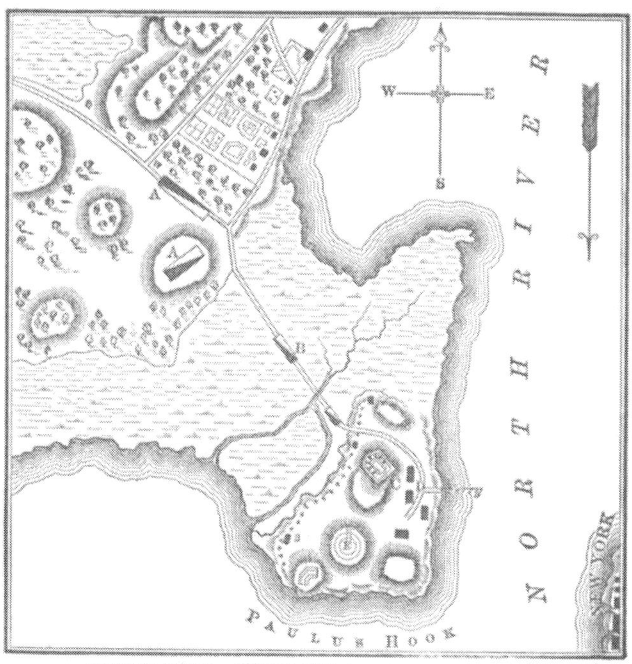

PAULUS HOOK.—(FROM THE LIBRARY AT CASSEL.)

PLAN

of the surprise of an English post at Paulus Hook, in the Province of Jersey, at half-past two in the night of the 18th–19th of October, 1779.

A. Approach and position of the rebels on the heights of Bergen, to cover the retreat.

B. Attack on the bridge and the blockhouses 1, 2, and 3, and on the fort C, which mounted seven 6-pounders. These did not succeed in firing.

D. Barracks in which the English garrison, one hundred and ten strong, were taken prisoners.

E. Work which a Hessian captain and one officer with twenty-five men occupied; whereupon the rebels retired at daybreak, with their prisoners.

Scale of 800 Paces.

saved their side from the appearance of a complete and shameful disaster.*

* Marshall, vol. iv. pp. 87-92; Washington, vol. vi. pp. 317, 326, 332, 333, 336, 376; Bancroft, vol. x. p. 229; Ewald's "Belehrungen," vol. ii. pp. 295-299; MSS. journals of Chasseur Corps, Regiment von Lossberg (Piel and Heuser), Wiederhold's Diary. See also the "Life of General Henry Lee," by General Robert E. Lee, prefixed to Lee's "Memoirs of the War," etc. General R. E. Lee says that Paulus Hook was entered by a stratagem, but this statement is not confirmed by any German account, nor by Marshall.

CHAPTER XX.

WIEDERHOLD'S VOYAGE—AN EPISODE—SEPTEMBER, 1779.

ON the 4th of September, 1779, the Regiments von Knyphausen and von Lossberg received orders to make ready to embark with all their baggage, and with such of their sick as could support a journey. Their destination was Quebec, though the men did not know it at the time. The Knyphausen and Lossberg regiments were two of those which had been captured at Trenton. The prisoners taken on that occasion had been exchanged, and the regiments, which had at one time formed part of a combined battalion, were now acting independently again.

Wiederhold had received a commission as captain in the Regiment von Knyphausen. The two regiments were embarked on the 8th of September on six vessels. Wiederhold's quarters were on the *Triton*, a brig armed with six small cannon and two swivels. The brig was crowded and uncomfortable, and had at first a crew of only seven men, counting the captain, cook, and steward. The Hessians on board were a lieutenant-colonel, who was sick, two captains, a lieutenant, an ensign, and a surgeon, and nearly two companies of infantry.

The brig put to sea on the evening of the 8th of September, but ran immediately into a gale of wind, and was separated from the fleet. The master, having received no orders as to his destination, was obliged to put back towards Sandy Hook on the morning of the 10th. On that day a vessel was made out ahead, and preparations were made to meet her in case she should be an American privateer. The cannons were cleaned and loaded, and a non-commissioned officer and six men ordered to take charge of each of them. The vessel, however, turned out to be a friend, a transport-ship with part of the Forty-fourth English regiment on board. The *Triton* kept in company with this ship, and on the morning of the 11th fell in with the convoy, consisting of twenty-three transports and trading sloops, protected by two small vessels of twenty and fourteen guns. From one of these vessels the *Triton* obtained two additional sailors—young, inexperienced fellows.

The fleet sailed immediately on the arrival of the *Triton*, and during the 11th and 12th all went well. On the 13th, however, the weather began to be stormy, and on the 14th it was the same. On the 15th the wind was rising, and in the evening it blew a hurricane. The fleet was completely scattered, and the night was pitch dark. About nine o'clock in the evening the mainmast broke off below the main yard, and before the wreckage was entirely cleared away the foremast went overboard, breaking just above the deck. The brig was now tossed about at the mercy of the waves, and was sometimes on her beam-ends. While the captain was nailing up a dark-light, and Wiederhold standing by with a candle to help him, the sea burst in and threw them both head over heels in the cabin.

Presently a new peril arose. One after another the cannons on the deck broke away from their fastenings, rolled hither and thither, and burst through the bulwarks into the sea. Four of them in succession were lost in this way, carrying with them the great iron kettle, which was large enough to cook for the whole ship's company and passengers at once. The fifth cannon, in rolling about, loosened the hatch, then broke away from its own carriage, and fell through on to the lower deck, where it alighted on a large chest belonging to Captain Wiederhold, and containing wine, spirits, mustard, vinegar, and the like. The chest and its contents flew into a thousand pieces, but the fall of the gun was broken, and the hull of the brig escaped injury.

The sixth cannon, however, was still running about the after-deck just over the cabin. It had already smashed the wheel and everything else that came in its way. Four of the sailors could or would work no longer, and lay helpless in their bunks. None of the others would go near the cannon, for fear of being crushed. The soldiers were lying about sighing, weeping, or praying. The lieutenant-colonel was too sick to do anything. Wiederhold tried to encourage the men, and told them that God, who had brought them into this great danger, could also bring them out of it, if they would do their part, and try in the first place to get the cannon overboard, and then work at the pumps and keep the ship afloat until morning; when, perhaps, Heaven would lend them aid, and either give them better weather or send a ship to their assistance.

Wiederhold's entreaties were useless at first. Some

of the soldiers were stunned or stupid with fright; others said they were sick. Wiederhold reminded them that he had himself been suffering for four weeks from a fever, but as there was no one else to render any help, he had tried to do something for the common safety. He did not doubt, he said, that there were some men there who were stronger than he, and who had enough affection for him to follow him and to do what he should tell them. He promised to stay on deck with them, lend a hand to their work, and share their fate, hoping to save the ship and all on board. No one would come, until at last Wiederhold cried out, "Is there no under-officer who is in health, and has ambition and a Hessian heart, who will follow and help me?" Hereupon a sergeant and two corporals started up, and were followed by fifteen or twenty men. "Well, then," said Wiederhold, "come along! Let us first try to pitch the cannon into the sea." After several attempts, during which they were in constant danger of being crushed, or of being carried overboard with the gun, they succeeded in mastering it, and pushed it over the side. In doing this a soldier had his arm broken in two places, and Wiederhold's little finger was crushed.

Now they went to work at the pump, in relays of four men. Each relay could only work for six or eight minutes at a time, and the men had to be tied, or cling to the stump of the mainmast, not to be washed away. About three or four o'clock in the morning the pump broke, and could not be mended in the dark, so they fell to bailing, which they kept up until daylight, when they managed to repair the pump.

While the men were working in the darkness a soldier fell overboard, but succeeded in seizing a rope, and called and shrieked for help. No one could see him, or knew just where he was. "Where are you?" asked Wiederhold. "Hanging on to the ship," answered the soldier; "I can't hold on much longer. Help me quickly, or I shall fall into the sea and drown." His comrades tried to get to him, but before they could reach him a wave was quicker than they, and washed him aboard again; and, says Wiederhold, in his narrative, "he's alive and healthy yet."

While the work was going on, Wiederhold noticed the master and some of the sailors, with a lantern, moving about the boats which were fastened to the ship, and, as he thought, preparing to launch one of them. Wiederhold asked the master what he was doing. "Oh, nothing," answered the master; "I am only seeing if they are fast enough." Wiederhold then asked for the lantern, on a pretext, and when he had got it and given it to one of his soldiers, he took the master by the arm, led him down to the cabin, and put him under arrest, in charge of two officers. This was done for fear the master should abandon the brig with his sailors, and leave the soldiers to their fate. When morning broke the boats were found to be past service. They were thrown overboard, and the master was released.

During the 16th of September the storm was abating, and the 17th was a clear day. The observation taken at noon showed 37° 19′ north latitude, so that the brig had drifted nearly as far south as the capes of Virginia. Of the longitude they had no idea.

The wreckage of the masts and bulwarks was now cleared away, and the hull of the brig examined, but no leak found. The soldiers came on deck and dried their clothes, for there was not a dry stitch on the brig, even in the knapsacks, but everything had been soaked in salt water and slime. The sailors rigged a jury-mast on the stump of the mainmast, and on the following day another on that of the foremast.

On the 19th prayers were offered by the Hessian soldiers, to thank God for their deliverance in the storm. A hymn was sung and the 107th Psalm was read. Even the sailors, who could not understand a word of what was said by the Germans, showed much reverence and seemed to be praying themselves.

The *Triton* now slowly made her way to the northward, meeting with tolerable weather. Several vessels were seen, but none came to her assistance. Wiederhold elaborated a plan of action by which, in his hardly manageable hulk, he was to resist any privateer that should attack him. He proposed to hide his men, decoy a boat-load of Americans on board the *Triton*, and capture them. The privateer would now be unwilling to fire into the brig for fear of hurting her own men, and could not board it, on account of the superior numbers of the Hessians. It was, perhaps, fortunate for Wiederhold and his party that circumstances prevented them from trying to put this ingenious scheme in action.

On the morning of the 25th of September the capes

of Delaware were in sight. Knowing now exactly where they were, the crew of the *Triton* put out to sea again, to keep out of the way of privateers. The wind was fair, and the Hessians hoped to see Sandy Hook in forty-eight hours. The morning of the 26th was fine. At daybreak two sails were seen in the distance. Wiederhold sprang joyfully into the cabin and reported the sight to the lieutenant-colonel and the other officers. All dressed and hurried on deck, hoping that these were ships sent out from New York to cruise before the harbor, or to assist vessels injured in the late storm. The strange sail, which were to windward, bore down on the *Triton*, and proved to be a schooner and a sloop. "But oh! how were our hopes betrayed!" cries Wiederhold; "for when they came near and hoisted their flags of thirteen stripes, our joy was turned into sorrow."

The schooner carried fourteen guns and was called the *Mars*. The sloop, named the *Comet*, carried ten guns, and was commanded by Captain Decatur. By eight o'clock in the morning they were alongside of the *Triton*. They ordered the master of the latter to lower one sail and bind the helm to starboard. Then each privateer sent an officer and five men aboard, and the *Mars* took the *Triton* in tow, and brought her into Barnegat Inlet, where she was anchored. The *Mars*, which had taken on board the master and several seamen from the *Triton*, presently got among the breakers and capsized. Only two of her crew were drowned, but all had to swim for it. This happened within two gun-shots of the place where the *Triton* lay at anchor. The captain of the

Mars had previously ordered the Hessian lieutenant-colonel to come on board of that vessel, but had fortunately excused him from doing so on account of his sickness.

On the 29th of September the *Triton* was brought into Little Egg Harbor. Here the prisoners were disembarked. They passed through Philadelphia and were at last quartered at Reading. The officers were exchanged and returned to New York in December, 1780.

Of the six vessels in which the Knyphausen and Lossberg regiments were embarked, one returned safely to New York with her passengers; the fate of one I have not been able to trace with certainty; one was lost at sea with all hands; two were disabled in the storm and afterwards taken by American privateers.

The remaining vessel, the *Badger*, with part of the Lossberg regiment, lost her fore and main masts in the storm. She was afterwards attacked by two small privateers, which followed her for two days and fired at her, but drew off on account of the determined attitude of the Hessians. On the 9th of October, however, a privateer mounting twelve guns attacked the *Badger*, and the latter, having no cannon, was obliged to surrender. A lieutenant, three ensigns, and twenty men were taken on board the privateer, together with the equipment of the remaining Hessians. The privateer seems, moreover, to have retained at first some hold on the *Badger* herself, on which a Hessian captain, who was sick, with a surgeon and most of the privates, still remained; for it is stated in the journals that the frigate *Solebay*, on the following day, freed the *Badger* from the privateer, and subsequently brought her safely to New York.*

* MSS. Wiederhold's Diary, Journals of the Regiment von Lossberg (Heuser and Piel), of the Jäger Corps, and of the Grenadier Battalion von Platte.

CHAPTER XXI.

SAVANNAH, CHARLESTON, AND PENSACOLA, 1778 TO 1781.

THE alliance between France and the United States increased the probability of the final independence of the latter. It therefore became important to diminish the amount of territory held by the Americans, even if their main army could not be destroyed. Lord George Germaine hoped that the thinly inhabited southern provinces might speedily be reduced to obedience, and the royal authority established from the Gulf of Mexico to the Susquehanna River.*

There was a further advantage to be gained by occupying at once the Northern and the Southern States. The summer and autumn were the season of activity in the former, the winter and spring in the latter. The British general, who could move his troops by sea, might thus leave each department with only soldiers enough to act on the defensive when the weather limited the operations that could be conducted, and maintain a superiority in each, when such a superiority was most important.

On the 6th of November, 1778, about thirty-five hundred men, under Lieutenant-colonel Campbell, were embarked at New York. Two Hessian regiments were of the expedition. The transports, delayed by bad

* Bancroft, vol. x. p. 284.

weather, did not clear Sandy Hook until the 27th, and arrived in the Savannah River on the 24th of December, after a stormy passage. The party landed on the 29th, and put to flight some eight hundred Americans who attempted to oppose them, killing and wounding about eighty, and taking four hundred prisoners. Nearly fifty cannon, a considerable quantity of stores, and several ships fell into the hands of the British, whose loss, including Hessians and Tories, was twenty men killed and wounded.

The town of Savannah was composed of about six hundred lightly built houses. Most of the inhabitants had run away with the rebels, taking with them such valuables as they could carry. Mahogany furniture was lying about broken in the streets—a sad sight to see. The Hessians are said not to have plundered, like the other invading troops. They were quartered in the fine barracks of the town.*

In January General Prevost arrived from St. Augustine to take command of the army. Then began the interminable series of marches that distinguished these southern campaigns. Augusta was occupied, then abandoned. General Lincoln, with an American army, marched towards Augusta, and General Prevost gave him the slip and threatened Charleston. Lincoln returned from Georgia, and Prevost withdrew to John's Island, on the coast of South Carolina. At last Beau-

---

* Schlözer's "Briefwechsel," vol. v. p. 1 *et seq.;* MS. journal of Regiment von Wissenbach. See, also, a description of the State of Georgia in 1776, Sparks's "Correspondence," vol. i. pp. 148–151. Many of the troops with the expedition were Tories, the least disciplined soldiers in the British army.

fort was occupied and John's Island abandoned by the British, and their main army returned to Savannah.

One or two incidents occurred during this campaign which especially concerned the Hessians. At a place called Stono Ferry a small fortification had been erected, originally as a *tête de pont*. It was separated by an inlet from John's Island, and the bridge which it once protected had been removed. The fortification was occupied by the Hessian Regiment von Trumbach and by one battalion of Highlanders, in all about five hundred men. This post was attacked on the 19th of June, 1779, by Lincoln's army. The Hessians at first gave way, but were supported by the Highlanders. They then rallied and renewed the battle. The Americans retreated before the arrival of German and Scotch reinforcements.*

It was about this time that two different engagements occurred in the inlets about John's Island between Hessians, using their field-pieces, and small vessels or galleys of the enemy. On each occasion the Hessians were successful, and caused the retreat or destruction of the vessels engaged. It is said that on one of these, named the *Rattlesnake*, were retaken sundry cannon and flags which had been captured at Trenton with Rall's brigade. How these trophies came to be in South Carolina is not mentioned.†

* Stedman, vol. ii. pp. 115–119; Lee's "Memoirs," pp. 130, 131; Eelking's "Hülfstruppen," vol. ii. pp. 26–28; MS. journal of the Regiment von Wissenbach.

† Eelking's "Hülfstruppen," vol. ii. p. 28, where the diary of the non-commissioned officer Reuber is given as authority. The story told by Eelking does not agree as to dates, etc., with the journal of the Regiment von Wissenbach. The Regiment von Trumbach, which fought at Stono Ferry, was Rall's old regiment.

On the 4th of September, 1779, the French fleet, under Count d'Estaing, appeared suddenly off the mouth of the Savannah River. Immediately all the outlying detachments of the British army were called into Savannah. On the 23d Lincoln and his men joined the French from Charleston, and volunteers from South Carolina flocked into their camp. But while d'Estaing was opening regular approaches, the soldiers of the garrison and the negroes of the town were busily strengthening the fortifications. It was too late in the season for the French fleet to remain with safety on the coast. D'Estaing determined to try an assault. This should have been done earlier, before reinforcements had been received by the British from Beaufort, and before their works had been strengthened, or it should have been postponed until those works had been crippled. The assault was undertaken on the 9th of October. Both Frenchmen and Americans behaved with spirit, and planted their banners on the parapets of Savannah, but both were repulsed with great slaughter. Colonel von Porbeck, of the Regiment von Wissenbach, was complimented in Prevost's report. A week later the French sailed away, while some of the Americans returned with Lincoln to Charleston, and others dispersed to their homes.*

* According to the "Histoire de la Derniere Guerre," 101 n., the French and American army numbered five thousand five hundred and twenty-four. The British had—white men, three thousand and eighty-five; Indians, eighty; negroes, four thousand. Stedman (vol. ii. p. 127) gives the number of the garrison at less than twenty-five hundred white men. The French loss was about seven hundred; the American loss not far from two hundred and fifty. The journal of the Regiment von Wissenbach

In the summer of 1779, Sir Henry Clinton planned an expedition against Charleston. The execution of the design was postponed on account of the neighborhood of the French fleet, but when this had sailed for Europe a corps of about eighty-five hundred men was prepared in New York. This corps was made up of Englishmen, Tories, and Hessians. The Hessians chosen were the four battalions of grenadiers, a regiment of infantry, and about two hundred and fifty chasseurs. With the last-mentioned were Captain Ewald and Lieutenant Hinrichs. Lieutenant-general von Knyphausen was left in command at New York. Sir Henry Clinton commanded the expedition in person. The soldiers were embarked about the 19th of December, but on account of the weather they did not put to sea until the 29th. The voyage was a very stormy one, and when, in the first days of February, 1780, the main body of the fleet arrived in the mouth of the Savannah River, many transport ships were missing. A bark, the *Anna*, containing thirty Hessian and Anspach chasseurs, and other soldiers, had been dismasted early in January and taken in tow by a man-of-war. In a subsequent storm the tow-line snapped, and the *Anna*, a sheer hulk, was left to the fury of the waves. For eight weeks this bark, with two hundred and fifty souls on board, was driven before the westerly gales. She was provisioned only for a month and for a hundred men, and famine presently set in. The dogs were eaten; bones were ground up and boiled with shavings from salt-beef barrels.

---

gives the British loss, killed and wounded, at fifty-six; about one half of the number usually given.

The master proposed that the crew and passengers should feed on each other, beginning with the women. This inhuman proposal was rejected with disgust. At last the Irish coast came in sight. The vessel grazed on a rock and sprang a leak. It was noticed that the master was putting out to sea, and, on inquiry, it was discovered that he was afraid of having to pay thirty guineas for a pilot. The master was thereupon sent below and the boatswain took command of the bark. He brought her to St. Ives in Cornwall, where, in answer to her signals of distress, two boats with a pilot and a carpenter put out to her assistance. The carpenter was so frightened at the sight of the famished Hessians that he started off again for the shore as fast as his oars would take him. The pilot succeeded in beaching the bark just as she was about to sink, and the crew and passengers were saved at last.*

The English fleet waited at Tybee Island until the 9th of February, 1780, for the scattered transports to reassemble. It then put out to sea again, and on the 11th all but the heavy men-of-war entered the mouth of the North Edisto River, and the troops were disembarked on Simon's Island. For a month the soldiers were busily landing stores and artillery, making good their footing, and advancing over the sandy islands southwest of Charleston Harbor. It was not until the 12th of March that fire was opened on the town

* The above particulars are taken from Eelking's "Hülfstruppen," vol. ii. pp. 63, 64. As usual, Eelking gives no reference. Bancroft, however, gives the outlines of the story, and there are various contemporary authorities for the fact that the ship was separated from the fleet and driven to England.

from Wappoo Neck, and only on the 29th did the British army cross the Ashley River. Meanwhile fortifications had been springing up like mushrooms in the Charleston sand.

No serious opposition was offered to the landing, nor to the advance of the army. Yet the opportunities for resisting or, at least, for annoying the British, must have been such as to have tempted a more able and energetic commander than Lincoln. The invaders were landing from a long and exhausting voyage, and were without horses to drag their cannon and stores. Lincoln's true course would probably have been to imitate Washington in the campaign before Philadelphia. He might have risked a battle, and, if defeated, have abandoned Charleston and preserved his army for the protection of the Southern States. Those states were now to be given up to plunder and blood. The war in the Carolinas and Virginia was marked by a degree of barbarity which had no parallel in the Eastern and Middle States, except in the small plundering expeditions in the neighborhood of New York. Already in the preceding year Prevost's soldiers had begun this barbarous style of warfare. The marks of their plundering were visible in every house on the islands they had occupied near Charleston.

While Lincoln was throwing up his sand-works in the town, the English were receiving reinforcements from Savannah. The men-of-war, all but the heaviest, were lightened, brought over the bar and refitted. Fort Moultrie, however, still defended the town, and the American and French ships in the harbor, and between it and Charleston the besieged had sunk vessels to impede further navigation. Small parties of Americans watched the movements of the British. On the 26th of March Sir Henry Clinton and several of the generals rode out to meet Colonel Patterson, who was bringing reinforcements from Savannah. They returned safe, though without an escort; but a Tory colonel and a hospital inspector, who rode a short way behind them, were taken prisoners.*

Ewald tells with glee how, at John's Island, in South Carolina, in the spring of 1780, he reconnoitred a position by calmly lounging up to an outpost of the enemy, taking off his hat, and falling into conversation with the officer in command. The outpost was made up from Pulaski's Legion, which was officered by Poles and Frenchmen, in whose gallantry the German captain confided—a kind of gallantry which the native Americans either could not or would not understand.†

On the 30th of March, 1780, the English army was encamped some three thousand yards from the lines of Charleston. Towards evening the Hessian chasseurs on the picket line stood about a mile from the city. Before them lay a flat, sandy plain, unbroken by a house, tree, or bush. The only possible shelter consisted in a few ditches. On the night of the 31st of March the first parallel was opened. The next morning the inhabitants began to move off their families and their valuables, going in boats up the Cooper River, the only way left open. Down this river, on the 7th of April, came seven hundred Virginian Continentals to reïnforce the garrison. They were received

* Eelking's "Hülfstruppen," vol. ii. pp. 67, 68; Lee's "Memoirs," p. 146.
† Pulaski himself had been killed at the siege of Savannah.

with ringing of bells and with salvoes of artillery. Night by night the work on the trenches continued. The artillery of the city tried in vain to stop it.

The afternoon of the 8th of April was cloudy, the tide was on the flood, and a strong breeze was blowing from the south. Nine men-of-war and a transport ship approached Fort Moultrie, sailing in line, one behind the other. Before them all came Admiral Arbuthnot, in a jolly-boat, with the lead in his hand, piloting the fleet. The fire from the fort was terrific. The *Roebuck*, leading the line, sailed close to the works, gave a broadside, and passed on into the harbor, uninjured. The second ship lost a piece of her foremast. Another luffed before the fort and kept up a continuous fire, so that the whole ship seemed like a long flash of lightning. The whole squadron entered the harbor except the transport ship, which ran aground and was set on fire. The beautiful sight was watched by thousands of deeply interested spectators. The Americans covered the ramparts of the town. The Englishmen and Germans leaped on their siege-works. So absorbing was the interest of the operations in the bay, that fighting on land ceased for the time. As soon as the second ship had passed the fort, the Americans disappeared from the walls of Charleston, and presently a crowd of small boats was seen on the Cooper River, carrying off the more timid of the inhabitants.*

---

* See the MS. journals of the Jäger Corps (this part by Lieutenant Heinrichs) and of the Grenadier Battalions von Minnigerode and von Platte. A singular discrepancy exists in the original accounts as to the day on which the British fleet passed Fort Moultrie. For the 8th of April we have Clinton's official report, Lincoln to Washington, Laurens to Washington, and the MS. journals above quoted. For the 9th of April

Communication between Fort Moultrie and Charleston was now cut off. The British fleet, however, found its progress further barred by a line of sunken hulks, and could not sail up the Cooper River and take the American works in their rear. As some of the ships in that river interfered with the operations of the besiegers, several large row-boats were hauled overland to operate on it, the vehicle used for this purpose being dragged by one hundred and thirty-four negroes. Work on the approaches went on unceasingly, but the siege was somewhat delayed by the fact that some of the heavy artillery and most of the horses had been lost at sea. The place of the siege-train was supplied by cannon from the ships, brought with great labor overland from James Island. On the 13th of April hot shot were fired by the Hessian artillery, and several houses caught fire. Sir Henry Clinton ordered his batteries to slacken their fire, that the flames might be extinguished. On the following night the second parallel was opened, and soon after this counter-approaches were begun by the Americans, so that not only artillery, but musket-balls, could be brought to bear. On the 20th, however, the siege-works had so far advanced that the chasseurs were able to pick men off in the embrasures of the fortifications, and render the service of the guns very dangerous. The third parallel was opened in the following night, and on the 21st, Lincoln, who had refused to surrender on the day after

---

we have Admiral Arbuthnot's official report, Tarleton, Ewald, and Stedman. See Tarleton, pp. 11, 39, 49; Sparks's "Correspondence," vol. ii. pp. 434, 436; Ewald's "Belehrungen," vol. iii. p. 252; Stedman, vol. ii. p. 180.

Fort Moultrie had been passed by the fleet, offered to capitulate. Hostilities were suspended for six hours, but at the end of that time they were renewed, as the generals had not agreed on terms. On the 24th the Americans made a sortie, and penetrated in some places as far as the second parallel, but were presently driven back into the town. On the 26th the British took possession of a fort commanding the Cooper River, and the besieged were completely shut up in Charleston.

On the night of the 3d of May, a party of men from the besieging camp rowed silently up to a three-masted vessel lying close to the town. They climbed on to the deck, which they found undefended, cast off the moorings, and took back the ship within the British lines. Next morning they examined their prize, and on going below found her to be a hospital-ship, full of small-pox patients.*

The end of the siege was approaching. On the night of the 7th of May, 1780, Fort Moultrie was taken by sailors from the fleet. On the 8th, negotiations for a surrender of the town were renewed and again broken off; but on the 11th, Clinton's terms were agreed to. These were that the garrison should march out with colors cased and bands playing, but not an English or Hessian tune, and lay down their arms outside the town. The Continentals were to be prisoners of war, the militia were to return to their homes on parole. In consequence of this capitulation the Continentals marched out on the 12th, the bands playing a Turkish march. The officers were allowed to retain their

* Journal of the Grenadier Battalion von Platte.

swords, but were deprived of them a few days later, on the pretext that they were making "disorders" in the town. The garrison had been reduced to a very ragged and pitiable condition. They were not much more than half as numerous as the besiegers, even counting the American militia. Of the Continentals there were about twenty-five hundred, and the English army can hardly have numbered less than twelve thousand men. The town was defended only by earthworks, and was a fortified camp rather than a fortress. The loss of the besiegers, in killed and wounded, is set down in a Hessian journal at two hundred and sixty-five men.

The town of Charleston contained about fifteen thousand inhabitants, and had been one of the richest and gayest towns in North America. The large and handsome houses were not set close together as in other towns, but much free space was left for the circulation of air. They were well furnished with mahogany and silver-ware, and great attention was bestowed on keeping them clean. The streets were unpaved and sandy, but had a narrow foot-path at the sides. Even in May, the dust was intolerable. Most of the rich families had fled at the approach of the British. There were many Germans and German Jews in the town, and many doctors, on account of the unhealthy climate. The women, at least most of those that remained, were sallow and ugly. The place, of course, was full of negroes, who formed quite half of its population.

The negroes had been accumulating in the British camp. Two companies of them had been brought from Savannah at the end of February. The slaves of rebels had been confiscated. These slaves, in South Carolina, were the most degraded on the continent, and had been the worst treated by their former masters. The field hands among them, according to a Hessian journal, usually received a quart of rice or Indian corn a day. This they ate half-cooked, finding it more nourishing in that condition than if fully boiled. Many of them had hardly a rag to cover their nakedness. Few could understand English.* On the 31st of May ten slaves were given to each regiment starting for New York. The negroes formed a part of the booty of the campaign, and thousands of them were shipped to the West Indies to be sold.

Early in June, Sir Henry Clinton sailed for New York. With him went the Hessian grenadiers and chasseurs, but some of the Hessian regiments remained behind.

The expeditions to Savannah and Charleston were not the most distant in which the German auxiliaries were engaged. In the autumn of 1778 about twelve hundred men, Waldeckers and Provincials, under Major-general John Campbell, were sent to reinforce the garrisons of West Florida. Sailing early in November and touching at Jamaica, these troops were landed at Pensacola at the end of January, 1779. Pensacola was then a town of about two hundred wooden houses, defended by forts built of logs and sand. It stood in a sandy desert, surrounded by thick and interminable forests. It was a four weeks' journey overland to Georgia by the old trading path. The woods were in-

* MS. journal of the Grenadier Battalion von Platte.

fested by Indians, who received three pounds sterling from the British for every hostile scalp. Among the Indians the Waldeckers found a countryman of their own, one Brandenstein, who had deserted in his youth from the Waldeck service, and after many adventures had assumed the manners and the costume of an Indian warrior.

The garrison of Pensacola was at first occupied in fortifying the town. Lieutenant-colonel Dickson, an English officer, held Baton Rouge. In the course of the summer of 1779 three companies of Waldeckers were sent to reinforce him. Meanwhile war had broken out between England and Spain. Don Bernardo de Galvez, the Spanish governor at New Orleans, was young and energetic. He seized several small vessels in the Mississippi and the waters near its mouth. In September fifty-three Waldeckers were taken prisoners on Lake Pontchartrain. The Spaniards advanced against Baton Rouge, and after two attempts to carry the works by assault began a regular siege. Dickson capitulated, and the garrison marched out of the fort with all the honors of war. They numbered over four hundred, and the besiegers under Galvez between fourteen hundred and two thousand men. Nearly one half of the capitulating garrison were Waldeckers, and more than thirty of the regiment had been killed or wounded.

The news of Dickson's surrender reached Pensacola on the 20th of October, but was at first received with incredulity. "Is not this a cursed country to make war in?" writes the Waldeck chaplain, "where the greater part of a corps may be prisoners for five weeks, and twelve hundred miles of country taken by the enemy, and the commanding-general not know it with certainty."

In March, 1780, a part of the garrison of Pensacola marched to the relief of Mobile, but arrived too late to save the latter place. Soon after the return of the troops to Pensacola, a Spanish fleet of twenty-one sail was seen off the harbor, but three days afterwards it disappeared again. The Spaniards held the country as far as the Pertido River, and once crossed it in April, but were driven back by the Indians. The latter, however, were but unruly auxiliaries. The remainder of the year 1780 passed without any important occurrence in Florida.

Early in January, 1781, Colonel von Hanxleden, with one hundred and fifteen white men and three hundred Choctaws, made an expedition against French Village. They met with a determined resistance, and were repulsed. The number of killed and wounded on the English side was considerable, and among the killed was Colonel von Hanxleden.

On the 9th of March a Spanish fleet of thirty-eight sail appeared before Pensacola, and during the night following that day a body of troops was landed on the island of Santa Rosa, which lies at the mouth of the harbor. From this time the siege of the place went on steadily. On the 19th the fleet, profiting by a favorable wind, ran past the fortifications into the bay. Reinforcements were received by the Spaniards from time to time. On the 25th of April a deserter reported that Galvez had ten thousand men with him. The writer of the Waldeck journal speaks of this force as being fifteen times superior to that in Pensacola, whence we may infer that General Campbell commanded between six and seven hundred white men. The Indians, though drunken, barbarous, and undisciplined, were useful to the British. At last, on the morning of the 8th of May, a shell exploded in the powder-magazine of one of the redoubts, killing many of the Pennsylvania Tories who occupied the work, and causing great confusion. The Spaniards hereupon increased the fury of their fire, and in the afternoon of the same day General Campbell hung out the white flag, and surrendered on terms in accordance with which the garrison were all shipped to New York on condition of not serving against Spain, or her allies, until exchanged. As the United States were not at the time allied with Spain, the Waldeckers could be immediately employed against the Americans.*

* For the Waldeckers in Florida, see Eelking's "Hülfstruppen," vol. ii. pp. 135-153. Eelking had access to two MSS. The MS. now in the library of the Prince of Waldeck at Arolsen is a fragment beginning April 11th, 1780. See, also, Schlözer's "Briefwechsel," vol. v. p. 112, and an article by George W. Cable in the *Century Magazine* for February, 1883.

CHAPTER XXII.

NEW YORK IN 1780 AND 1781.

WHEN Sir Henry Clinton set sail for Charleston in December, 1779, he left the command of the garrison of New York to Lieutenant-general von Knyphausen. The regular troops in and about the city numbered some six thousand—Englishmen, Hessians, and Anspachers. By arming the inhabitants and the sailors from the ships that were icebound in the harbor, Knyphausen succeeded in nearly doubling the number of his men, and the new recruits were such as could do good service behind fortifications. Washington, meanwhile, commanded a small, ill-fed, and unpaid army, which in the spring of 1780 contained less than seven thousand regulars, only half of whom could be spared from garrison duty and made available for active operations.

The winter was an unusually cold one. The North and East rivers and Long Island Sound were frozen over, as was also the channel between Staten Island and the New Jersey shore. This state of things was favorable to expeditions, and these were constantly undertaken by both sides. In January, Lord Stirling landed on Staten Island, but found that the garrison there was expecting him, and returned to New Jersey, many of his men having suffered from frost-bites. Knyphausen was preparing to send reinforcements to the island through the floating ice of the harbor. At the end of this month and early in February the British made expeditions against Elizabethtown, Newark, and Young's House, and took a number of prisoners.

Before the year 1780 a new spirit was brought into the conduct of the war. Howe and Burgoyne had hoped not only to conquer, but to conciliate. The homes and property of non-combatants had been spared, at least to some extent. Clinton and Cornwallis, acting under the instructions of Lord George Germaine, abandoned this conciliatory policy. Expeditions were undertaken with no other purpose than robbery and destruction. In these, also, the Hessians were employed. On the evening of the 22d of March, 1780, for instance, a body of four hundred men, British and German, was set across the Hudson. About three in the morning they reached Hackensack, then a beautiful and rich village. No resistance was made. Not an American soldier was in the place. There was no one to withstand the barbarities that were committed. The British and Germans broke into the houses and loaded themselves with spoil. They made prisoners of all the male inhabitants they could lay hands on, and having completed their robbery, they set fire to the Town-house and to some of the principal dwellings. At daybreak five or six hundred Americans came to the rescue from Pollingtown, and it might have gone hard with the invaders had not another detachment of about four hundred men, under the partisan Emmerich, advanced to support them. As it was, they were chased back to the Hudson. From the journal of the Anspach musketeer Doehla, Eelking makes the following quotation: "We took considerable booty, both in money, silver watches, silver dishes and spoons, and in household goods, clothes, fine English linen, silk stockings, gloves, and neckerchiefs, with other precious silk goods, satin, and stuffs. My own booty, which I brought safely back, consisted of two silver watches, three sets of silver buckles, a pair of woman's cotton stockings, a pair of man's mixed summer stockings, two shirts and four chemises of fine English linen, two fine table-cloths, one silver table-spoon and one teaspoon, five Spanish dollars and six York shillings in money. The other part, viz., eleven pieces of fine linen and over two dozen silk handkerchiefs, with six silver plates and a silver drinking-mug, which were tied together in a bundle, I had to throw away on account of our hurried march, and leave them to the enemy that was pursuing us."*

Knyphausen claimed to have inflicted on the Americans a loss of sixty-five killed and three hundred and twenty prisoners during the winter.† The beginning of the summer brought round the time for more important action. On the evening of the 6th of June, 1780, the first of the five divisions of a British expeditionary force was landed in New Jersey at Elizabethtown Point, and the four other divisions followed the next day. They comprised almost all the regular soldiers at Knyphausen's disposal. The first and second divisions pressed on through Elizabethtown and Connecticut Farms, meeting with some resistance. At the latter place the army halted, and the chasseurs

* Eelking's "Hülfstruppen," vol. ii. p. 86. † Ibid. p. 87.

were thrown out towards Springfield. The chasseurs were but three hundred strong at this time, a part of the corps being at Charleston, and another part being turned into cavalry, or, more properly, mounted chasseurs. On these three hundred fell the brunt of the fighting on that day. The Americans showed great pertinacity, and charged repeatedly with the bayonet. About one o'clock the chasseurs received reinforcements, and the enemy were driven back to Springfield. A cannonade was now begun, but at about four in the afternoon the chasseurs were ordered back to their first position, and the army encamped. The pickets were posted in some houses in front of the line, but were presently attacked. The chasseurs charged and drove the Americans back a long distance, and the houses were burned. Three cannon were brought up, but the enemy did not renew the attack. The chasseurs lost fifty-five men killed and wounded during the day. At dusk news was brought by deserters that Washington with his main army was expected at Springfield during the night. Thereupon Knyphausen started at eleven in the evening and returned to Elizabethtown Point. On the following day Lord Stirling, with the American advanced guard, attacked an English regiment, but this was supported by two regiments of Germans, and the Americans were driven back to Elizabethtown. During the days that followed there was continual skirmishing. On the 13th, the mounted chasseurs made an attempt to surprise and capture an American cavalry picket, but their purpose was betrayed and the picket escaped. "It is almost impossible to surprise the enemy on any occasion," says the journal of the Jäger Corps, "because every house that one passes is an advanced picket, so to speak; for the farmer, or his son, or his servant, or even his wife or daughter fires off a gun, or runs by the foot-path to warn the enemy."

On the 19th of June Sir Henry Clinton, who had just returned from Charleston with the Hessian grenadiers and detachment of chasseurs, the British grenadiers and light infantry, and the Provincial Queen's Rangers, reviewed Knyphausen's army. Preparations were made for an advance, and on the 23d, four German regiments besides the chasseurs, and six regiments of Englishmen and Tories marched out towards Springfield. For a time the Americans held their ground at Connecticut Farms, but soon they fell back to the battlefield of the 7th, and the English army was drawn up on the heights on this side of Springfield. The Passaic River lay between the opposing forces, and the Americans, under Major Lee, held the bridge. The Hessian chasseurs waded through the stream in the face of a brisk fire, while an English regiment charged on the bridge, and Lee was driven back to the heights beyond the town, where he joined a larger corps. The town of Springfield was occupied, and for an hour the chasseurs in the advanced guard were skirmishing with the enemy beyond it. Then the British set fire to the town and retreated. The chasseurs now formed the rear guard, and could hardly pass between the burning houses. The Americans pressed hard upon them and harassed their retreat. About two miles from Elizabethtown the chasseurs were relieved by an English regiment, and the retreat continued to Elizabethtown Point. Here the troops took up their old positions, but were, during the night, ordered to break camp and pass over to Staten Island. This was done, and the bridge of boats which had been built on the 11th between the island and the mainland was immediately broken up, one Hessian regiment remaining in the *tête de pont* on the Jersey shore until the operation was completed. At about three o'clock in the morning the whole army had crossed. The loss of the chasseurs during the day was considerable, twenty-four being killed and wounded at the attack on the bridge over the Passaic, and perhaps as many more beyond the bridge and during the retreat.*

This expedition to Springfield was the last attempt made by Sir Henry Clinton to attack Washington's main army in New Jersey. The remainder of the year was uneventful in the Northern States, except for the treason of Arnold and the execution of André; nor was the first half of 1781 marked by any engagement in that region more important than a skirmish.

On the evening of the 2d of July, 1781, the partisan Emmerich, with a hundred men, had marched out to the Phillips House. During the night word was brought to Lieutenant-colonel von Wurmb that the American army was approaching New York in force, and that its advanced guard had been seen at Sing Sing. A lieutenant-colonel, with two hundred chasseurs and thirty cavalrymen, was, therefore, sent out at dawn to bring in news and to cover Emmerich's re-

* See MS. journal of the Jäger Corps; also Greene's report to Washington, Washington, vol. vii. p. 506 *et seq.*, and Lord Stirling's report, Sparks's Correspondence, vol. iii. p. 5.

treat. The lieutenant-colonel passed over Kingsbridge and continued on his march along Harlem Creek, sending a non-commissioned officer and ten men to explore the ruins of Fort Independence, which commanded his road. On reaching the heights on which the fort was built, Rübenkönig, the sergeant in command of the scouting party, saw men at a little distance. Unable to distinguish what they were in the gray of the morning, he advanced alone to meet them, and thought he recognized the blue coats and straw-colored trimmings of the Regiment von Donop, a part of which was with Emmerich's command. He had hardly wished them good-morning, when half a dozen men sprang at him, seized him by the hair and by the straps of his cartridge-box, and tried to choke him. Rübenkönig twisted himself out of their hands, and with cries of "Rebels! Rebels!" made off to his own party.

The advanced guard of the chasseurs was already in the narrow pass between the hill on which the fort stood and Harlem River. The men had to make their way back across the morass. The ground where the main body was drawn up was narrow and unfavorable, and the first assault on the Americans was repulsed, the Germans falling back in a disorderly mass. The cavalry then attacked without success, but the Americans retreated to the ruins of the fort, and the chasseurs had time to form properly and on good ground. The Americans were at last driven from their position, perhaps by the approach of reinforcements to the Germans, for Lieutenant-colonel von Wurmb arrived at about this time. They fell back to high ground, about one thousand yards off, and appeared to be some six or seven hundred strong. Emmerich and his party, meanwhile, had retreated across Spyt den Duyvel Creek, and were cut off from the chasseurs, as the bridge was in the hands of the enemy. The whole corps with the cavalry therefore advanced to clear the bridge, and the Americans retreated slowly. Wurmb having accomplished his first object, and believing that the enemy was trying to draw him into an ambuscade, halted his command and reported to headquarters. In the afternoon the American army advanced and encamped on Valentine's Hill, extending over Courtland's Reach to Spyt den Duyvel. The Hessian loss in the engagement was thirty men killed and wounded.*

On the 6th of July, 1781, the French army, under Rochambeau, joined that of Washington before New York, and for more than a month a skirmishing warfare was kept up, Sir Henry Clinton expecting to be besieged in New York whenever the French fleet should arrive from the West Indies. At last, on the 18th of August, 1781, the enemy was reported to be crossing the North River. Still Clinton's eyes were not opened. In vain did Lieutenant-colonel von Wurmb of the chasseurs, who had permission to send out spies on his own account, warn the commander-in-chief that the allied army was on its way to Virginia. The lieutenant-colonel had two grounds for believing this. The first was that preparations had been made to provide the Americans and Frenchmen with food and forage on the road across New Jersey; the second, that the lieutenant-colonel had been informed that an

* MS. journal of the Jäger Corps; Ewald's "Belehrungen," vol. i. p. 5–8.

American woman, who was the mistress of a French officer of distinction, had been instructed to go to Trenton. General Clinton was not convinced until it was too late to oppose the movement.*

Even after Washington's plan had become clear to him, Sir Henry Clinton was unwilling to employ his whole available force in any operation important enough to have served as a diversion in favor of Lord Cornwallis. It is probably now impossible to say whether an expedition in force against Philadelphia, or up the Hudson, might not have caused the return of the allied army from their southern expedition.† Clinton, however, contented himself with preparing to embark a corps for Yorktown, and sending a party under Benedict Arnold, who had lately returned from Virginia, to the coast of Connecticut. Arnold, at the head of two English regiments and one hundred Hessian chasseurs, reached New London on the 6th of September and stormed the fort, whose small garrison made an obstinate resistance. Arnold burned part of the town, the magazines, and the ships on the stocks. Those in the harbor escaped up the river.

It was not until the 19th of October that the British fleet put to sea to go to the assistance of Lord Cornwallis. The Hessian grenadiers and the other troops were carried as passengers on the men-of-war. On the 28th of October the fleet was off the mouth of Chesapeake Bay, and received from the shore the news of Cornwallis's surrender. "This second Burgoynade,"

---

* MS. journal of the Jäger Corps, August 18th.

† See Clinton's letters to Cornwallis, Tarleton, chap. vi. Notes A, M, O, Q, S.

writes a Hessian officer, "will probably contribute much to bring the war to an unhappy issue." The prediction was certainly verified from its author's point of view, and we must now turn our attention to the events which led up to the catastrophe at Yorktown.

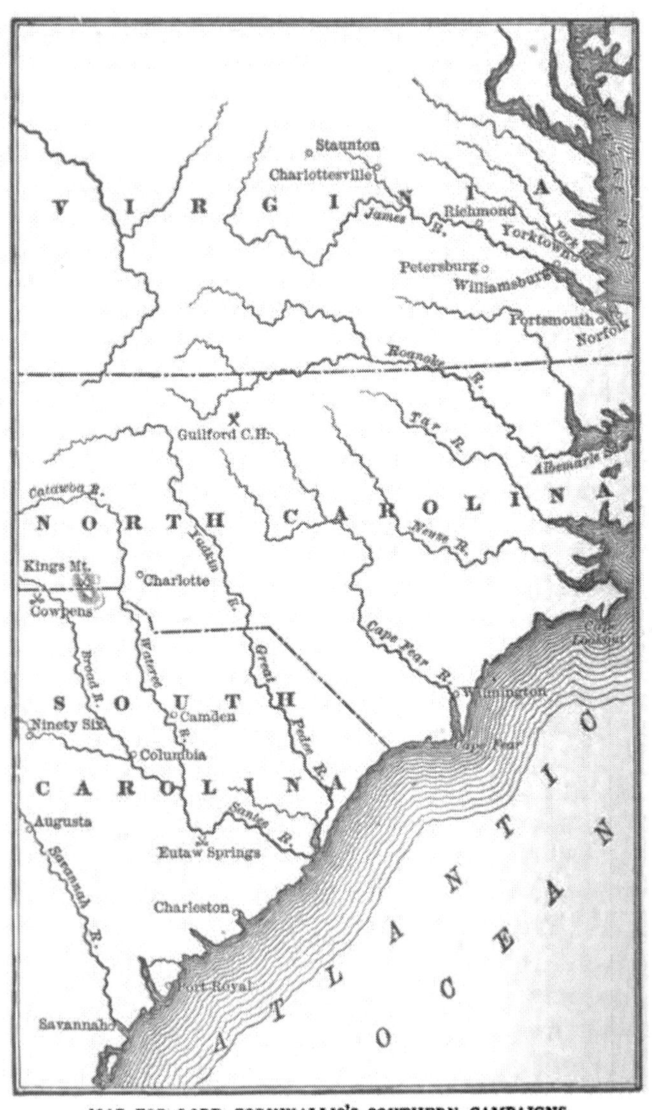

MAP FOR LORD CORNWALLIS'S SOUTHERN CAMPAIGNS.

CHAPTER XXIII.

THE SOUTHERN CAMPAIGN OF 1781.

WHEN Sir Henry Clinton sailed away from Charleston in June, 1780, two Hessian regiments were included in the garrison which he left behind him, and one more such regiment was brought from Savannah soon afterwards. I do not find any record of an active part taken by these regiments in the campaigns which Lord Cornwallis conducted in South and North Carolina. On the 16th of August, 1780, the American army under General Gates was routed at Camden, and on the 18th Tarleton surprised a party under Sumter. Six weeks later the tables were partially turned by the brilliant engagement at King's Mountain, where about fourteen hundred backwoodsmen surrounded and stormed a hill held by an equal number of British regulars and Provincials, killing and wounding two fifths of them, and taking the remainder prisoners.

In the month of October, 1780, General Leslie, with several English regiments, the Hessian Regiment von Bose, and a detachment of one hundred chasseurs left New York for the Southern States. They landed at Portsmouth, in Virginia, but shortly afterwards abandoned this post and proceeded to Charleston, where they arrived in the latter part of the year.

Having this reinforcement within reach, Lord Cornwallis started from Wynesborough, west of Camden, and marched against General Greene, who, at Washington's desire, had been appointed Gates's successor. The British army numbered about thirty-five hundred. Learning that Morgan, with a separate force,* was on the south side of Broad River, Cornwallis determined to cut him off from Greene's main army. For this purpose he detached Lieutenant-colonel Tarleton, with about a thousand men. Tarleton was to attack Morgan in front, while Cornwallis was to follow up the left bank of Broad River and capture the fugitive Americans. Tarleton came up with Morgan on the morning of the 17th of January, 1781. Hardly waiting to form his army, the gallant cavalry colonel rushed on his despised enemy. The American militia forming the first line gave way. The second line, formed largely of Continentals, stood firm. Tarleton ordered up his reserves. The Americans gave ground, then turned and poured in a vigorous and well-directed fire. This unexpected resistance threw the British into confusion. They wavered. Two companies of Virginia militia charged with the bayonet. The British gave way on all sides. Tarleton rallied about fifty horsemen, and, for a moment, checked the pursuit. Most of the British infantry were taken, but the cavalry escaped, and the baggage was destroyed. The Americans took about five hundred prisoners, and about a hundred Englishmen were killed. The American loss did not exceed seventy-five. Two standards, two cannon, thirty-five wagons, eight hundred muskets, and one hundred horses fell into Morgan's hands. The cannon had already been captured by Gates at Saratoga

* Morgan had from eight hundred to one thousand men.

and by Cornwallis at Camden. Morgan's battle, fought almost in the wilderness, is called Cowpens, after the place where the inhabitants of that part of the country collected and salted their roving cattle.

Soon after his victory General Morgan was laid up with rheumatism and forced to leave the army.* Few men engaged in the Revolutionary War had done better service to their country.. There is a legend which tells that the house he built for himself near Winchester, in the Valley of Virginia, was constructed of stones quarried by Hessian prisoners, who carried them for miles on their shoulders. The story is picturesque and not impossible, but I know of no German authority for it.

Cornwallis was disappointed but not daunted by the rout of his ablest subordinate, and of nearly a third of his soldiers. On the day after the battle of Cowpens he was joined by Leslie's division. In a few days he was marching across North Carolina, and Greene was retreating before him. The latter was driven out of the state and across the Dan River. Cornwallis called on the Tories to rise, and these at first showed an inclination to do so, but a party of them was attacked and dispersed by a superior force under Henry Lee and Pickens, and the others became discouraged and went home again.

At last General Greene, having received reinforcements, advanced again to Guildford Court House, in North Carolina, and prepared to give battle. His army consisted of sixteen hundred and fifty-one Con-

* Lee, however, blames Morgan for leaving the army at this time.—"Memoirs," pp. 237, 583.

tinentals and more than two thousand militia. Lord Cornwallis commanded eighteen hundred and seventy-five veterans. On the 15th of March, 1781, Greene drew up his army in three lines. The foremost of these was composed of North Carolina militia, posted in the woods behind a fence. A portion of this line was on the edge of a clearing. Its left was supported by a body of riflemen under Lieutenant-colonel Henry Lee and Colonel Campbell. Greene's second line, stationed three hundred yards behind the first, was composed of Virginia militia. They stood in the thick woods. The third line contained all the Continentals of the army.

Opposite to this force, after a skirmish of the advanced-guards, Lord Cornwallis drew up his army in two divisions. The left wing was under Lieutenant-colonel Webster, the right under Brigadier-general Leslie. The right wing first came on the North Carolina militia, which fled at its approach. Lee and Campbell, however, with their riflemen, continued in action. The British advanced against the Virginia militia. The whole English line was now engaged, and the Virginians defended themselves so well that Lord Cornwallis was obliged to call up his reserves. The American second line was finally driven back, and the British pressed forward to meet the Continentals. By this time a good deal of confusion had been caused among the English, fighting in the thick woods. It was Lieutenant-colonel Webster, with his brigade, who first met the Continentals. Attacking them rashly, he was driven back behind a ravine. The Second Maryland regiment, however, was broken by an attack of the second battalion of English guards, and two 6-pounders were taken. The First Maryland regiment and Colonel Washington's cavalry charged the guards, drove them back in confusion, and recaptured the guns. Then Lieutenant Macleod of the British artillery opened fire with two 3-pounders on friend and foe alike. Washington's dragoons were checked, Webster advanced again and was supported by a part of Leslie's division, and General Greene drew off his army, abandoning his artillery, whose horses had been shot.

The Hessians engaged in this battle were a detachment of chasseurs and the Regiment von Bose. This regiment was on the right of the British line. It was opposed throughout the action to the riflemen under Lee and Campbell, who attacked it with great determination, both in front and rear. In this position the regiment behaved with great valor, and, at one time, relieved the first battalion of English guards, which had been thrown into confusion. A decisive share in the victory is claimed for the Hessian regiment by Eelking and Bancroft. This share can hardly be conceded to it, but the soldiers, and Lieutenant-colonel du Puy, who commanded them, deserved the favorable mention in despatches which they obtained from Lord Cornwallis.

The whole engagement lasted about two hours. The total loss of the British was five hundred and thirty-two, of whom eighty belonged to the Regiment von Bose.* Cornwallis was so crippled by his victory

* For Guildford Court-House, see Bancroft, vol. x. pp. 475–480; Eelking's "Hülfstruppen," vol. ii. pp. 101–104; Marshall, vol. iv. pp. 368–

that he turned away from the Virginian border and marched down to Wilmington to rest his army, leaving his severely wounded behind him.

Lord Cornwallis having retired to the coast, General Greene overran the states of North and South Carolina. Before the middle of September the Americans had lost three battles and conquered three provinces. Successively defeated at Camden, Ninety-six, and Eutaw Springs, Greene and the partisan leaders that co-operated with him took many smaller posts by siege, or storm, and caused the capitulation of Augusta, and the evacuation of Camden and Ninety-six. In the autumn of 1781 the British held no part of the three most southern states, except Savannah, Charleston, and Wilmington.

On the 10th of December, 1780, Benedict Arnold, now a British brigadier-general, sailed from New York at the head of about sixteen hundred men, including one hundred Hessian chasseurs under Captain Ewald. Arnold reached James River early in January, 1781. There was no one to oppose him but a small force of militia, under Baron Steuben. Arnold burned the town of Richmond, with its stores of tobacco, and then retreated to Portsmouth, at the mouth of the James. It was soon after this that the chasseurs gave another proof of their valor. On the 19th of March, 1781, the American General Muhlenberg, with a party reckoned at five hundred men, advanced against the British line,

379; Sparks's "Correspondence," vol. iii. p. 266; Tarleton, pp. 271–278 and (Lord Cornwallis's official report) pp. 303–310; Stedman, vol. ii. pp. 337–345; Lee's "Memoirs," pp. 274–286; Ewald's "Belehrungen," vol. ii. p. 135; vol. iii. p. 322; MS. journal of the Regiment von Bose.

scattered and partially captured a picket of chasseurs, and approached the position held by Captain Ewald. This was at first defended by a non-commissioned officer and sixteen men. The captain and nineteen more men hastened to assist them. The Americans had to advance over a narrow dyke, some thirty paces long, and on this they were crowded together. Every shot told in their ranks, and twenty-nine were killed or wounded. The chasseurs lost but two men, and Muhlenberg drew off his force. "On these occasions," says Ewald, "we must screw the heels of our shoes firmly to the ground and not think of moving off, and we shall seldom find an adversary who will run over us in such a position." Ewald was wounded in the knee in this skirmish. Eelking relates that Arnold came to see the captain after the fight. Ewald reproached the general for not reinforcing the chasseurs. Arnold answered that he had thought the position was lost. "So long as one chasseur lives," cried the angry captain, "no —— American shall come over the dyke." Arnold, who still considered himself an American, took this in bad part, and showed his pique by omitting to mention the conduct of the chasseurs in the orders of the day. Ewald complained of this to Arnold's aid, and the general came to him the next day with apologies, and rectified the omission.*

Meanwhile Lafayette, with twelve hundred Continentals, had been ordered to Virginia. The young general marched at once with a part of his force, leaving Wayne to follow with the remainder. Ten French

* MS. journal of the Jäger Corps; Ewald's "Belehrungen," vol. ii. p. 169; Eelking's "Hülfstruppen," vol. ii. pp. 107, 108.

ships of war were sent to co-operate with the marquis. These fell in with the English squadron, on the 16th of March, off the capes of Virginia. After an engagement, which lasted two hours, the French fleet sailed back to Newport and the English entered Chesapeake Bay. The defence of Virginia was thrown on the land forces exclusively, and these were unequal to the task.

On the 19th of March Major-general Phillips, the same who had been taken prisoner with Burgoyne at Saratoga, sailed from New York to assume command of the English forces in Virginia. He took with him a reinforcement of two thousand men, and nearly as many more followed him six weeks later. Soon after his arrival General Phillips sallied out from Portsmouth, went up the James River burning and plundering on both banks, carried off the negroes and shipped them to the West Indies, destroyed the magazines at Manchester, under the nose of Lafayette, who remained on the north side of the river, and on the 9th of May took possession of Petersburg, where his army was to make a junction with that of Lord Cornwallis, advancing from Wilmington. Four days later General Phillips died of malignant fever, and Arnold was again in command of the army. On the 20th, however, Lord Cornwallis arrived at Petersburg, and the traitor was shortly afterwards sent back to New York.

Cornwallis left Petersburg on the 24th of May, crossed the James River twenty-five miles below Richmond, and on the first of June was at Cook's Ford, on the North Anna River, near Hanover Court House. Thence he sent Tarleton on a raid to Charlottesville, where the Legislature of Virginia was in session. Tarleton scattered the legislature, and took a few of its members. Meanwhile Simcoe was sent to take or destroy some magazines and stores at Point of Fork, where the Rivanna and Fluvanna rivers unite to form the James. He found that the stores, which were under the guard of General Steuben, were on the south side of the James River. There was no ford, and Simcoe had but a few small boats. He, therefore, resorted to a stratagem. By drawing out his four hundred men in a long line, and half displaying and half concealing them, he succeeded in making Steuben believe that his command was the advanced guard of Cornwallis's main army. Not reflecting that with only a few skiffs in which to cross the river a whole army was hardly more formidable than a detachment, Steuben retreated, leaving a part of the stores behind him. Twenty-four men were, thereupon, set across the river, and while half of them kept watch the others destroyed the stores without being disturbed.*

Lafayette retreated as far north as the Rappahannock, where Wayne joined him with reinforcements. The marquis then made a rapid march to the southward and westward and placed himself between the British army and the stores in the western part of the state. He was still too weak, however, to risk a battle. Cornwallis did not advance against him, but on the 15th of June turned towards the seaboard. This gave Lafayette an apparent advantage. He followed

* Ewald, vol. ii. pp. 194–199; Stedman, vol. ii. pp. 389, 390. Kapp says that the stores destroyed were of small value, and believes that Steuben acted wisely.—Steuben's "Leben," pp. 429–436. See, also, Lafayette's "Mémoires," vol. i. pp. 97, 150.

Cornwallis on the march, but at a respectful distance. The army under Lafayette at the time numbered forty-five hundred men, of whom only one thousand five hundred and fifty were regulars.*

But two engagements occurred during this return march. The first of them was on the 26th of June. A party under Simcoe and Ewald, forming the rear guard of the British army, was attacked, and in a measure surprised by a detachment of Wayne's division. The British and Hessians were resting at noon not far from Williamsburg, when the Americans made a spirited attack upon them. The cavalry were soon mounted, however, and the chasseurs under arms, and the Americans were beaten off, with a loss on either side of thirty or forty men.†

At Williamsburg Lord Cornwallis received orders to send back three thousand men to New York, which Clinton supposed to be threatened by the combined forces of France and the United States. For the purpose of carrying out this order, Cornwallis proceeded on his march to Portsmouth. On the 4th of July he left his camp at Williamsburg and marched to Jamestown, with the intention of crossing the James River. The rangers under Simcoe and the chasseurs under Ewald crossed the same night. A part of the baggage was taken over the next day. On the 6th of July Cornwallis, with the army, remained at Jamestown,

* Johnston's "Yorktown Campaign," p. 55; Lafayette to Washington, June 28th, 1871, in "Mémoires de Lafayette," vol. i. p. 150.

† Ewald's "Belehrungen," vol. iii. p. 474; Tarleton, pp. 301, 302; Johnston's "Yorktown Campaign," pp. 56, 190, with official return of the American loss.

and the general received intelligence that Lafayette was marching to attack him. This was what Cornwallis wished, as he had a good position and a much larger number of regular soldiers than Lafayette.

On the afternoon of the 6th of July Lafayette drew near, uncertain whether the main army of Lord Cornwallis was on the left bank of the James, or only the rear guard. The Americans came on cautiously. Wayne attacked with about five hundred men. The British pickets had received orders to make a stubborn resistance and then fall back. Encouraged by this, Wayne brought the rest of his brigade into action, having thus more than one thousand men in line. The remaining Continentals of the army formed a reserve. It seemed to Cornwallis that the moment to strike had come. His army was drawn up in two lines. The first consisted of about twenty-five hundred men. The second, in which was the Regiment von Bose, was about one thousand strong. Wayne and Lafayette discovered their error, and saw that it could best be redeemed by boldness. Wayne advanced with his brigade. This checked the British. The hostile lines halted about seventy yards apart, and a brisk fire was kept up for fifteen minutes. Then, as the British were beginning to outflank them, the Americans fell back. Two cannon, taken from the Brunswickers at Bennington, were left on the field, their horses having been shot. The loss of the Americans was reported at one hundred and thirty-nine, that of the British at seventy-five.*

* For Green Spring, see Johnston's "Yorktown Campaign," pp. 60 *et seq.*, 190; Bancroft, vol. x. p. 507; Eelking's "Hülfstruppen," vol. ii.

After arriving at Portsmouth, Cornwallis received counter-orders, and retained the whole of his army. He was to occupy and fortify Old Point Comfort and, if he considered it expedient, some other situation on the peninsula, suitable for a naval station. The engineers having reported adversely on Old Point Comfort, Cornwallis, in the first week in August, occupied Yorktown, and the small village of Gloucester, opposite to it. Here he soon collected his whole force, and went busily to work fortifying his position, while Lafayette waited and watched him.

Just at this time Washington was informed that the French fleet, under Count de Grasse, was preparing to assist in the operations near Chesapeake Bay. Preparations were quickly and secretly made to move the American and French armies from New York to Virginia. We have seen that on the 18th of August it was already reported in the city of New York that the allies were crossing the North River. There were so few boats that this operation lasted a week. Sir Henry Clinton, although warned of Washington's design, was still under the impression that an attack on Staten Island might be intended. It was not until the 29th that he was undeceived. Leaving less than four thousand men under General Heath to guard the Highlands, Washington and Rochambeau were in full march against Cornwallis.

The allied army which was crossing New Jersey,

---

p. 114; Ewald's "Belehrungen," vol. ii. p. 332–335; Wayne to Washington, Sparks's "Correspondence," vol. iii. p. 347–350; Tarleton, pp. 353–357; MS. journal of the Regiment von Bose. Also a letter from Ewald to Riedesel, Eelking's "Riedesel," vol. iii. p. 336.

and on which the fate of the war depended, was a very small one. It consisted of four thousand Frenchmen and two thousand Americans. Passing through Philadelphia, it arrived at Head of Elk on the 6th and 8th of September, 1781. Already the Count de Grasse had arrived in the Chesapeake with twenty-four ships of the line, carrying seventeen hundred guns and nineteen thousand seamen. Against him, on the 5th of September, came Admiral Graves, with an inferior force. The battle lasted two hours, and the English, though not decidedly beaten, were not in a condition to undertake anything more against the French. They sailed off to New York four days later, leaving de Grasse master of Chesapeake Bay.

The Frenchmen and Americans who had come from New York were now brought down the bay, and joined with Lafayette's corps and the French troops brought by de Grasse. The united army at Williamsburg on the 27th of September, 1781, consisted of about seven thousand Frenchmen, fifty-five hundred Continentals, and thirty-five hundred Virginian militia. In the ranks of the Continentals were companies from all the states north of the Carolinas. The English army at Yorktown numbered some seven thousand soldiers. Of these, not quite eleven hundred were subjects of the Margrave of Anspach-Bayreuth, rather more than eight hundred and fifty were subjects of the Landgrave of Hesse-Çassel, and the remainder, or about five thousand men, were subjects of the King of Great Britain, to whom all in this army had sworn obedience. About eight hundred marines fought on each side during the siege. The French fleet was not within range, but the English ships were actively engaged.

Yorktown was not a strong position, and was defended only by field-works. On the 30th of September, 1781, the British abandoned their outer line of defences, perhaps prematurely. On the night of the 6th of October the first parallel was made. On the afternoon of the 9th the parallel opened fire, and from that time to the end of the siege the cannonade was nearly continuous.

Almost the first fighting that occurred was a skirmish, on the Gloucester side of the river. Here were posted Simcoe's rangers, Tarleton's dragoons, Ewald's chasseurs, and an English regiment. Opposed to them were more than a thousand Frenchmen under Choisy and de Lauzun, and twelve or fifteen hundred militia under General Weedon. Tarleton and Simcoe had discarded the use of carbines by their cavalry, and this aided in their discomfiture. On the morning of the 3d of October it was reported to Lauzun that there were English dragoons outside the works of Gloucester. Advancing to reconnoitre, he saw a pretty woman at the door of a small house by the roadside. Lauzun would not have been Lauzun if he had passed a pretty woman unquestioned. She informed him that Colonel Tarleton had just been at her house, and desired very much "to shake hands with the French duke." "I assured her," says Lauzun, "that I had come on purpose to give him that satisfaction. She pitied me much, thinking, I suppose, from experience, that it was impossible to resist Tarleton; the American troops were in the same case."

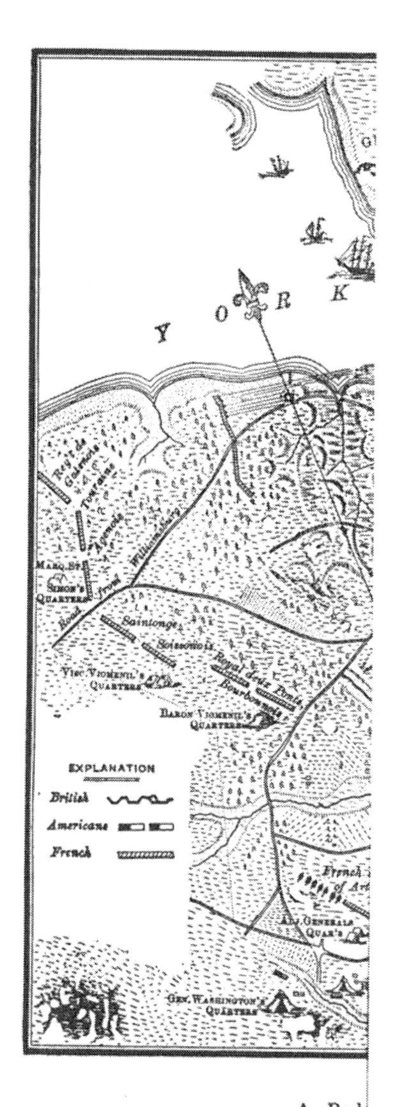
Y O R K
Reg't de Gatenois
Touraine
Agenois
Williamsburg
Marq. St. Simon's Quarters
Road from
Saintonge
Soissonois
Royal deux Ponts
Bourbonnois
Visc. Viomenil's Quarters
Baron Viomenil's Quarters
EXPLANATION
British
Americans
French
Gen. Washington's Quarters

A. Rede
B. Redo

Presently the French and English dragoons met. Tarleton raised his pistol and approached Lauzun. A single combat was imminent, when Tarleton's horse fell. The English dragoons covered the escape of their colonel, but his horse was taken by Lauzun.*

The 10th of October was marked by a deed of valor. Major Cochrane had left New York in a small vessel with despatches for Lord Cornwallis. He arrived at Chesapeake Bay in broad daylight, ran the gantlet of the French fleet, which fired briskly at him, and reached Yorktown in safety. This brave man had, however, seen the last of his good fortune. Two days after his arrival he pointed a gun with his own hands. As he looked over the parapet to see the effect of his shot, his head was carried off by a cannon-ball. Lord Cornwallis was standing by his side, and narrowly escaped sharing his fate.†

On the night of the 11th of October the second parallel was opened. Two redoubts, facing the right wing of the allied position, were so placed as to interfere with this parallel. It was necessary to take them. The work of storming the larger one was intrusted to the French. The redoubt was manned partly by Germans. The French, under command of the Baron de Vioménil, were discovered and challenged at one hundred and twenty paces from the redoubt. Some time was spent in making an opening in the abatis. When

* "Mémoires du Duc de Lauzun," p. 245; Ewald's "Belehrungen," vol. ii. p. 391; Tarleton, pp. 376–378; Lee's "Memoirs," pp. 496–498; Rochambeau's "Mémoires," pp. 291, 292.

† Ewald's "Belehrungen," vol. i. p. 11; Johnston's "Yorktown Campaign," p. 138, quoting a statement by Captain Mure in a letter published in appendix to vol. vii. of Lord Mahon's "History of England."

this was passed the work was stormed. Ninety-two Frenchmen were killed or wounded in the attack. The loss of the enemy was fifteen killed and fifty prisoners. The Americans were equally successful in taking the smaller redoubt, and, as they were less delayed by the abatis, their success was more rapid. Nine men of their column were killed and thirty-one wounded, including five officers.

Early in the morning of the 16th of October a sortie was made against the second parallel. For a few moments it was successful, and several cannon were spiked, but the British were presently driven back by a charge of the French grenadiers, and the cannon were bored out within a few hours. On the following night Cornwallis made an attempt to take his army across the York River, with the intention of trying to get off into Virginia.* A violent storm of wind and rain, which drove all his boats down the river, prevented him from carrying out this design, and such of the troops as had already crossed to Gloucester were brought back the next morning, leaving only the regular garrison of that place.†

The British artillery was now completely silenced, and Cornwallis saw that he could hold out no longer. On the 17th of October, 1781, negotiations were opened, and on the 19th the capitulation was signed,

* See this plan discussed at length, Tarleton, pp. 379–385; and in Lee's "Memoirs," pp. 503–506.

† Cornwallis's report to Clinton, in Johnston's "Yorktown Campaign," p. 181. There were one hundred and forty-two Hessians killed and wounded at Yorktown (Knyphausen to the Landgrave, November 6th, 1781); this does not include the chasseurs at Gloucester, nor the Anspachers.

the terms being substantially those accorded to General Lincoln at Charleston in the previous year. On the afternoon of the same day the British and Germans marched out of their intrenchments with cased colors, and with their bands playing an old English tune, "The World Turned Upside Down."

CHAPTER XXIV.

CONCLUSION.

CORNWALLIS'S surrender at Yorktown decided the fate of the Revolutionary War. The armies remained quiet through the winter, and in the spring of 1782 General Clinton and General von Knyphausen returned to Europe. Sir Guy Carleton assumed the command in New York, and Lieutenant-general von Lossberg became chief of the Hessian division. On the 14th of December, 1782, Charleston was evacuated, and on the 25th of November, 1783, two years after the fall of Yorktown, the last Hessians sailed down the Bay of New York. "About two in the afternoon we weighed anchor," says the journal of the Jäger Corps, "and as the fleet fell down to Staten Island we saw the American flag hoisted on several houses. None was raised on Fort George, however. At sunset we passed Sandy Hook, and at nightfall the land disappeared from our sight."

The force of German mercenaries which England maintained in America from 1776 to 1783 averaged not very far from twenty thousand men. In the course of that time about thirty thousand soldiers were brought over, and seventeen thousand three hundred and thirteen returned to Germany when the war was ended. For the services of these men England paid in levy-money and subsidies to the princes more than

£1,770,000 sterling. This was in addition to the pay of the soldiers and to all expenses except those of recruiting and equipment.

There can be no question that for this large sum of money Great Britain obtained the services of excellent soldiers. It is true that the Germans were several times unsuccessful when left to themselves and not accompanied by English troops. Breymann's Brunswickers at Bennington found it impossible to get over the ground with reasonable speed, but the whole of Burgoyne's army was singularly slow in its movements. That general, in a private letter, speaks of the Germans at Saratoga as "dispirited and ready to club their arms at the first fire." Yet they had fought with valor in the earlier part of the campaign, and had rendered essential services both at Hubbardton and Freeman's Farm. At Saratoga the Brunswick regiments held the most exposed part of the line. Turning now to the war in the Middle States, we see the Hessians taking the leading part and behaving with great gallantry at White Plains and Fort Washington. We see them, made over-confident by success, surprised at Trenton and defeated at Red Bank. On the former occasion they were thrown into confusion, their commander was killed, and the men "never made any regular stand." On the latter occasion they fought with desperation, suffering a loss of three hundred and seventy-one officers and men, in a force that cannot have exceeded twenty-five hundred. It would lead us too far to consider minutely those actions in which the Germans did not form the principal part of the king's forces, but I think that it would be found that on few occasions during the war did the Hessian soldiers show either a want of courage or a want of discipline. One difficulty was inevitable in the employment of troops of different nationalities. Jealousy and ill-will arose between the officers and between the soldiers. We have seen how Heister was recalled, because he could not get on with Sir William Howe, and how Riedesel felt himself injured by Burgoyne. The British were, moreover, accused of acting unfairly in the matter of the exchange of prisoners, and of exchanging their own officers while they left the Germans in captivity. Riedesel went so far as to write to Washington on the subject, and was politely reminded that it was not a matter within the latter's control.*

We may take it for granted that the jealousy felt by the superior officers was shared by the subordinates. In a letter from Brookland (Brooklyn), dated the 7th of September, 1776, a Hessian chaplain writes: "Our dear Hessians learned to bear their hardships, and I endeavored in my prayers and sermons to strengthen them in their Christian heroism. The loitering of the English general made them impatient, but still more the proud and insulting looks which the English are wont to cast on the Germans. This often led to bloody scenes. A non-commissioned officer to whom an Englishman said over their cups, '—— —— you, Frenchman, you take our pay,' answered coldly, 'I am a German and you are a ——.' Both drew, and the Englishman was so badly wounded that he died. Not only was the good German pardoned by the English general, but orders were given that the English

* Eelking's "Hülfstruppen," vol. i. p. 340.

should treat the Germans like brothers. All this happens since our teachable Germans have learned a little English." *

Too much weight must not, however, be given to such stories, many of which, undoubtedly, obtained circulation in America during the war. "It is astonishing," writes Ewald, many years afterwards, "what stuff deserters often tell in order to please their new friends and obtain a good reception. After I had been taken prisoner at Yorktown, and had made the acquaintance of several French officers, a French general, then chief of the Deux Ponts Regiment,† asked me quite in confidence whether the Hessians were not very discontented with the English service, as it was very hard that these troops should always be employed in the most doubtful battles; that they should often be wantonly sacrificed; that they should always have the worst quarters assigned to them; that they should receive the worst provisions; that they should be improperly paid and allowed to suffer want of all sorts. I could not help laughing at his story, and assured him that not a single word of all this was true, but quite the contrary; whereupon the general was very much astonished, for every deserter had assured him that it was so."

It has sometimes been said that the German soldiers deserted in great numbers in America. This assertion is only partially borne out by facts. At the time

---

* Schlözer's "Briefwechsel," vol. vii. p. 362.

† The colonel of the Deux Ponts Regiment was the Count de Deux Ponts. I suspect that he was the "general" alluded to.—Ewald's "Belehrungen," vol. ii. p. 424.

when the first Hessians arrived at Staten Island, Congress caused papers to be distributed among them, encouraging them to desert. Washington was busy with such papers within a few days of their landing.* The promises then made were renewed from time to time. One proclamation, dated on the 29th of April, 1778, promises fifty acres of land to every soldier that will come over, and any captain who brings forty men with him shall receive eight hundred acres of woodland, four oxen, one bull, two cows, and four sows. Deserters were not to be obliged to serve on the American side, but might devote themselves at once to the improvement of their estates. Such officers, however, as would accept service in the army of the United States should receive a rank higher than that which they had enjoyed in the army they were leaving, and should be appointed to a corps composed of Germans, to be employed on frontier or garrison duty exclusively, unless at its own request.†

These promises were not entirely without result. In August, 1778, two Hessian lieutenants came to Washington's camp, and held out hopes that other officers would follow them. These hopes were illusory for the most part. Ewald asserts that no other born Hessian officer deserted, but I have reason to suppose that some few officers of the smaller German contingents went over.‡

Even among the privates the desertion was less than

* Washington, vol. iv. pp. 66, 67. See in the MS. journal of the Regiment von Huyn a copy of a proclamation addressed at this time to the Hessian officers.

† Eelking's "Hülfstruppen," vol. i. pp. 344-347.

‡ Ewald's "Belehrungen," vol. ii. pp. 425-427.

might have been expected. It was proportionally large among the prisoners of war. The army that surrendered at Saratoga in October, 1777, numbered five thousand seven hundred and ninety-one men, of whom two thousand four hundred and thirty-one were Germans. From this army six hundred and fifty-five Englishmen and one hundred and sixty Germans had deserted by the 1st of April, 1778. There is no doubt that continual efforts were made to induce these and other prisoners to desert and enlist in the American army. Washington was very much opposed to this system. On the 27th of November, 1776, he writes to the President of Congress: "By a letter from the Board of War on the subject of an exchange, they mention that several of the prisoners in our hands have enlisted. It is a measure, I think, that cannot be justified, though the precedent is furnished on the side of the enemy; nor do I conceive it good in point of policy. But as it has been done, I shall leave it with Congress to order them to be returned or not, as they shall judge fit."* And again, on the 30th, he expresses the same opinion to the Board of War, and adds: "Before I had the honor of yours on this subject, I had determined to remonstrate to General Howe on this head. As to those few, who have already enlisted, I would not have them again withdrawn and sent in, because they might be subjected to punishment; but I would have the practice discontinued in future."†

* This letter is not given by Sparks, from whose edition the other quotations from Washington's writings are made. This is from an old London edition of "Washington's Official Letters."

† Washington, vol. iv. p. 196.

In a letter written on the 8th of October, of the same year, he had gone still further, and said that mechanics and other prisoners who wished to remain should be obliged to return.* On the 12th of March, 1778, he says that if prisoners have been enlisted by the Americans he has not known it. "We have always complained against General Howe, and still do," writes he, "for obliging or permitting the prisoners in his hands to enlist, as an unwarrantable procedure, and wholly repugnant to the spirit at least of the cartel."† A few days later, however, he refers Pulaski to Congress. "I have informed him," writes Washington, "that the enlisting of deserters and prisoners is prohibited by a late resolve of Congress. How far Congress might be inclined to make an exception, and license the engaging prisoners in a particular detached corps, in which such characters may be admitted with less danger than promiscuously in the line, I cannot undertake to pronounce."‡

It is probable that Pulaski did, in fact, enlist deserters, and it is certain that the so-called Chevalier Armand (in fact Marquis de la Rouerie) did so. Wiederhold, when in captivity at Reading, early in 1780, saw two squadrons of Armand's corps pass through that town. He says that the corps had been four hundred strong and composed entirely of German deserters.

On the 22d of May, 1778, Congress passed a resolu-

---

* Washington, vol. iv. p. 147. † Ibid. vol. v. p. 270.

‡ Ibid. vol. v. p. 278. See, also, Washington's letters to James Bowdoin and to General Heath against enlisting deserters.—Washington, vol. v. pp. 287, 346.

tion advising the states to declare all deserters and prisoners free from militia duty, and to forbid their serving as substitutes in the militia. On the 29th of the same month a singular scene is said to have taken place at Cambridge. Some Brunswick officers caught a deserter, one of the prisoners on Prospect Hill. He was making off to Watertown, where Colonel Armand had a recruiting station. The poor wretch was brought back to camp, and, as he was the first that had been caught, it was determined to make an example of him. He was tied to a post and flogged with a rod, three hundred strokes. His hair was then cut off, and he was dishonorably dismissed from the service. The Americans are said to have looked calmly on, but to have received the man with kindness after the punishment, and led him away in triumph.* Eelking gives no authority for this story, and we may hope that it is apocryphal. At any rate, the punishment, if it really took place, did not prove very effectual, for some fifty Brunswickers deserted in the course of the next five months, and the loss of men from desertion during the journey to Virginia was heavy.

Some of the desertion among the prisoners was only apparent. The German captives sometimes left the dreary huts in which they were confined and wandered away, in hopes of reaching New York, or one of the British armies. On the 18th of May, 1779, Governor Clinton writes to Washington concerning "an alarm on the frontiers of Ulster County, occasioned by the appearance of about one hundred Indians and Tories. They were joined at this place by twenty-

* Eelking's "Riedesel," vol. ii. p. 262.

seven Tories from east of Hudson's River, mostly Hessian deserters from the Convention troops. The sudden assembling of the militia deterred them from penetrating farther into the country, and prevented them from doing any material injury."* And in February, 1781, General Greene wrote that thirty-eight out of a detachment of forty men in Armand's legion had deserted to the enemy, and that Baron Steuben had been obliged to order a number of them to join their regiments, who were prisoners at Charlottesville.†

If it be true, as the German writers assert, and as seems to be the case, that the German soldiers deserted less than the English in this war, the cause is not far to seek. The troops were employed for the most part in neighborhoods where the inhabitants could speak no German. Moreover, the "Hessians," as the auxiliaries were indiscriminately called, were objects of peculiar abhorrence to the natives. Their name might probably be sometimes heard as a term of reproach to this day in country districts. The English deserter became indistinguishable from the moment when he took off his red coat. The German could speak no word that did not betray him.‡

Neither among the English nor among the Germans was desertion so prevalent as among the Americans. But in saying this, one great difference must be noted. The British or German soldier could only desert to the enemy. The American militiaman generally returned to his home. The Revolutionary militia were, in some important respects, more like the clans of

* Sparks's "Correspondence," vol. ii. p. 298.

† Ibid. vol. iii. p. 247.

‡ Ibid. vol. iii. pp. 142, 154.

Scotch Highlanders in the civil wars of the seventeenth and eighteenth centuries than like modern soldiers. They came or went, as patriotism or selfishness, enthusiasm or discouragement, succeeded each other in their breasts. Often intrepid in battle, they were subject to panics, like all undisciplined troops, and were such uncomfortable customers to deal with that it was equally unsafe for their generals to trust them or for their enemies to despise them.

We have seen that seventeen thousand three hundred and thirteen Germans, or about fifty-eight per cent. of those who came over as mercenaries, returned safely to Europe. Of the twelve thousand five hundred and fifty-four that remained, a small proportion had been killed in battle or had died of their wounds, many had died of sickness, many had deserted, some had remained in America, after peace was concluded, with the consent of the authorities. Hessian officers and privates received grants of land in Nova Scotia, and the Duke of Brunswick, with characteristic inhumanity, ordered that not only soldiers guilty of crimes and disorderly conduct, but those who were bodily unfit for military duty, should be left in Canada.*

The Landgrave of Hesse-Cassel has not failed to find apologists. These dwell, in the first place, on the general wickedness of the Americans, and on their criminality in revolting against the King of England, under whose government they were only too happy; and, secondly, maintain that the letting of troops was in accordance with the customs of the last century, that the money received by the Landgrave was used

* MS. journal of the Grenadier Battalion von Platte; Eelking's "Hülfstruppen," vol. ii. pp. 253–255; Appendix D.

for the benefit of his people, and that these approved of the transaction. Into the first contention I do not propose to enter further than is necessary to point out its irrelevance. Had the Landgrave gone into the Revolutionary War on its merits, an argument drawn from the depravity of the rebels and the wickedness of rebellion would have been pertinent. It has no force when applied to a prince who, in accordance with a policy that was hereditary in his dynasty, let out his troops to the highest bidder. As to the second argument, it is true that public morality in the matter of the employment of mercenaries was and is deplorably loose. A nation engaged in a great struggle can hardly be expected not to take help where it can find it. The individual soldier of fortune has long been looked on with too much indulgence. But to be a soldier of fortune by proxy, to coin money out of other people's blood, and by perils which he who profits by them does not share, has never been considered a manly occupation; and those who say that the Hessian people approved of Landgrave Frederick's bargains condemn his subjects without excusing himself. A better argument was found by his minister, Schlieffen, in the close connection between the English court and the courts of Hesse and Brunswick. The American provinces might conceivably be inherited by a Hessian prince. Did we, therefore, see Hessian soldiers serving in English pay against American rebels without pecuniary compensation to the Landgrave, we might believe that they were sent for political reasons. This argument loses its force in the face of the subsidies. The Landgrave entered into a sordid bargain, and it is in the light of this bargain that he must be judged.

APPENDIX.

A.

LIST OF GERMAN AUTHORITIES USED IN PREPARING THIS WORK.

PRINTED.

FRIEDRICH KAPP.—Der Soldatenhandel deutscher Fürsten nach Amerika. Berlin, 1864.

The same.—The same. Berlin, 1874. (*The first edition contains in its appendix much interesting material omitted in the second edition. The second edition is enlarged and corrected. References in this volume are to the second edition unless stated to be otherwise.*)

The same.—Geschichte der Deutschen im Staate New York. New York, 1869.

The same.—Friedrich der Grosse und die Vereinigten Staaten von Amerika. Leipzig, 1871.

The same.—Article in Sybel's Historische Zeitschrift. II. 6=42. 1879.

The same.—Leben des Amerikanischen Generals Friedrich Wilhelm von Steuben. Berlin, 1858.

MAX VON EELKING.—Die deutschen Hülfstruppen im nordamerikanischen Befreiungskriege, 1776 bis 1783. Hannover, 1863. 2 vols.

The same.—Leben und Wirken des Herzoglich Braunschweig 'schen General-Lieutenants Friedrich Adolph von Riedesel. Leipzig, 1856. 3 vols.

GENERALIN VON RIEDESEL.—Die Berufs-Reise nach Amerika. Berlin, 1801.

CHRISTIAN LEISTE.—Beschreibung des Brittischen Amerika zur Ersparung der englischen Karten. Wolfenbüttel, 1778.

F. B. MELSHEIMER.—Tagebuch von der Reise der Braunschweigischen Auxiliar Truppen von Wolfenbüttel nach Quebec. Minden, 1776.

The same.—Erste Fortsetzung. (*These are two small pamphlets.*)

J. VON EWALD.—Belehrungen über den Krieg, besonders über den kleinen Krieg, durch Beispiele grosser Helden und kluger und tapferer Männer. Schleswig, 1798.

Folge derselben. Schleswig, 1800.

Zweite und letzte Folge derselben. Schleswig, 1803.

Briefe eines Reisenden über den gegenwärtegen Zustand von Cassel, mit aller Freiheit geschildert. Frankfurt und Leipzig, 1781.

Hochfürstl. Hessen-Casselischer Staats- und Adress-Calender auf das Jahr Christi 1779. Cassel.

KARL BIEDERMANN.—Deutschland im Achtzehnten Jahrhundert. Vol. I. Deutschlands Politische, materielle und sociale Zustände im Achtzehnten Jahrhundert. Leipzig, 1880.

FERDINAND PFISTER. — Der Nordamerikanische Unabhängigkeits-Krieg. Kassel, 1864.

Friedrich II. und die neuere Geschichts-Screibung.—Ein Beitrag zur Widerlegung der Märchen über angeblichen Soldaten-Handel hessischer Fürsten. Zweite mit eine Beleuchtung Seumens vermehrte Auflage. Melsungen, 1879.

I. G. SEUME.—Sämtliche Werke. Leipzig, 1835. (Mein Leben.)

The same.—Article in I. W. v. ARCHENHOLTZ's Neue Literatur und Völkerkunde. Für das Jahr 1789. Zweiter Band. (Schreiben aus Amerika nach Deutschland, Hallifax, 1782.)

AUGUST LUDWIG SCHLÖZER's, &c., Briefwechsel meist historischen und politischen Inhalts. Göttingen, 1780 to 1782. (*A reprint in* 10 *vols. of this interesting magazine, dating from* 1776 *to* 1782, *and containing a large number of articles on the Revolutionary War, and of letters from America.*)

The same.—Stats-Anzeigen. (*A continuation of the above-mentioned magazine under a new title.*) 18 vols.

Die neuesten Staatsbegebenheiten mit historischen und politischen Anmerkungen. Frankfurt am Mayn und Mainz, 1775, 1776, 1777. 3 vols.

KARL HEINRICH RITTER VON LANG. — Geschichte des vorletzten Markgrafen von Brandenburg-Anspach. Anspach, 1848.

J. B. FISCHER.—Geschichte von Anspach oder Onolzbach. Anspach, 1786.

Reglement für Hessische Infanterie. Cassel, 1767.

Von den Hessen in Amerika, ihren fürsten, &c., 1782. (The pamphlet attributed to Schlieffen.)

MANUSCRIPTS.

(From originals or copies in the Ständische Landesbibliothek at Cassel.)

(1.) Journal von dem Hochlobl: Hessischen Grenadier olom Battaillon von Minnigerode, modo von Loewenstein vom 20ten Januarii, 1776, bis 17ten May, 1784.

(2.) Journal vom Hochfürstlich Hessischen Grenadier Battaillon Platte. Vom 16 Februar, 1776, bis den 24 Maij, 1784. Geführt durch dem Regiments Quartier Meister Carl Bauer.

(3.) Journal des Hochlöblichen Fuselier Regimentes von Alt-Lossberg. Geführt durch den Regiments Quartier Meister Heusser, vom Ausmarsch aus der Garnison Rinteln an, bis zur Zurückkunft des gedachten Hochlöblichen Regiments aus America vom 10ten Merz, 1776, bis den 5ten October, 1783.

(4.) Geschichte des hochlöblichen Fuselier-Regiments von Lossberg in Form eines Tagebuchs angefangen 1776–1783 (by Adj. Piel).

(5.) Journal vom Löblichen Garnisons-Regiment von Huyn, nachher von Benning de ao. 1776, bis medio November, 1783 geführt durch mich dem Regiments Qtiermstr G. Kleinschmidt.

(6.) Journal geführt bei dem Hochlöblich Hessischen Feld-Jäger Corps während denen Campagnen der Konigl. Grossbrittanischen Armee in North Amerika. Angefangen den 23ten Juli, 1777, von dem Tage wo der Oberstlieutenant Ludwig Johann Adolph von Wurmb das Commando über das Corps übernahm und geendigt den 20ten April, 1784, bei der erfolgten retour derer sämtlich Hochfürstlich. Hessischen Truppen aus America.

(7.) Tagebuch des Hauptmannes Wiederhold, v. 1776–80. (*The copy in the library at Cassel is made from the original by the husband of Wiederhold's granddaughter, and contains several interesting appendices.*)

(8.) Journal von dem Hochfürstl. Hessischen Hlöbl. Infanterie Regiment von Trümbach, modo General Lieutenant von Bose, seines in ao. 1776 aus Hessen nach Amerika gethanen Aus Marches, und in ao. 1783 wieder gehabten Ein Marches zur Garnison Hofgeismar.

(9.) Journal von dem Hochfürstlichen Hessischen, des General Major von Knoblauch Löbl. Garnisons-Regiment, seit dem Amerikanischen Krieg von anno 1776 bis Ende 1783.

(10.) Briefe des General-Majors von Riedesel. Tagebuch vom Capit. Pausch.

(From the library of his Serene Highness the Prince of Waldeck.)

(11.) Fragment of a diary of the Waldeck Regiment, April 11, 1780, to July, 1782.

(From the archives at Marburg.)

(12.) Berichte Sr Excellentz des Herrn General Lieutenant von Knyp-hausen au Serenissimum.

(Of the above-named MSS. I have copies. I have also consulted a collection of papers concerning Regt. von Mirbach in the library at Cassel, and sundry documents in the archives at Marburg.)

B.

THE HESSIAN REGIMENTS AND THEIR NAMES.

The Landgrave of Hesse-Cassel sent fifteen of his regiments to America. Each of these regiments was composed of 650 officers and men, in five companies. This was less than the normal strength of a Hessian regiment. Fourteen of the fifteen regiments had given up one company of grenadiers each, and these fourteen companies, with two more from the Landgrave's bodyguard, were formed into four battalions of grenadiers, with a strength of 524 officers and men for each battalion. A corps of chasseurs (Jägers), originally consisting of two companies, accompanied the army. It was augmented in 1777 to a nominal strength of 1067 officers and men, but I think it never much exceeded six or seven hundred effective. There were three companies of artillery, together numbering 588 (Kapp's Soldatenhandel, I. ed., p. 280). Thus the Hessian force (Cassel) was composed of 15 regiments of infantry, 4 battalions of grenadiers, 1 corps of chasseurs, and 3 companies of artillery. There was no cavalry, but a few of the chasseurs were mounted.

A Hessian regiment was usually named after its "Chef." This "Chef" was sometimes the colonel of the regiment, but more frequently a prince or superior officer. As the "Chefs" were frequently changed or transferred, it is often difficult to identify a regiment. The battalions of *grenadiers* in America were named after their lieutenant-colonels. The following list of the regiments and battalions that served in America, and of the changes in their names, is taken partly from a list appended to the copy of Wiederhold's diary, in the library at Cassel. I believe it to be generally correct. I have added the names of the principal battles and expeditions in which the various regiments and battalions were engaged. (Those regiments which came over with von Heister are marked "I. div." Those which came with von Knyphausen are marked "II. div."

Gren. batt. von Linsingen. (*I. div.—Long Island, Chatterton Hill, Brandywine, Redbank, Charleston.*)

Gren. batt. von Block; 1777, von Lengerke. (*I. div.—Long Island, Chatterton Hill, Brandywine, Redbank, Charleston.*)

Gren. batt. von Minnigerode; 1780, von Loewenstein. (*I. div.—Long Island, Chatterton Hill, Brandywine, Redbank, Charleston.*)

Gren. batt. von Koehler; 1778, von Graff; 1782, von Platte. (*II. div.—Fort Washington, Charleston.*)

Leib Regiment. (*I. div.—Chatterton Hill, Brandywine, Germantown, Newport, Springfield.*)

Regiment Landgraf (sometimes called Wutgenau). (*II. div.—Fort Washington, Newport, Springfield.*)

Regiment Erbprinz. (*I. div.—Long Island, Fort Washington, Yorktown.*)

Regiment Prinz Carl. (*Newport.*)

Regiment von Dittfurth. (*I. div.—Newport, Charleston.*)

Regiment von Donop. (*I. div.—Long Island, Fort Washington, Brandywine, Germantown, Springfield.*)

Fuselier Regt. von Lossberg (sometimes Alt von Lossberg). (*I. div.—Long Island, Chatterton Hill, Fort Washington, Trenton, Brandywine.*)

Fuselier Regt. von Knyphausen. (*I. div.—Long Island, Chatterton Hill, Fort Washington, Trenton, Brandywine.*)

Grenadier Regt. Rall; 1777, von Woellwarth; 1778, von Trümbach; 1779, d'Angelelli. (*I. div.—Long Island, Chatterton Hill, Fort Washington, Trenton, Brandywine, Savannah.*)

What remained of the three last-mentioned regiments after Trenton formed the "Combined Battalion" in the campaign of 1777. In December of that year two battalions were formed, under Colonels von Loos and von Woellwarth. The three regiments subsequently resumed their separate organization, but the two first of them again suffered heavily by storm and captivity in September, 1779 (see Chapter XX.).

Regiment von Mirbach; 1780, Jung von Lossberg. (*I. div.—Long Island, Fort Washington, Brandywine, Redbank.*)

Regiment von Trümbach; 1778, von Bose. (*I. div.—Fort Clinton, Springfield, Guildford Court-House, Green Spring, Yorktown.*)

Garnisons Regt. von Stein; 1778, von Seitz. (*II. div.*)

Garnisons Regt. von Wissenbach; 1780, von Knoblauch. (*II. div.—Savannah.*)

Garnisons Regt. von Huyn; 1780, von Benning. (*II. div.—Fort Washington, Newport, Charleston.*)

Garnisons Regt. von Bünau. (*II. div.—Fort Washington, Newport, Springfield.*)
Feld Jäger Corps. (*Detachments of this corps were concerned in almost every operation.*)

(The above-named regiments are from Hesse-Cassel.)

With the army commanded by Howe and Clinton, commonly served the following German regiments, in addition to those above-mentioned:

Regiment Waldeck. (*Fort Washington, Pensacola.*)
Regiment Anspach. (*Philadelphia, Newport, Springfield, Yorktown.*)
Regiment Bayreuth. (*Philadelphia, Newport, Yorktown.*)

(The two last-mentioned are generally called the two Anspach regiments. The Anspach chasseurs made a part of the Hessian Jäger Corps.)

The BRUNSWICK contingent, serving in Canada and northern New York, was composed of the

Regiment of Dragoons (dismounted). (*Bennington under Baum.*)
Battalion of Grenadiers. (*Bennington under Breymann, 1st Stillwater, 2d Stillwater, Saratoga.*)
Regiment Prinz Friedrich. (*Remained at Ticonderoga during the Saratoga campaign.*)
Regiment von Riedesel. (*1st Stillwater, Saratoga.*)
Regiment von Rhetz. (*2 companies at 1st Stillwater, Saratoga.*)
Regiment von Specht. (*Saratoga.*)
Jäger battalion, or Battalion Barner. (*1st Stillwater, Saratoga.*)

The Hanau regiment and the Hanau artillery served with this army, and shared its fate. The artillery had done good service in the campaign of 1776, on Lake Champlain, as well as in 1777.

The Hanau chasseurs, or some of them, took part in St. Leger's expedition.

The regiment from Anhalt-Zerbst reached Canada after active hostilities in that province were over.

C.

"He is, at this time, transporting large armies of foreign mercenaries to complete the works of death, desolation, and tyranny already begun with circumstances of cruelty and perfidy scarcely paralleled in the most barbarous ages, and totally unworthy the head of a civilized nation."—*Declaration of Independence.*

D.

TABLE OF THE NUMBER OF TROOPS SENT TO AMERICA BY EACH ONE OF THE GERMAN STATES, AND OF THE NUMBER THAT RETURNED.

The numbers originally given in Schlözer's "Stats-Anzeigen" (vi. pp. 521, 522), were corrected by Kapp as to the Anspach contingent. They form, perhaps, the nearest approximation attainable.

BRUNSWICK sent in 1776	4,300
" " March, 1777	224
" " April, 1778	475
" " April, 1779	286
" " May, 1780	266
" " April, 1782	172
Total	5,723
Returned in the autumn of 1783	2,708
Did not return	3,015

HESSE-CASSEL sent in 1776	12,805
" " December, 1777	403
" " March, 1779	993
" " May, 1780	915
" " April, 1781	915
" " April, 1782	961
Total	16,992
Returned in the autumn of 1783 and the spring of 1784	10,492
Did not return	6,500

HESSE-HANAU, under various treaties	2,038
" recruits sent in April, 1781	50
" " April, 1782	334
Total	2,422
Returned in the autumn of 1783	1,441
Did not return	981

ANSPACH-BAYREUTH sent in 1777	1,285
" " " the autumn of the same year, recruits	318
" " " 1779	157
" " " 1780	152
" " " 1781	205
" " " 1772	236
Total	2,353
Returned in the autumn of 1783	1,183
Did not return	1,170

WALDECK sent in 1776	670
" " April, 1777	89
" " February, 1778	140
" " May, 1779	23
" " April, 1781	144
" " April, 1782	159
Total	1,225
Returned in the autumn of 1783	505
Did not return	720

ANHALT-ZERBST sent in 1778	600
" " April, 1779	82
" " May, 1780	50
" " April, 1781	420
Total	1,152
Returned in the autumn of 1783	984
Did not return	168

Total number sent	29,867
Total number returned	17,313
Total number of those who did not return	12,554

Of the 12,554 who did not return my own estimate is as follows:

Killed and died of wounds	1,200
Died of illness and accident	6,354
Deserted	5,000
Total	12,554

E.

LIST OF THE LOSSES SUSTAINED BY THE GERMANS IN THE PRINCIPAL BATTLES OF THE REVOLUTIONARY WAR.

	Killed.	Wounded.	Missing.
Long Island	2	25	
September 15th, 1776*	2	16	
September 16th, 1776	1	1	
October 9th to October 23d (including Chatterton Hill)	13	63	23
Fort Washington	56	276	
Trenton	17	78	
Assanpink (January 2d, 1777)	4	11	
Burgoyne's Campaign to October 6th, 1777	164	284	
Burgoyne's Campaign from October 7th to 16th	25 (?)	75 (?)	
Skirmish, September 3d, 1777	1	19	
Brandywine, Chasseurs	7	39	
" other Hessians	2 (?)	16 (?)	
Redbank	82	229	60
Newport	19	96	13
Stono Ferry	9 (?)	34 (?)	
Charleston	11	62	
Springfield	25 (?)	75 (?)	
Baton Rouge	25	8	
Pensacola	15 (?)	45 (?)	
Guildford Court House	15	69	4
Yorktown	53	131	27
Total	548	1652	127

* Although the British landed on New York Island without opposition, as stated on page 72, there was a skirmish on the day of their landing, in which the Hessian grenadiers suffered the loss stated above.

INDEX.

A.

B.

C.

D.

E.

F.

G.

H.

L.

M.

N.

O.

Q.

R.

S.

W.

Y.

Z.

THE END.

Curtis's Life of James Buchanan,

Fifteenth President of the United States. By GEORGE TICKNOR CURTIS. With Two Steel-Plate Portraits. 2 vols., 8vo, Cloth, Gilt Tops and Uncut Edges, $6 00.

Memoirs of General Dix.

Memoirs of John Adams Dix. Compiled by his Son, MORGAN DIX. With Five Steel-plate Portraits. 2 vols., 8vo, Cloth, Gilt Tops and Uncut Edges, $5 00.

Charles Carleton Coffin's Works.

The Boys of '76.

A History of the Battles of the Revolution. Illustrated. 8vo, Cloth, $3 00.

Old Times in the Colonies.

Illustrated. 8vo, Cloth, $3 00.

Building the Nation.

Events in the History of the United States from the Revolution to the Beginning of the War between the States. Illustrated. 8vo, Cloth, $3 00.

Helps's Spanish Conquest in America,

And its Relation to the History of Slavery, and to the Government of Colonies. By Sir ARTHUR HELPS. 4 vols., 12mo, Cloth, $6 00; Half Calf, $13 00.

Warburton's Conquest of Canada.

By ELIOT WARBURTON. 2 vols., 12mo, Cloth, $3 00.

Draper's American Civil War.

History of the American Civil War. By JOHN W. DRAPER, M.D., LL.D. 3 vols., 8vo, Cloth, $10 50; Sheep, $12 00; Half Calf, $17 25.

Foote's War of the Rebellion.

Consisting of Observations upon the Causes, Course, and Consequences of the late Civil War in the United States. By H. S. FOOTE. 12mo, Cloth, $2 50.

Robertson's America.

History of the Discovery of America. By WILLIAM ROBERTSON, LL.D. 8vo, Cloth, $2 25.

A Century of Dishonor.

A Sketch of the United States Government's Dealings with some of the Indian Tribes. By "H. H." With a Preface by Bishop Whipple and an Introduction by President Seelye. 12mo, Cloth, $1 50.

The First Century of the Republic.

A Review of American Progress. 8vo, Cloth, $5 00.

Hudson's History of Journalism.

Journalism in the United States, from 1690 to 1872. By FREDERIC HUDSON. 8vo, Cloth, $5 00; Half Calf, $7 25.

General Beauregard's Military Operations.

The Military Operations of General Beauregard in the War between the States, 1861 to 1865; including a brief Personal Sketch and a Narrative of his Services in the War with Mexico, 1846–48. By ALFRED ROMAN, formerly Colonel of the 18th Louisiana Volunteers, afterwards Aide-de-Camp and Inspector-General on the Staff of General Beauregard. 2 vols., 8vo, Cloth, $7 00; Sheep, $9 00; Half Morocco, $11 00; Full Morocco, $15 00. (*Sold only by Subscription.*)

Carroll's Twelve Americans:

Their Lives and Times. By HOWARD CARROLL. Containing Sketches of Horatio Seymour, Charles Francis Adams, Peter Cooper, Hannibal Hamlin, John Gilbert, Robert C. Schenck, Frederick Douglass, William Allen, Allen G. Thurman, Joseph Jefferson, Elihu B. Washburne, Alexander H. Stephens. Portraits. 12mo, Cloth, $1 75.

Johnston's Yorktown Campaign.

The Yorktown Campaign and the Surrender of Cornwallis, 1781. By HENRY P. JOHNSTON. Illustrated. 8vo, Cloth, $2 00.

Cushing's Treaty of Washington:

Its Negotiation, Execution, and the Discussions relating thereto. By CALEB CUSHING. Crown 8vo, Cloth, $2 00.

Baldwin's Ancient America.

Ancient America, in Notes on American Archæology. By JOHN D. BALDWIN, A.M. Illustrated. 12mo, Cloth, $2 00.

Made in the USA
Lexington, KY
05 August 2014